AFTER TOAST

AFTER TOAST

recipes for aspiring cooks

kate gibbs

FAIRFAX BOOKS
ALLEN&UNWIN

First published in 2012

Fairfax Books, an imprint of
Allen & Unwin
Sydney, Melbourne, Auckland, London

83 Alexander Street
Crows Nest NSW 2065
Australia
Phone: (61 2) 8425 0100
Fax: (61 2) 9906 2218
Email: info@allenandunwin.com
Web: www.allenandunwin.com

Cataloguing-in-Publication details are available
from the National Library of Australia
www.trove.nla.gov.au

ISBN 978 1 74237 941 8

Photography credits:
Food photography by Louise Lister, Kristin Hove and Kate Gibbs
All other photography by Kristian Taylor Wood and Kate Gibbs

Design by Lindbjerg Graphic Pty Ltd
Set in 11/14 pt AFBattersea
Printed in China by 1010 Printing Limited

To my amazing mum and dad, who taught me love of food, the world and everything.

To Margaret Fulton, most inspiring grandmother a girl could have. You'll forever be the leader of our pack, in life and in food.

And for Ben, my great culinary dreamer-upper.

CONTENTS

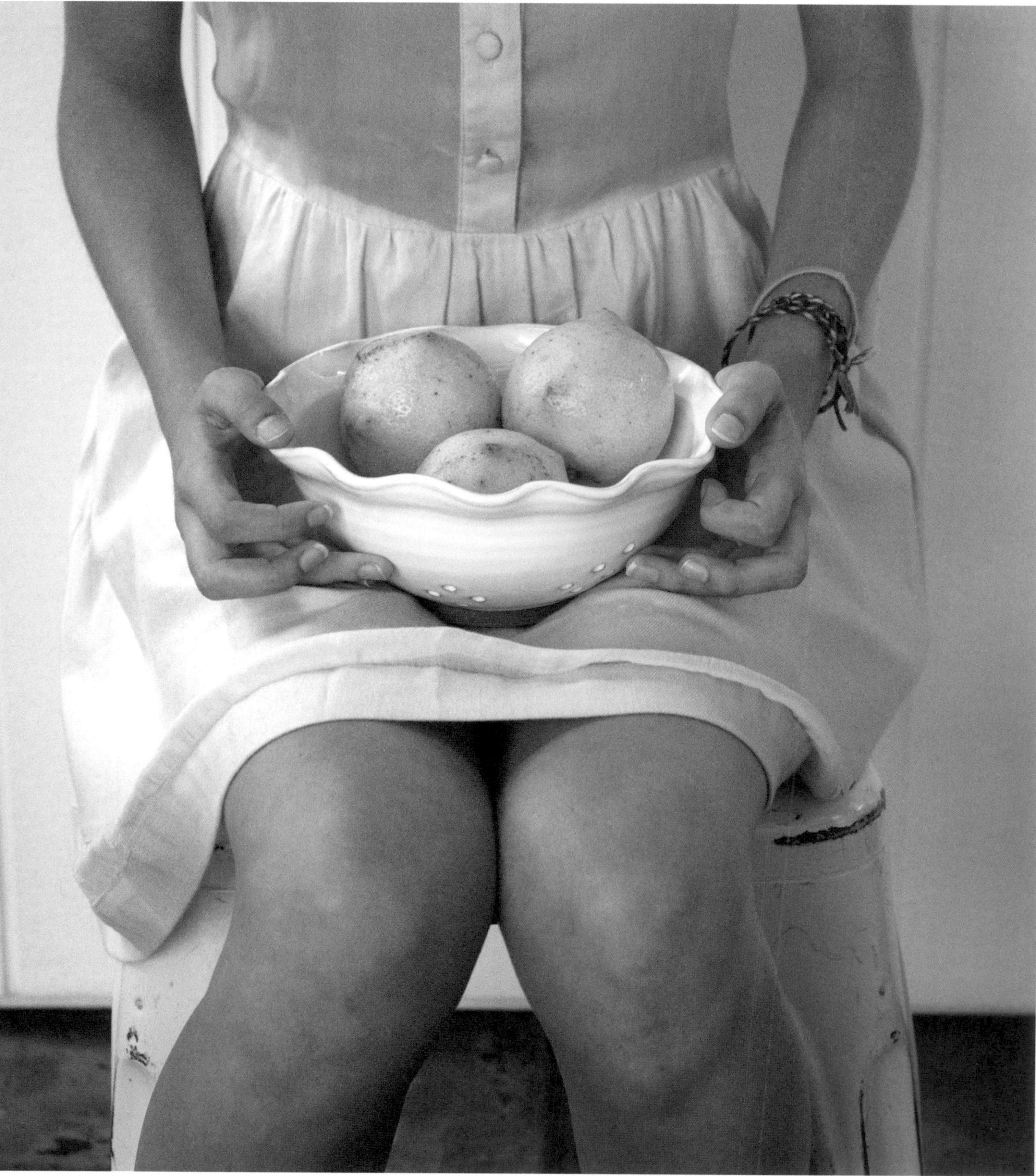

In AFTER TOAST, Kate Gibbs visits the culinary lives of young, aspiring cooks. She relives her own cooking steps at a teenager and young adult, and delves into the lives, interests, language, expressions and fresh ideas of the young for food.

We start with Breakfast, with recipes such as Not-quite huevos rancheros and Frog in the hole–'round egg, round hole'. It all seems like great fun. What a good idea to have a Great-fast smoothie or a Peaches and cream smoothie, and with Hash browns and Bacon and corn muffins, breakfast presents as a meal you just wouldn't want to miss.

Kate offers good, sensible advice, too. 'This book kind of demands a love of food,' she writes. 'I just don't believe you can cook well unless you love to eat.' There's no hint of the school marm about this–it's knowing the realities of bad habits, the mistakes that many of us make in our early years when cooking and eating.

Snacks are given a healthy spin with the likes of Holy moley guacamole. Lunch and Dinner is appropriate with the same enthusiasm. The chapter Parties & Friends is a cheerful way to say 'what-to-cook through any social spell, while eating well'.

Hints scattered through the book shed light on complicated subjects for the culinary novice. 'How to host a sophisticated gathering' tells you: 'First tidy up, but remember, you're having friends over, not the Queen. So sure, clean the bathroom. Get a bunch of flowers if you like and pop them in a large glass jar.' It's good advice for even the more established host.

With so many mouth-watering photographs and simple-to-follow recipes, it will be easy to spoil family and friends, and yourselves. You will enjoy the many expert tips on cooking, life and the world that are scattered through the book. The design also warrants a mention, it just adds to the excitement.

Rarely have I read a book that invades and expresses an age and era so completely. And not only that–these words and recipes make such good reading. This book has cast a magic spell over me, taking me back in time to my own youth, to a time that wasn't quite so forward-thinking and exciting as this book offers. May I say, I want to be 20 again!

Congratulations, my granddaughter, Kate.

MARGARET FULTON

Love food, can cook

... There's a sound that happens when you run your finger along the spines of books packed into a bookshelf. Tap tap tap tap click click tap tap. The sound changes depending on whether they're little paperback novels or those hard-cover, thick-bound, seriously big books. Or a long row of cookbooks, say. Don't let this book become one of those books that just sit there gathering dust. Instead, keep it with you to actually use.

This book is about how to make food. Food to eat. Food you can cook. Food that you'll want to eat, and that you will like, and that your friends and family will like. Food you'll be really, really proud to tell your mates you cooked.

I am not entirely sure I buy in to the idea of kids' or young people's food, in the sense that the more you restrict the sorts of food you eat, the less adventurous you'll be with food for the rest of your life.

You can scale a wall. You can tell your little brother what to do. You've heard of trigonometry and can spell words like 'Mississippi' and 'hyperbole'. You can do a very cool dance in your room by yourself and you know how to upload videos to YouTube. You can text as fast as you can talk. You can do mini peace talks between friends, you can surf, and you know one to ten in another language. Dude, you can cook pots de creme.

My parents have a whole room in their house full of cookbooks. My mother's a professional cook, so that makes sense. I grew up surrounded by amazing, healthy and real food—my mum and dad had me stirring pots and chopping herbs and deglazing pans once I was tall enough to see over the kitchen bench. I knew what a roux was and I knew 180° Celsius was a reasonable temperature to bake many things. But it wasn't until I was much older that I actually cooked an entire meal. By myself.

As a self-declared 'foodie' as a teenager, I once told my friends I'd make roast chicken for them while my parents were away. Easy? Um, no, not actually. It's not at all easy if you've never cooked a whole meal by yourself. I mean all the shopping, all the chopping, all the stuffing herby butter under the chicken's skin, avoiding burns on the oven or the hot roasting tin, timing the vegetables to be cooked and done about the same time as the chicken—in other words, proper cooking.

My advice then, as someone who once only knew how to make toast or the more daring sandwich or salad, but then gradually learned how to cook, is just to start cooking. Make pikelets today. Then, tomorrow, make a grilled quesadilla. In a week, bake a cake. By next month, you can serve a whole meal. True.

And that is what this book is about. It's about giving you, the discerning young eater, the mini gastronome, well-informed choices about what you eat. But this means you're doing the cooking. You can have your cake, as they say, but you have to bake it.

What you choose to eat is of course up to you. But please, please, let's not be dull. Let's be interesting about it. Let's be a bit adventurous. Let's open ourselves to a world of really good food. Here are some things you should know:

cooking is something you can do
cooking is creative
cooking is scientific
good food wins you friends
healthy food makes you smarter
food you make at home is cheaper
eat better now, look better your whole life
eat more veg—it's good for you and the planet

I hope you take this cooking-and-eating-really-awesome-food thing seriously, and happily. And I hope you discover the joy of cooking, too.

TO START

STARS AND YOU

Recipes are given stars to denote difficulty levels. One star is totally do-able. Two may need a little more focus, and three is what to make when you're really getting the hang of this cooking malarky.

A COOK'S TOOLS

A bad workman blames his tools when something goes wrong. But chefs simply can't do their best work without a decent set of gadgets, knives and things. Here's a list of things you really need on hand if you're going to take this cooking caper seriously.

Microplane grater
Wooden spoons
Stainless steel mixing bowls
Whisk
Baking trays
Heavy-based frying pans (2 sizes)
Heavy-based saucepans (2–3 sizes)
A few very sharp knives (and a knife sharpener)
At least 2 thick plastic chopping boards
1 thick butcher's block or large wooden board
Sieve
Colander
Steamer that sits inside a saucepan with a lid
Mortar and pestle
Metal spatula, rubber spatula, ladle
Metal tongs (a few small ones)
Small ceramic mixing bowl
Heavy-based baking dish
12-hole muffin or cupcake tin
23 cm (approx. 9 inch) springform round cake tin.

SAUCEPAN Near the top of any good cook's must-have list is a decent saucepan. It should be heavy to ensure even cooking and avoid burning. I prefer cast-iron, whether unlined or lined with Silverstone or some other non-stick surface. Copper is brilliant because it's heavy, plus it looks stunning if you look after it, though it is pricey. I'm not a fan of stainless steel because, while it's quite easy to clean, it's too light and is very likely to cause burning. Three saucepans will do you nicely—a small, medium and large—and make sure they all have matching lids with steam outlets to prevent boiling over.

FRYPANS As you develop your gastronomic and culinary skills, you'll want a battery of pans. This must include a frying pan for browning meats and for general frying and sautéing. It should have a fairly long handle and sloping sides of about 5 cm depth.

WOODEN SPOONS Keep a few wooden spoons in your kitchen. Have one especially for highly flavoured foods such as garlic, onions and curries. Keep another for sweet delicate dishes like custards. This stops the flavour transferring and avoids curry-flavoured custards. Dab a little bright pink nail polish at the handle end of one to identify which is which, though the smell should make it pretty obvious.

TEA TOWELS So incredibly useful for moving hot pans around the kitchen, in and out of ovens and the like. But, a HUGE warning note—when handling hot cooking utensils, make sure never to use a wet tea towel. This is particularly true when getting something hot out of the oven. As the moisture from the tea towel comes into contact with the heat, steam forms and rushes through the cloth, bound to give a very painful and nasty burn. Oven mitts or thick dry tea towels are a much safer bet.

A COOK'S TRICKS

Cooking is a bit like a science project: you really need to pay attention or you'll end up with a mess on your hands. It just doesn't work if you do it half-heartedly. I've seen many a mini chef pay only a bit of attention to what's cooking, and mostly check their iPhones, and so things end up a bit of a disaster.

Cooking is a full-attention thing to do. You do it completely, and finish it completely, before being distracted by something else. It's great fun, but you still need to take it a bit seriously.

Here are some tips and notes to help you do all this cooking malarky better.

BLANCH. A healthy method for cooking vegetables as things only get partly cooked, so less vitamins come out. Boil water over a high heat and just pop the vegetables in for a minute or less.

CHOP. What do the words 'finely chopped' or 'roughly chopped' really mean? Chopping is a very general word for cutting food into chunks, basically. The exact shape usually doesn't matter. 'Finely chopped' things should be pretty small—say, 2 mm (1⁄16 inch) chunks. 'Roughly chopped' can be a little bigger, say double that size or bigger. Practise chopping on herbs. Place the herbs on a board, hold the knife handle in one hand and place the other hand, very flat, on top of the blunt side of the blade, at the other end. Keep the knife's point on the board and bring the handle up so the blade goes over the herbs. Your flat hand holds down the tip-end of the knife, while the handle end rocks and chops the herbs. Careful of your fingers!

GRILL. Get the pan or barbecue very hot to grill something. You want things browning nicely to add flavour, without cooking them forever.

MISE EN PLACE. This is one of the most useful skills I learned at culinary school. *Mise en place* is a French term, meaning 'put in place'. Basically, have everything ready to go—chopped, diced, weighed and measured. Before any stoves are turned on, before any bubbling or simmering begins, all ingredients should be measured and ready to go. This turns messy, distracted, frantic cooking into something that's actually fun. It also means you don't realise halfway through your recipe that you're missing a vital ingredient. Whether you're making scrambled eggs or baking a chocolate cake, get everything ready first. Read through the ingredients list and if it says ½ cup flour, then measure it out. If it says '2 carrots, finely chopped', then finely chop two carrots before you do anything else.

GRIND. We often grind things in a mortar and pestle. This very old, traditional cooking tool is still very much in vogue. The mortar is a very heavy stone bowl, and a pestle is a heavy bat-shaped object that is used to pulverise things in the mortar. Larger, heavy ones are generally better, because they make less work for you.

PURÉE. This really common kitchen term means to turn something solid into something loose in texture. So, for example, whole carrots become an orange, carrot-flavoured slop. Depending on the food, purées can be made in many different ways. Often a food processor or blender is used to really pulp an ingredient, or it may be ground up really fine using a mortar and pestle or by pushing it through a sieve. It's often how we make soups, dips and even some sauces.

REDUCE. First we build the dish up with lots of ingredients, then we reduce it down. When we 'reduce' a stock or sauce, we simmer it down so the water evaporates a little and we're left with something stronger and richer in flavour. If you reduce a sauce or stock too much, and it's just too strong in flavour and there's not enough of it, just add a little water to the pot. Makes sense.

REFRESH (SHOCK). Technically speaking, to 'refresh' is how we rejuvenate yesterday's leftovers by adding a fresh ingredient—some herbs or fresh stock, for example. But many cookbooks, including this one, use the term 'refresh' in another way—meaning to plunge cooked food (usually vegetables) under cold water, or in a bowl full of ice and water, to stop it cooking. Technically the term 'refresh' isn't correct for this procedure, but you'll see and hear it used a lot. In proper culinary circles, plunging hot cooked vegetables into cold water is actually known as 'shocking' the vegetables.

SAUTÉ. Taken from the French word 'jump', this cooking method requires food to be cooked in a small amount of butter or oil. The food is thrown around in the pan either by tossing the pan or moving things around with a spoon.

SCALDING POINT. This refers to the point at which liquid (usually milk or water) is heated just a moment before it boils or simmers. The liquid may shimmer a little, like it's about to burst with bubbles.

SEAR. A term often used for meats, it means to quickly brown something over a high heat. The heat shouldn't permeate the food too much. Did you know there is a myth about searing meat? Check it out on page 4.

SEASONING. In the ingredients list, you won't always see salt and pepper listed, even though they are often used in the method. So, as always, it's a good idea to read a recipe through first so you know exactly what you're doing. Always use good-quality sea salt—I like sea salt flakes best. And always use freshly ground black pepper, unless instructed otherwise. Always taste a dish you're about to serve for seasoning, before you take it to the table. You can always add seasoning at this point, and a tiny pinch of salt makes a big difference. Be careful with seasoning though—add a little bit at a time—you can always add a little more salt and pepper, but you can't take it out. And remember people can always add a little more salt at the table if they like.

STEAM. Food is placed above simmering water so the steam actually cooks it. The nutrients don't all come out in the water, so it's a healthy way to cook. Fish and vegetables are great steamed. Just season the water with salt and then drizzle with a little olive oil, salt and pepper after cooking.

STIR-FRY. A healthy method of cooking because not much oil is added, and food is tossed around (usually in a wok) at a high temperature, so a lot of the nutrients stay inside the food.

TOAST. Recipes often ask for nuts or seeds to be toasted. Heat a dry, heavy pan over a moderately low heat. Add the nuts or seeds and 'toast', tossing occasionally until fragrant, about 5 minutes. Use your nose as a guide, and look for a toasty, golden colour. Be careful, they will continue to toast in the hot pan even after the heat has been turned off. The microwave is also a great way to toast nuts and seeds. Place in a microwave cooking dish on top of kitchen paper and cook on high, stirring and moving frequently until required toastiness.

ZEST. Zest is the colourful, oil-rich, very outer peel of citrus fruit. It has a wonderful, strong flavour used in sweet and savoury dishes. Zest can be taken off the fruit using a zester or microplane, which removes zest in a finely grated form and leaves behind the white pithy part, which tastes bitter. So when a recipe asks for zest, you want the coloured bit of the peel, without any of the white pith.

MEAT and CHICKEN

PORTION SIZE

We eat a lot of meat. In previous generations the famous Sunday Roast was often the only time a family would eat meat in a week, and all the bones and trimmings would be used through the week to pad out other meals—as leftovers in soups, stews and the like.

- Estimate about 150–200 grams (5½–7 ounces) per person for lamb, beef, pork and chicken.
- Supermarkets do a roaring trade on packed meat that is portioned out for one-meal use. Be it steaks, mince or a couple of chicken breasts, this is all about convenience. Be careful to only buy what you need and will eat, though.
- Don't use the excuse of high cost for buying low-quality meat. Best to buy excellent meat and have it less often.

HOW TO CHOOSE . . .

STEAK should be a little marbled with fat, which adds a lovely texture when cooked. If you want a very lean fat-free steak, go for a thick-cut **eye fillet steak**, which you should cook medium-rare or rare so it's lovely and juicy. I love a **scotch fillet steak**, which has a ribbon of fat through it but is packed with flavour and is extremely tender. A **porterhouse** or **sirloin steak** is quite lean and has fat running along one side, which is easy to cut off after cooking. It's a top quality cut, relatively lean with a lovely tender texture. A rump steak is always boneless and quite fatty, and although it's not as tender as others, it's very juicy and tasty.

ROAST BEEF comes in many forms. Just drizzle with olive oil and season with salt and pepper, then cook carefully and you can't go wrong. A **fillet of beef** is the long muscle that comes from deep inside the cow, not around the edge like most cuts. It's arguably the most tender (and most expensive) cut, but is amazing roasted. It's best seared in a pan then roasted for a short time so it's quite rare. **Brisket** is quite tough, until it is slow roasted in a low temperature oven. It's amazing value and it's really tasty. **Standing rib eye** (or prime rib of beef), is that glorious Flintstones-style roast done on the bone. If you love to gnaw a giant bone after a roast beef that's intense with flavour, this is your best bet.

BEEF STEW and slow-cooked dishes like Beef Provençale are about long, slow braising. So you want a beef cut that is fatty and not too expensive. The long cooking time makes fat disappear and the meat go meltingly soft and delicious. Beef cheeks and chuck steak are great for stews, cut into large cubes. Beef shin and oxtail are on the bone, but will become all soft and delicious and fall-off-the-bone when cooked for hours.

by the way

THE SEARING MEAT MYTH

Many people assume (and steadfastly argue) that searing meat is how we seal in the juices, thus making a more succulent steak or whatever. This turns out, actually, to be untrue. The juiciness of meat is determined by the 'doneness' to which it is cooked. The less cooking time, the juicier the steak. The more you cook it, the less water (and juice) will be inside. Searing is still really necessary though—a very hot pan will cook the meat right away and thereby intensify its flavour by browning the juices which flow from it. So browning is about adding lots of flavour, which is only a good thing.

BARBECUE is about cooking at really high temperatures either over hot coals or flames. The smoke really penetrates the meat and gives it an amazing aroma and flavour. But the trick is to get the barbecue really hot first and to cook the meat for a really short time—barbecue meat is often overcooked!

- # If you're doing beef, go for a sturdy, fatty, thick-cut beef from the butcher that won't cook too quickly, like rump.
- # Barbecued chicken is amazing, but can dry out quickly. Ask your butcher to butterfly a whole bird for you so it's flat—just marinate in olive oil, lemon juice, chilli flakes and loads of garlic, season well, then cook flat on a hot plate. Otherwise choose thighs over breast, because they don't dry out as quickly.
- # Lamb, marinated in rosemary, garlic, grated lemon rind and olive oil, makes a brilliant barbecue. I ask my butcher to butterfly a whole leg of lamb for me, so it's easy to slice for everyone. Chops and cutlets are good too, just be careful not to overcook lamb on the barbecue or it will go really dry and grainy.

STIR-FRY cooking is fast and hot hot hot. You want that wok very hot before you cook, and everything should be done in a flash. Things should brown, and quickly. Use chicken thighs, cut into pieces. You can use chicken breast but be careful not to overcook or it will dry out. I use rump steak in stir-fries because it's so full of flavour and can take the high heat.

IS THE STEAK COOKED?

Before you cook a steak, it should be at room temperature. This way, it will cook more evenly.

- # RARE OR WELL-DONE We all have our preferences, though to me a well-done steak is ruined, too tough and with a grainy texture. I prefer a rare to medium-rare, which has an almost crispy exterior and is still pink instead but definitely warm all the way through. Rare looks the same from the outside, but inside it's close to raw and still bloody.
- # GRILL a 4 centimetre (1½ inch) thick fillet steak for 2 to 3 minutes on each side for medium-rare. Minus a minute each side and it's rare, and add a minute more and it's well done.
- # REST THE MEAT Remember the meat continues to cook and relax once you've taken it off the heat. So it's always best to cook it less and let it rest for 5 minutes. Resting is really important with meat—it makes it more tender and keeps the juices inside.

IS THE CHICKEN COOKED?

When cooked, chicken juices should run clear. Whether you've roasted a whole bird or pan-fried a chicken breast, just slide a knife into the thickest part and watch the juices run out. They should be clear or close to it. If they're red or pink, cook the chook a little longer. Organic chicken is often more pink in colour. That's because they haven't been pumped with chemicals that make the meat white. Don't worry about this pink and brown colour, it's how it's supposed to be. While the juices should run clear, the meat may still be quite pink, especially near the bone.

GRASS OR GRAIN-FED BEEF?

There are HUGE differences between meat produced from animals fed and raised on these different diets. I only ever eat and buy grass-fed beef, I find it more ethical and I prefer the flavour. I also buy organic because I don't like to have hormones with my steak. But do try both and see which you prefer.

- # Grass-fed, or pasture-fed, beef generally has a better, cleaner flavour. These beasts roamed pastures and got to hang out with other cows in a relatively natural environment. Their muscles got a decent work out, so their meat is often less fatty.
- # Grain-fed beef comes from cattle that was fed for a specified number of days on high-energy feed. So 100-day grain-fed cattle spent the last 100 days of its life being fed grain in a feedlot. Grain-fed cattle tends to have high levels of fat marbled through the meat, which impacts the flavour and texture.

FISH PLEASE

Fish can be a daunting thing for the beginner cook. The first tip you need is to get over the 'err yuk' factor. I like to think that since a little creature has given up its life for our dinner, we owe it respect and professionalism when cooking it.

HOW TO SELECT FISH

Slapping, flipping fresh fish is the best sort. Any fish that's more than a day old will start to taste a little stronger, a little fishy.

STRONG FISH Fish such as tuna, salmon and ocean trout are stronger in flavour because they're rich with healthy oils. If you find them too strong, they taste milder when slightly undercooked, so they're quite a deep, dark pink inside.

LIGHT, FLAKY FISH is often a good way to go for fish-eating beginners because the flavour is not as strong. In Australia we have flathead and whiting, which can both be filleted so they're close to boneless. These are great pan fried.

ROBUST WHITE FISH A firm white fish is great wrapped in prosciutto and herbs and pan fried in olive oil, it holds up well against the strong flavours. It's also lovely sliced and 'cooked' in lime juice and olive oil. Wild John Dory and wild leatherjacket are firm, meaty white fish that grill, roast and barbecue well, and their flavours are mild. The white and meaty yellowtail kingfish (always go for the sustainable wild one) is lovely as a sashimi, or just lightly grilled.

HOW FRESH IS THAT FISH? Rely on your senses. It shouldn't smell too strong or bad, and should have a fresh smell of the sea. If you've got a whole fish, the eyes should be clear (not glazed) and not sunken.

MY FISH, MY EARTH Only ever buy sustainable fish. Generally, sardines and small fish are the most environmental. Be aware that a lot of shark, what we often call 'flake', is not sustainable.

HOW TO STORE FISH

Fish should be eaten the day it's bought (preferably the day it's caught). Keep it one day in the fridge at the most. To store, remove fish from any packaging you bought it in and place on a clean plate. Cover with plastic wrap and place in the fridge.

Or, if you know you're not going to eat it straight away, wrap it well and freeze it.

HOW TO COOK FISH

There are as many ways to cook fish as there are fish in the sea. Well, almost. But here are some quick and easy ideas to get you started.

PAN FRY The speedy way. Toss light, flaky fish fillets in seasoned plain flour, heat olive oil in a pan on high, and lightly pan fry. Squeeze a lemon over the top.

CRUMBED Dust firm fish fillets in seasoned plain flour, then dip in a lightly beaten egg then Panko bread crumbs. Heat 4 tbsp rice bran oil in large frying pan over high heat and fry fish until crispy. Squeeze lemon over the top.

OVEN BAKED Fish in a bag, in the oven, rich with herby flavours. Try this with John Dory or fillets of salmon or kingfish. Preheat oven to 220°C (425°F) and tear off a piece of foil or baking paper that will wrap around fish two times. Lay fish in the middle and cover with sliced tomatoes, 1 thinly sliced garlic clove, a glug of olive oil, 1 tsp balsamic vinegar, torn basil leaves, salt, pepper and 1 tsp water. Fold foil or paper around the fish a few times so it's airtight. Place in a baking tray and cook for 10–20 minutes (whole fish will need longer, a fillet less time). Remove bag from oven, let it rest for 5 minutes and serve.

CRISPY SKIN Many of us love some crispy skin on our fish. Season fish, drizzle with olive oil. Get the pan really hot and place the fillet in the dry pan, skin side down. Don't poke it and don't overcrowd the pan. Cook until skin goes crispy, then turn it over and cook for much less time, until just done.

SALAD GREENS & VEGETABLES

Eat your greens. Grrr! The reason we keep banging on about greens is because they're so darned healthy. But also, they're really lovely. We're not talking those grey green beans your Aunt Jean makes you eat, we're talking crunchy, sweet, fresh and completely awesome. Don't overcook your vegies or overdress your salads (see page 91)—it's just a crime to serve something soggy and overdone. A drizzle of olive oil and a squeeze of lemon on some steamed vegetables, a crunchy chopped salad of iceberg lettuce, cucumber, parsley leaves, some shaved Parmesan cheese and a drizzle of dressing over the top . . . suddenly the eternal vegetable nag doesn't seem so bad.

STEAMED VEGIES Unless we're talking ratatouille or a vegetable stew, vegetables should be soft, but still bright and clean, with a subtle firm bite. Most green vegetables require 3–5 minutes for steaming, so get the water boiling and do this as your last task before plating up.

TO BOIL OR NOT TO BOIL? Vegies that grow above the ground should be added to boiling water and those that grow below the ground should be put into cold water which you bring to the boil. This stops them overcooking on the outside before the inside is cooked.

NOT IN THE FRIDGE! Number one rule about tomatoes? Not in the fridge. A chilled tomato is a sorry sight. It has less flavour and the texture is just odd. If you're tired of those half-cut tomatoes you wrap in plastic wrap, store in the fridge and never use, here's a good idea—buy cherry tomatoes instead.

HOW TO STORE SALAD GREENS The high water content of salad greens makes them highly perishable, but properly stored they can last up to a week. First, wash them thoroughly in several changes of cold water to remove any sand or grit. Be careful not to bruise and batter them, as any bruising will show up as brown the next day. Then dry them thoroughly in a salad spinner or wrap in a cotton tea towel and shake the water off. Don't pack them too tightly, and wrap in kitchen paper before putting them in plastic or storage bags. Press all the air out of the bags and store them in the crisper of the refrigerator.

VEGIES AND SCOURERS The humble plastic scouring pad has a second great use—to scrub vegetables! Use it to scrub potatoes, carrots and other root vegetables. You'll find there's no need for peeling, so more nutrients are left in (just under the skin). Another useful hint is to hold vegetables with the scourer when grating or slicing on the mandoline. It will help to protect your knuckles.

by the way

CANNED, FROZEN OR FRESH?

Fresh is usually best, but if isn't just picked, canned or frozen may be better. A lot of goodness can be lost in the time between picking and cooking at home. Think about it—a tomato is picked and from grower it goes to the market, then to a greengrocer or supermarket in a massive refrigerated truck. This is why people often argue food from markets, sold directly by the farmer, is best. Canned or frozen fruits and vegetables are great convenience foods and they lose little of their natural goodness in the processing. I always buy fresh green vegetables, but love a can of tomatoes for cooking. Canned stone fruits and pulses such as kidney, borlotti, cannellini and chickpeas cope pretty well in a can. Plus, there is something to be said for convenience.

HERBS & SPICES

HERBS

Pots of basil, rosemary, thyme, mint, parsley, sage, coriander, chervil and tarragon sit on windowsills the world over. In Italy, a sprig of oregano lifts a simple grilled fish, while in Sweden some chopped dill gives gravlax its unique flavour. In Britain, a roast lamb is turned into something genius with a mint-packed sauce. Herbs are the easiest way to give a fresh twist to leftovers, and they're the miraculous secret ingredient in kitchens across the globe. Try growing your own herbs in pots in the garden, balcony or windowsill.

BASIL is perhaps the most popular and famous herb for Italian cooking, but is also used in the Far East. It goes perfectly with tomato. It's best fresh, not dried, torn over pasta or pizza, used to make pesto, or thrown into a salad.

BAY is a small tree with sturdy and shiny green leaves that you can use dried or fresh. A single leaf will add depth of flavour to stocks and stews.

CHERVIL has small delicate leaves and has a very slight aniseed flavour. It's lovely fresh, just tossed into a salad or sprinkled whole over a dish to decorate it.

CORIANDER is two in one—it's a herb and a spice. The pungent green herb, which looks but tastes nothing like parsley, is also known as cilantro, or Chinese parsley. It's used in Mexican, Indian and Asian cooking. The roots are packed with flavour; just wash them well and finely chop with the stalks and fry with onions and garlic for a curry or stir-fry, then add the leaves later. Coriander has a strong distinct flavour.

MINT is often associated with sweet things, like chocolate. But fresh it's lovely with stone fruits such as peaches and nectarines. It's also great tossed into a green salad, used to make mint sauce for roast lamb, or in a salty watermelon salad (see page 91).

PARSLEY is a common, soft herb that comes as either flat-leaf (also known as Italian parsley) or curly. The leaves are great chopped and scattered through salads, over pasta, vegetables or most grilled meat. Stalks can be finely chopped and used to flavour stocks and soups.

ROSEMARY is a shrubby wooden bush that looks a lot like lavender. Its thin leaves resemble pine needles and are amazing with lamb. It's often used in bread, as well as with beef and other strong Mediterranean flavours like olive oil, garlic and olives.

SAGE is a pretty herb with long, slightly furry leaves. It's great pressed into pork before grilling or chopped and added to stuffings. You'll often find it in sausages. It's great fried in butter until crispy, and then drizzled over ravioli.

TARRAGON has long slender green leaves and tastes a lot like aniseed, which is similar to licorice. It goes brilliantly with chicken, especially tucked under the skin of a roast chook with butter.

THYME is a woody herb that's totally easy to grow yourself. Its tiny perfumed leaves are great in stews, stocks and pressed into steaks before grilling. It goes well with all sorts of vegetables.

HOW TO

STORE HERBS The best way to store herbs is in the garden, still fresh and growing. Grow herbs in pots on the balcony or by a windowsill, and just pick them as needed. But, if you only have bought ones, you can store them in the refrigerator. Wash them thoroughly and then shake till fairly dry. Wrap them in kitchen paper, then place in an airtight plastic container. Herbs often dry out in the fridge, so dampen the kitchen towel lightly if this happens.

DRY YOUR OWN HERBS Love herbs, hate waste. Here's how to keep that massive bunch of dill, thyme, or oregano you can't use up right now. Use the microwave. Simply wash, remove from stems and lay in a single layer on kitchen towels. Microwave on high for about 2 minutes and they will be dried ready for storing airtight by the time they have cooled. If not, repeat for another 30 seconds in the microwave.

SPICE GIRLS AND CHAPS

Nothing drives me crazier than hesitant diners who shy away from spice—'Ooh no thanks, I don't like things too spicy.' WHAT? I think what people often mean by this is that they don't like too much chilli-based heat in their food, which is fair enough. But spice? Spice is about flavour, aroma, colour, sourness, texture and deliciousness. Spice reacts with the flavours of meat and vegetables in different specific and incredible ways—cumin added to lamb is very different to cinnamon added—a dish can completely change depending on which of these two you add. Remember that spice doesn't always make a dish hot. If you're not sure about a spice, have a sniff, and use it in moderation at first.

CARDAMOM is an aromatic spice of a plant from the ginger family, generally sold in its pod. It's amazing with milk-based desserts as well as in savoury dishes. There are two varieties—the large, dark brown cardamom is more pungent than the small, pale green variety. The seeds can be used ground or whole.

CHILLI POWDER Indian chilli powder is made from ground chillies. It is much hotter than the Mexican-style chilli powder, which is a spice mixture that includes ground cumin seeds.

CINNAMON is available in 7 centimetre (2¾ inch) long dried quills or sticks and in ground form. The whole spice is often left in curries and pilafs as a garnish. But it can also be used in sweet dishes. It has a delicate, sweet taste and a heady fragrance.

CLOVES are dark brown little spears that have a sharp, pungent taste and fragrant aroma. Biting on a whole one can make your mouth go a little numb (so they're great for toothaches!). They are used whole, are great on a glazed ham, or ground in curries and pilafs.

CORIANDER SEEDS are an essential component of curries and can be used in baking cakes, gingerbread and biscuits. It has a strong distinct flavour.

CUMIN SEEDS are one of the key ingredients in prepared curry powders. It has a pungent sharp taste and is used ground or whole. It is a caraway-shaped seed, usually medium brown.

FENNEL SEEDS have a sweet licorice flavour but are usually used in savoury dishes.

NUTMEG has gentle aroma and a sweet taste. It goes very well with cardamom in milk-based desserts or rice pudding. Nutmeg is best purchased whole and grated when needed.

SAFFRON is the world's most expensive spice by weight and comes from a flower called the saffron crocus, which produce three vivid crimson stigmas each. The spice lends a richness and perfume that cannot be imitated. Saffron, as well as turmeric, is used to make curries. It turns any dish a pale red.

TURMERIC is a member of the ginger family and has bright yellow flesh. It's also extremely good for you and is said to help prevent many diseases. It's most readily available as a yellow powder. Good quality turmeric lends a characteristic yellow colour to a dish and gives a wonderful woody aroma.

in my world

NICE SPICE

Spice was used instead of money in many old civilisations, including in ancient Rome. Humans have been using spice since 50 000 BC. The Egyptians used it for embalming and by 1000 BC spice was used in medicine in China and India. In the Roman Empire, people would sometimes get paid in salt. This is where the term 'worth his salt' comes from. Some say the word 'salary' comes from these times, because soldiers would get paid a 'salarium' or salary so they could buy salt.

BAKING

Baking is chemistry first, poetry second. Apologies to creative geniuses out there, but the premier rule of baking is to follow the recipe. We have a saying in my house that sprouted from too many failed efforts to put IKEA shelves together without directions, and cakes together off the top of our heads: 'If all else fails, follow the instructions.' Baking is not some culinary scam meant only for gastronomic gurus. Actually, it's one of the simplest things you can do in the kitchen. And it's certainly one of the most satisfying.

PREHEAT OVEN Preheat the oven properly. Don't skimp by putting a cake in too early or it won't rise as it should.

CREAMING When a recipe says to 'cream the butter and sugar', it means literally that. Get the butter a little soft (though not melted or warm) by taking it out of the fridge an hour beforehand. Using electric beaters (or a wooden spoon and plenty of muscle), beat the butter by itself for a few seconds until it goes creamy, then add the sugar and beat them together at a high speed. After about 8–10 minutes (no sooner!) it will go quite pale and fluffy. Stop too soon and the cake will be dense. For the cake to rise and have a light, airy texture, creaming for long enough is essential. This is one of the most important steps for successful baking.

FOLDING The trick is combining ingredients without letting air escape. This term is common in recipes using egg whites. Use a large metal spoon to cut through the centre of the mixture, then fold half the mixture over the top of the other half. Repeat until mixture is combined. Use a large metal spoon because it deflates the mixture less.

SIFTING In recipes, 'sifted flour' is not the same as 'flour, sifted'. The first gives a measurement of flour that's already been sifted. The second gives a measurement of flour that is straight out of the packet, which you sift after it's been measured. There is usually less flour in the 'sifted flour' version.

MEASURING FLOUR Don't dip a cup measurement into a bag of flour, because that will compact it and you'll get too much. Precision is essential when baking. Instead, put the cup measurement on the bench and spoon flour into it so it overflows (messy but precise). Don't pack it down. Then, scrape the top of the flour off using a knife—this will give you a more accurate amount. However, the best way to measure flour and other dry ingredients is to weigh them.

UNCOOKED DOUGH Most uncooked biscuit dough can be rolled in a cylinder shape, wrapped in plastic wrap and frozen for up to 3 months. Then, when you need a few biscuits or cookies, just slice and bake.

WHAT SIZE TIN? Use the correct size tin for the job. Get it wrong and the recipe might not work.

NON-STICK TINS Non-stick tins are easier to clean, so I almost always use them. But always grease and line a tin as well rather than rely on its non-stick qualities.

LOAF TINS In recipes using a loaf tin, the measurements given refer to the base of the tin.

WHICH TIN TO BUY Invest in the best cake and loaf tins you can, because cheaper ones tend to warp in the oven heat. Also, the sturdier the tin the better it will conduct heat, making the result so much better.

STORE BISCUITS Cool biscuits and cookies completely before you store them in an airtight container so they don't go soft.

STORE CAKES Store cooled and un-iced cakes in an airtight container for about 5 days. You can freeze a cake for about 2 months, then bring to room temperature before you ice it.

ICING Let cupcakes and cakes cool completely before you ice them, or the icing will melt.

WHEN TO EAT Cupcakes and scones should be enjoyed the day they are made. But you can freeze un-iced cupcakes for up to 3 months, and then let them reach room temperature before you ice them.

HOW TO PLATE FOOD

Wonder why food in restaurants often looks so incredible? Sure, the actual food has a lot to do with it, but so does how they 'plate' it–how they put it on the plate and decorate it. One trick restaurants use is not to serve up too much food on a single plate (there's always seconds!). Create a wide, empty border on a plate by piling the food in the centre. Also, instead of laying food out in one layer, try stacking it–putting meat on top of veg or some leafy greens, making a pretty assortment of foods to one side (like some edible flowers from the garden or a pretty tangle of beans), and even 'painting' a sauce on the plate and then placing the food on just one small part of that. Experiment and practise. Notice how food is plated in cookbooks and in restaurants to get new ideas.

THE BIG FREEZE

Freezing is one of the most convenient methods of preserving food to make it last a lot longer. Extreme cold stops the growth of microorganisms and slows down chemical changes that cause food to spoil. Even so, food won't keep in the freezer forever. Here's a guide to freezing food safely.

COOL TRICKS

Get yourself a nice clean freezer to start. Chip away any major icicles or large puddles of frozen water. Throw out anything that was frozen more than about 8 months ago.

Get food to room temperature, no hotter, before freezing it.
Pop the food in a container that fits: not too big, not too small. There should be a little space, so the food can expand a little, but not loads of it.
If freezing more than one container, help them freeze more quickly by spreading them out on various shelves, rather than stacking them. Stack them after the food is frozen if you need to. (It also helps to set the freezer temperature to its coldest setting a few hours before.)
Don't overload the freezer all at once with unfrozen food. A few small containers at a time is okay.
Defrost food overnight in the fridge. Once it's defrosted, either use it immediately, or pop it in the fridge and use it that day. Never cook something while it's still a bit frozen, especially meat.
Never, ever, ever defrost something and then refreeze it. You'll get food poisoning!

HOW LONG CAN I FREEZE THIS FOR?

1 MONTH

Whole bananas / Vegetable soups and stews / Mashed potato / Cooked rice and pasta / Cooked green vegetables / Raw egg yolks

2 MONTHS

Baked goods (pies, quiche) / Raw egg whites / Cooked meat (stews, lasagne, bolognaise, casseroles) / Cooked burger patties and mince

3 MONTHS

Raw burger patties and mince / Milk and buttermilk / Bread rolls, bagels, tortillas / Fatty fish (salmon and tuna) / Cooked fish and most shellfish

4 MONTHS

Berries / Grated cheese / Ice cream and sorbet

6 MONTHS

Shellfish like lobster and crab / Raw green vegetables / Lean fish (like flathead, barramundi)

12 MONTHS

Raw beef, lamb, pork, chicken, duck / Butter / Cookie dough

NEVER FREEZE

Whole or hard-boiled eggs / Potatoes (raw or cooked) / Lettuce / Tomatoes / Onions / Sliced ham and cold cuts

LOVE FOOD, HATE WASTE

No self-respecting chef ever wastes a thing if they can help it. All the very best chefs are careful when shopping, buying only what they will use. If calculations go amiss and there are ingredients left over, they'll just find another way to use it. If the very best master chefs can do this in big commercial kitchens, you can do it at home too!

- Keep an eye on how much a recipe serves and how many you're cooking for, and alter the recipe to work for you.
- Meat, fish and chicken servings should generally be no more than 180 g (6 oz) per person. Allow for one potato or ½ cup (100 g/3½ oz) rice and 1–2 cups of salad or vegetables per person if you're having meat.
- Get some snap-lock bags and plastic containers with lids for keeping those yummy leftovers.
- Label and date dishes you're freezing, so you can remember when you made them. Check your freezer regularly so you can eat up meals before they're ruined.
- Avoid refrigerator clutter. Before you cook something from scratch, check there's not another delicious dish waiting to be eaten.
- Write a shopping list of everything you need. Check what's in the fridge and pantry, then cross off what you don't need to buy.
- Buying something in bulk may seem like a good deal, but think about when and if you'll use it. Ever thrown out half a bag of rice or flour because of weevils or pantry moths? It may seem more expensive to buy things as you need them, but there's usually much less waste.
- Rather than waste leftover ingredients, make double the quantity of dishes such as lasagne and curries and freeze for later.
- Help rid the world of landfill! Do you know where those containers and bags you throw in the bin go? They get squashed, packed up and thrown in a hole in the ground, and the rubbish then poisons the earth. This is land we could turn into playgrounds or parks, or just leave for other creatures to use and build lives on. When shopping, don't pop your various vegetables in separate bags—they're fine rattling around in your shopping basket for now. Choose brands with less packaging, and always recycle paper and plastic packaging where possible.
- Take your own non-plastic shopping bags to the supermarket so you can say 'No thanks' to more plastic bags. Hooray for you (and the environment)!

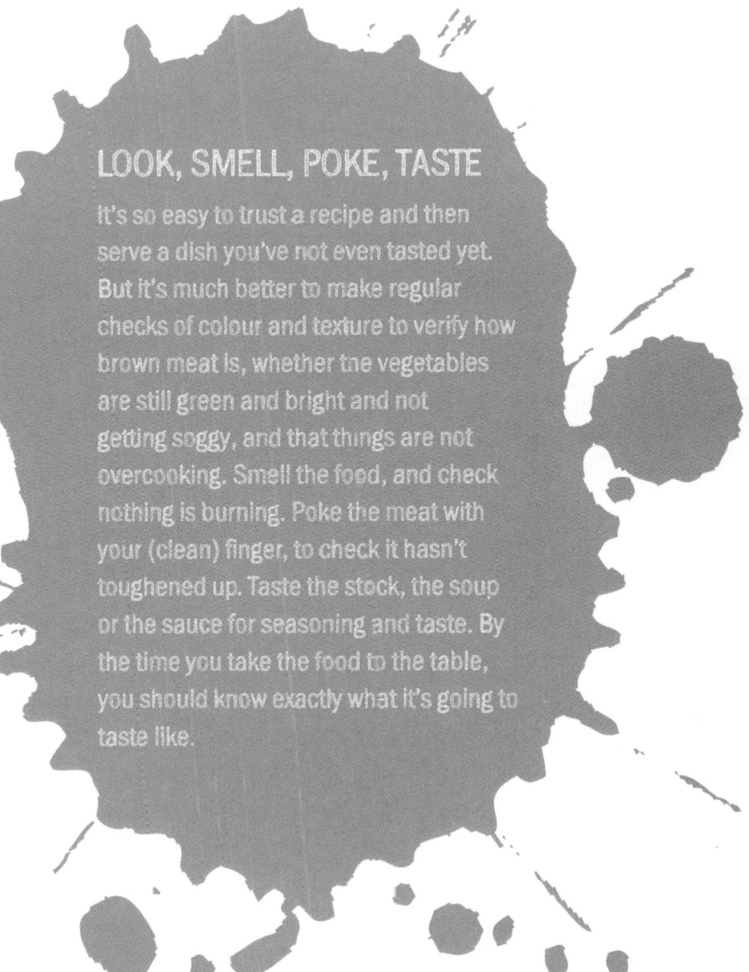

LOOK, SMELL, POKE, TASTE

It's so easy to trust a recipe and then serve a dish you've not even tasted yet. But it's much better to make regular checks of colour and texture to verify how brown meat is, whether the vegetables are still green and bright and not getting soggy, and that things are not overcooking. Smell the food, and check nothing is burning. Poke the meat with your (clean) finger, to check it hasn't toughened up. Taste the stock, the soup or the sauce for seasoning and taste. By the time you take the food to the table, you should know exactly what it's going to taste like.

KITCHEN CONFIDENT

AVOID FOOD POISONING

Food, bacteria, nasties; they're not a good mix. We've all heard horror stories of nights spent in bathroom after a questionable meal, so let's not make it happen after a meal you made. Good food preparation habits are important to avoid the spread of unhealthy bacteria. Here are some rules:

Wash your hands before, during and after preparation. Think of keeping a pump pack of antibacterial liquid wash on the kitchen sink and keep a hand towel for drying, rather than use tea towels for hands.
Always check the expiry date on food and refrigerate fresh food as soon as possible. If freezing meat and seafood, do so on the day of purchase.
Leave frozen food to thaw in the refrigerator rather than on the kitchen bench because bacteria multiply quickly at room temperature.
Use separate chopping boards to prepare meat and vegetables, and thoroughly clean and scald or disinfect the boards after use.
Separate raw foods from cooked, especially meat. Use different boards and knives for each.
Keep hot foods hot and cold foods cold.
Use paper towels for wiping food that is to be cleaned.
Regularly freshen up dishcloths and sinks by filling up the sink with diluted disinfectant and letting the cloths soak for a while.
Hang tea towels that have been washed in the sunshine to dry, rather than using a dryer—it kills more bacteria (and saves the environment!).
Cool hot food that is to be stored in the refrigerator as quickly as possible. Pack airtight and refrigerate as soon as cooled.

DIRTY DISHES

I firmly believe that if you're the one who cooked, you shouldn't have to wash up. It's a family rule at my place, and one I smugly remember whenever I cook. But, as someone who was once diabolically messy in the kitchen, I have literally been forced to learn how to clean up as I go. There were too many near washing-up mutinies, as flatmates were left reeling at the vast trail of pots and pans left behind in wake of my culinary genius. Anyone who works in a professional kitchen learns this lesson fast. There's just no room for messy cooks in there—imagine what Gordon Ramsay would say!

Here's how to minimise that pile of dishes in the sink, and keep the kitchen peace.

Learn the beauty of the one-pot meal. Where possible, bring the dish you cooked in to the table, and serve straight out from it. If this means investing in a decent-looking baking dish or a smart salad bowl, so be it.
Use your time efficiently. If the soup has to simmer for 20 minutes, use that time to wash the boards, knives and anything else you used. Now is not the time to check your emails.
Get a decent knife. You really need one sharp knife that fits your hand, and works for chopping and slicing. This saves using a different knife for every ingredient in the recipe.
Rinse measuring cups, spoons and mixing bowls as you cook. This means you use the same one-cup measure a few times when baking a cake, instead of using one for the sugar and then another one for the buttermilk or whatever.
Wipe up the benches as you go. A clear bench makes for a clear head, and you'll find it a lot easier to remember what step you're at in a recipe. It also means you can jump from marinating chicken to starting on dessert without worrying about food contamination.

Not-quite huevos rancheros * Soft-boiled egg with toast soldiers * Ramekin eggs (3 ways): Pizza topping eggs; Benedict's breakfast; Green eggs and ham * Asparagus soldiers * Poached eggs with rocket and prosciutto * Frog in the hole * I heart eggs omelette * Eggy crumpets with crispy bacon * Great-fast smoothie * Peaches and cream smoothie * Fruit-only frappe * Crunchy nut muesli * Poached peaches plums please * Breakfast blueberry quinoa * Apple maple bircher * Crunchy chewy muesli bars * Bacon and corn muffins * Potato hash browns * Baked beans * Wrapped-up breakfast burritos * Zucchini fritters with melty cheese * Mega tortilla Española * Spoonable French toast with maple berries * Raspberry pikelets * Eyes closed strawberry jam * Cinnamon berry muffins

BREAKFAST

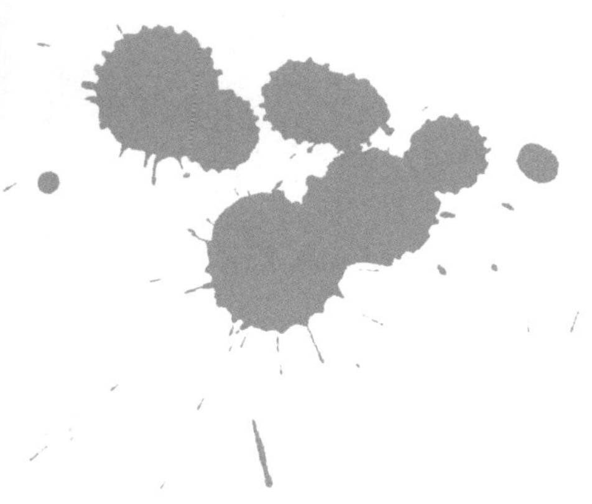

Weekday mornings hardly need a recipe book ...

... It's more of a toast-out-the-door kind of time. So, you can either wait for Saturday morning to read this chapter, or start making things like granola bars, muffins and bircher muesli ahead, so you've actually got some edible choices before you dash.

Otherwise, the essential consideration when thinking about breakfast is the gastronomic opportunities it opens up. I'm not a stickler for what to have for breakfast, in the same way I don't berate myself for eating cereal for dinner. I won't be bored, though. I just refuse to be. I want breakfast to be a proclamation of what sort of day I have planned—a note-to-self about potential. If the day starts well, surely that bodes well.

The habit of breakfast can take some training. I was eventually won over by the fact that I felt half asleep by 10 a.m. if I didn't eat breakfast, plus I was told—correctly!—that you're more likely to gain weight and feel generally unhealthy if you skip breakfast. Odd as it may seem, eating breakfast gets your metabolism going, and that's only a good thing.

I got through university fuelled on tortilla Española. My best friend and I would make it for breakfast, stir too many sugars into too many coffees and be on our way for the four hours of class a day. This is the sort of food you need to sit through an English exam, or flop on the lawn and watch boys play cricket all day in the sun while you try to read *Sense and Sensibility*. It's the fire of the studiers, for the players, for the hungry among us.

Breakfast says 'I can be bothered'. You know, with life. With exercise and energy and giddying activity packed into one expansive day. Breakfast says, 'I have things to do and people to meet.' It's a meal-driven epiphany we all need to have.

And if you need more convincing, make eggy crumpets with crispy bacon and maple syrup for brunch, and you'll never go back to skipping breakfast again.

VANS
"OFF THE WALL"

NOT-QUITE HUEVOS RANCHEROS **

This take on *huevos rancheros*, or ranch eggs, is a not-so-authentic version of a Tex-Mex breakfast tortilla.

1/3 cup (80 ml/2 1/2 fl oz) olive oil
1 red capsicum (pepper), seeds removed, cut in 4 lengthways
4 mini tortillas
1/2 cup (50 g/1 3/4 oz) grated cheddar cheese
4 free-range eggs
2 vine-ripened tomatoes, finely diced
1 red onion, finely diced
1/3 bunch coriander (cilantro), roughly chopped
400 g (14 oz) tin black beans, rinsed and drained
Tabasco sauce (optional)

01 Heat a heavy-based saucepan over medium heat. Add a few drops of oil and fry capsicum pieces for 3 minutes each side. Remove from heat, cut into julienne and set aside.
02 In the same pan, heat a little more oil, fry one tortilla until light golden, then flip. Sprinkle 1 tbsp cheese on the tortilla in the pan, then break 1 egg into the middle of the tortilla. Drag any egg white that has spilled out into the pan back onto the tortilla, and season with sea salt and freshly ground black pepper.
03 Flip the tortilla, being careful not to break the egg yolk. Fry for 30 seconds, or a little longer for a well-done egg.
04 Flip the tortilla, egg side up, out onto a plate. Sprinkle with a little tomato, onion, coriander, beans, more cheese, and a few drops of Tabasco if you like.
05 Repeat with remaining tortillas.
06 Roll the tortilla and eat with your hands, or leave it flat on a plate and devour using a knife and fork.
Serves 4 for breakfast or as a light snack

SOFT-BOILED EGG WITH TOAST SOLDIERS *

There are about as many techniques to soft-boil an egg as there are types of chicken in the world. But I use the method my grandmother taught me.

1 free-range egg
2 slices of wholegrain or seeded bread

01 Submerge a large egg in a small saucepan filled with enough cold water to cover it. Bring to the boil over medium–high heat. Once the water begins to boil, set a timer for 3 minutes.
02 When time's up, plunge the egg into cold water to stop it cooking.
03 While the egg is cooking, put 2 slices of bread in the toaster. When it pops, butter the toast, give it a grinding of sea salt and freshly ground black pepper, then cut into soldiers. Serve your egg in a little egg cup, with your toast soldiers on the side for dipping.
Serves 1

by the way

FRESH EGGS OR NOT?

They're covered in shell and smell like nothing, so how long has that egg been in the fridge? How do you tell whether an egg has gone off, without cracking it open? Float it in cold water. A freshly laid egg will basically sink to the bottom, while one that is too old to use will float on top of the water like a semi-sunk boat. If it's underwater, with a tiny bit poking through the surface, you're still OK.

how to

RETRIEVING BROKEN EGG SHELLS

If you've ever cracked an egg, then found bits of broken shell in the bowl and tried to pick the blooming things out with your fingers–after all, nobody likes egg shells in their food–you'll know how hard this is. Stop right there: just use the broken shell in your hand to fish out any broken bits in the bowl. I don't know why it works, but it does. We'll just chalk that one up to magic.

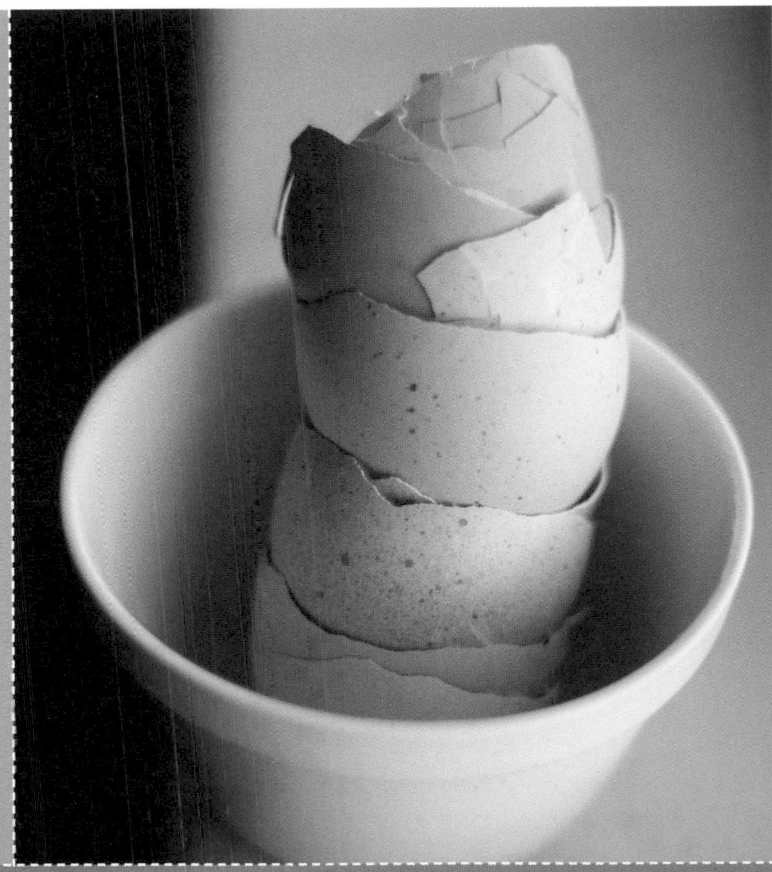

how to

SCRAMBLING *LES OEUFS*

Scrambling eggs, or *les oeufs* for our French friends, is trickier than it seems. You really don't want some spongy, grainy, dried matter atop your bread. Here's what you do.

Don't use a high heat. You need to be patient to cook the perfect scrambled curds. Use a medium-low heat, and stir constantly. Pull the pan off the heat if it gets too hot–the eggs should still be soft and wet, and will keep cooking a little even once the heat is off.

Ditch the fork. It will wreck your pan, and won't stop the eggs overcooking on the bottom. Instead, use a flat-bottomed rubber spatula or wooden spoon–or if you're using a non-stick or cast-iron pan, you can use chopsticks.

Adding water, milk and even cream to your eggs before you scramble them might make them a little watery, just because the liquid can separate from the egg. Add a dash of cream if you must, but a better bet is to stir a spoonful of crème fraîche through the eggs once they've been removed from the heat.

RAMEKIN EGGS {3 WAYS}

A gastro-dude must be flexible to the reality of what's in the fridge, and what's in the cupboard. But this eggy breakfast—or lunch, or dinner—is flexible to the wants and needs of the most discerning appetites and makes an easy and complete meal. All you need is a wide saucepan with a lid, which fits two ramekins inside. You can top these cool little egg pots with almost anything you fancy, like some herbs from the garden maybe, or try these ideas.

Pizza topping eggs *

1 golden shallot, finely chopped
1 medium tomato, cut into 5 mm (1/4 inch) dice, or 6 cherry tomatoes
4 basil leaves, thinly sliced
1/4 cup (25 g/1 oz) grated cheddar cheese
2 tsp olive oil
4 free-range eggs

01 Divide shallot, tomato, basil, cheese and oil between two ramekins, then crack 2 eggs into each ramekin. Do not stir or touch. Season with sea salt and freshly ground black pepper.
02 Place ramekins in a wide saucepan and pour about 100 ml (3½ fl oz) water into pan, being careful not to get water in the eggs. Cover pan with a lid and cook over medium heat for 10 minutes, or until egg whites are cooked but yolks are still runny.
03 Carefully remove ramekins from the pan. Serve on a plate with a teaspoon.
Serves 2

Benedict's breakfast *

1 large handful baby spinach, roughly chopped
1 spring onion (scallion), sliced
1 garlic clove, finely chopped
4 slices smoked salmon, roughly sliced
4 free-range eggs
2 tbsp pouring (whipping) cream
olive oil, for drizzling

01 Divide spinach, spring onion, garlic and salmon between two ramekins, then crack 2 eggs into each ramekin. Add 1 tbsp cream to each ramekin and season with sea salt and freshly ground black pepper. Drizzle with a little oil, but do not stir or touch.
02 Place ramekins in a wide saucepan and pour about 100 ml (3½ fl oz) water into the pan, being careful not to get water in the eggs. Cover pan with a lid and cook over medium heat for 10 minutes, or until egg whites are cooked but yolks are still runny.
03 Carefully remove ramekins from the saucepan. Serve on a plate with a teaspoon.
Serves 2

Green eggs and ham *

1 large handful baby spinach, roughly chopped
1/4 cup (35 g/1 1/4 oz) grated parmesan cheese
4 slices free-range ham or prosciutto, cut into strips
2 tsp olive oil
4 free-range eggs

01 Divide spinach, parmesan, ham or prosciutto and oil between two ramekins, then crack 2 eggs into each ramekin. Do not stir or touch. Season with salt and freshly ground black pepper.
02 Place ramekins in a wide saucepan and pour about 100 ml (3½ fl oz) water into the pan, being careful not to get water in the eggs. Cover pan with a lid and cook over medium heat for 10 minutes, or until egg whites are cooked but yolks are still runny.
03 Carefully remove the ramekins from the pan. Serve on a plate with a teaspoon.
Serves 2

ASPARAGUS SOLDIERS *

This is the toast-free equivalent of boiled eggs with toast soldiers. Dip the blanched asparagus into a runny egg yolk instead.

1 bunch (175 g/6 oz) asparagus
4 free-range eggs

01 First prepare the asparagus. Break off the tougher, non-pointy ends of the asparagus stalks, at the point where they will snap easily. Place asparagus in a frying pan two-thirds full of boiling salted water and cook for 4–5 minutes, or until tender. Lift out with a slotted spatula or tongs onto a paper towel and keep warm by covering with a plate or large bowl.
02 Meanwhile, place eggs in a saucepan with warm water over medium heat (see soft-boiled egg recipe page 20). Simmer for 3 minutes for soft-boiled eggs, or 4 minutes for medium-boiled eggs. Serve in egg cups on plates, with the asparagus alongside and sea salt and freshly ground black pepper to hand. Cut the top off the egg using a sharp knife.
Serves 2 hungry people or 4 not so hungry ones

POACHED EGGS WITH ROCKET AND PROSCIUTTO **

Poaching an egg is an essential skill for the chef-to-be . . . for the kitchen connoisseur . . . for *you*. You can totally do this.

2 tsp white vinegar
4 free-range eggs
1 handful baby rocket (arugula), stalks trimmed
squeeze of lemon juice
1 tsp olive oil
4 thick slices toast
4 slices prosciutto

01 Bring a medium-sized saucepan of water to the boil over high heat. Add the vinegar.
02 Crack 1 egg into a small bowl. Use a large spoon to swirl the boiling water to make a whirlpool. Carefully pour the egg into the centre of the whirlpool. Cook for 1–2 minutes for a soft egg, or to your liking. Use a slotted spoon to transfer the poached egg to a plate, then cover loosely with a bowl to keep warm. Repeat with remaining eggs.
03 Place the rocket, lemon juice and oil in a medium bowl. Season with sea salt and freshly ground black pepper and toss well. To serve, place a slice of hot toast on each plate and top with the rocket, a slice of prosciutto and a poached egg. Finish with a grinding of black pepper to taste.
Serves 4

FROG IN THE HOLE *

Round egg, round hole. The egg sits in a little bready nook, so you can delve into it with your knife and fork. I like mine with tomato sauce (ketchup) or homemade baked beans.

2 thick slices wholemeal (whole-wheat) or seeded bread
1 tbsp butter, for pan-frying
2 free-range eggs

01 Use a round, 6–8 cm (2½–3¼ inch) diameter cutter (or a small tumbler) to cut a hole in the centre of each slice of bread. Discard the cut-out holes. Lightly toast the slices in the toaster.
02 Meanwhile, heat a large frying pan over medium heat. Melt butter in pan and fry both slices of bread, turning once, until golden.
03 Crack an egg into each hole, then cook until egg whites turn white—about 3 minutes.
04 Transfer to a plate using a spatula. Season with sea salt and freshly ground black pepper and serve.
Serves 2

I HEART EGGS OMELETTE **

This is an oops-we've-run-out-of-everything lifesaver. If all you have are a few eggs sitting all lonely in the fridge, you'll still have a great breakfast, or dinner. Experts say that a traditional French omelette of 2–3 eggs per person should be beaten, cooked and served in 90 seconds. So make sure you have the filling completely ready before you cook the eggs. An omelette should be served *baveuse*, or frothy—never well-done. I've added asparagus, just because I think they're delicious sticks of green, but you don't have to. Maybe try some chopped herbs instead?

4 free-range eggs
1 bunch (175 g/6 oz) asparagus (optional)
2 tsp butter
⅓ cup (30 g/1 oz) grated cheese

01 Crack eggs into a bowl. Beat with a fork, just enough to blend the yolks and whites. Season with sea salt and freshly ground black pepper.
02 Meanwhile blanch the asparagus in a saucepan of boiling, salted water for 3–5 minutes, until just cooked. Refresh under cold water, cut stems in half acrossways and set aside.
03 Melt butter in a medium non-stick frying pan over medium heat, tilting the pan to lightly coat the base and sides with butter. When the butter just starts to colour, pour in the eggs. With a wooden spoon or silicone spatula, pull the edges of the egg towards the centre of the omelette as it thickens. Let the liquid run into the empty spaces in the pan. Quickly repeat so there is no more liquid, but the eggs are still soft. Scatter the cheese and asparagus over the eggs.
04 Lift the handle of the pan so the omelette rolls over itself and onto a warmed plate. Serve immediately.
Serves 2

EGGY CRUMPETS WITH CRISPY BACON *

Having rummaged through the cupboards in a frantic search for bread to make French toast, with no happy find, I still refused to give in. I did, perhaps oddly, have crumpets. Maple syrup and crispy bacon are perfect additions. These are great if you're not mad keen on eggs—the mixture completely soaks into the crumpets, rewarding you with soft, gooey-centred things.

2 large free-range eggs
2 tbsp milk
olive oil or rice bran oil, for pan-frying
4 slices free-range smoked bacon
4 crumpets
maple syrup, for drizzling

01 Crack eggs into a bowl. Add milk and whisk together with a pinch of sea salt and freshly ground black pepper.
02 Heat a few drops of oil in a large non-stick frying pan over medium heat, then fry the bacon, turning once, until crispy.
03 Meanwhile, drop crumpets into the egg mixture, and really drench them to absorb the mixture. Turn them a few times to soak up the egg.
04 Push the bacon to one side of the pan and tilt the pan to allow the fat to run around a bit. Add crumpets and fry until golden, about 3 minutes each side.
05 Top the eggy crumpets with bacon. Serve drizzled with maple syrup.
Serves 2

GREAT-FAST SMOOTHIE *

Here's a weekday special for people who have neither the time nor the inclination to eat much in the morning. The peanut butter or healthy almond butter adds protein, and the chocolate malt adds a sneaky treaty element that makes having breakfast not seem like such a chore at all. This is a great way to use up bananas, which you can cut into 4 chunks and store in snap-lock bags in the freezer for this throw-it-all-together smoothie.

1 peeled frozen banana, cut in four
1 cup (250 ml/9 fl oz) cold milk (or soy milk)
1 tbsp maple syrup
3 tsp chocolate malt powder
1 tbsp peanut butter or almond butter

01 Place all ingredients in a blender and whiz to mix. Pour into a tall glass and drink.
Serves 1

PEACHES AND CREAM SMOOTHIE *

This smoothie is easy and quick. You can use tinned peaches. Fresh is better but, come the early morning hours, I'd rather compromise on 'purity' than have nothing to eat at all. I often replace half the milk with coconut water, which you can buy from most decent supermarkets now.

1 cup (200 g/7 oz) peaches, stones removed, roughly chopped
1½ cups (375 ml/13 fl oz) milk
½ tbsp honey or maple syrup
¼ cup (25 g/1 oz) rolled (porridge) oats, finely chopped

01 Place all ingredients in a blender and whiz to mix. Pour into a tall glass and drink.
Serves 1

FRUIT-ONLY FRAPPE *

This super-quick breakfast is packed with cold-fighting nutrients—and is completely fat free. It's cold and summery and is great whizzed with a splash of cranberry or apple juice.

1 orange, peeled and white pith removed, cut into chunks
½ cup (125 g/4½ oz) frozen raspberries
½ cup (125 g/4½ oz) frozen blueberries

01 Place all ingredients in a blender and whiz until smooth. Serve immediately.
Serves 1

CRUNCHY NUT MUESLI *

⅓ cup (80 ml/2½ fl oz) vegetable oil
¾ cup (260 g/91/4 oz) honey or maple syrup
4 cups (400 g/14 oz) rolled (porridge) oats
1 cup (25 g/1 oz) puffed rice or barley
1 cup (125 g/4½ oz) slivered almonds
1 cup (155 g/5½ oz) raw pepitas (pumpkin seeds)
1 cup (75 g/2½ oz) wheatgerm
1 tbsp ground cinnamon
½ cup (125 g/4½ oz) roughly chopped dried prunes
½ cup (75 g/2½ oz) dried cranberries

01 Preheat oven to 180°C (350°F). In a large bowl, mix oil and honey or maple syrup together. Add oats, puffed rice or barley, almonds, pepitas, wheatgerm and cinnamon. Toss until combined with honey mixture, using a large spoon to stir until evenly coated.
02 Spread mixture evenly in a large baking dish. Bake for 25 minutes, or until golden brown, mixing every 10 minutes or so to ensure muesli browns evenly. Mix in prunes and cranberries and bake for another 10 minutes.
03 Remove from oven and set aside to cool. Store in an airtight container.
Makes enough for a week or two

try me *

POACHED PEACHES PLUMS PLEASE**

Sometimes I almost wish I had a family fraught with angst and drama, a sort of harmless catastrophe of bumbling and exuberance. And then I'd just sit them all down with a bowlful of this, maybe with custard or a great spoonful of vanilla-spiked yoghurt and brown sugar. And I'd say, 'Here you are family, have this, just relax, it's going to be OK.' Pending such calamitous relatives, I'll have to eat it myself.

5 peaches or nectarines, or about 6 plums
4 cups (1 litre/35 fl oz) cranberry juice
2 tbsp caster (superfine) sugar
1 cinnamon stick
2 wide strips lemon or orange rind (no white pith)

01 Put kettle on, place fruit in a large bowl and cover with boiling water. Leave for 1 minute, then strain and run under cold water for 5 seconds. Peel skin away from fruit, then cut each in quarters and discard the stones.
02 In a large saucepan, heat cranberry juice, sugar, cinnamon and citrus rind over medium heat, stirring gently until sugar dissolves. Bring to a gentle simmer for 5 minutes.
03 Add fruit and simmer for 5 minutes, until fruit can be easily pierced with a fork. Remove fruit from poaching liquid with a slotted spoon or tongs and set aside to cool in a large jar or container with a lid.
04 Meanwhile, reduce the poaching liquid. Bring it to a simmer and leave for 10 minutes until reduced by about half.
05 Set poaching liquid aside to cool, discard citrus rind and cinnamon stick, then pour liquid over the fruit. Chill in the fridge until ready to eat.
Serves 4–6

TIP: Toss these onto porridge or muesli (granola), or just have straight up with a great dollop of yoghurt.

BREAKFAST BLUEBERRY QUINOA *

Pronounced 'keen-wa', quinoa is a seed that is usually used in savoury dishes. But it's also great as a hot, creamy cereal for those not keen on porridge. I love it in winter, topped with poached fruits (see recipe to the left), or fresh blueberries and maple syrup. It's super healthy but also gives you loads of energy.

2 cups (500 ml/17 fl oz) milk or soy milk
1 cup (200 g/7 oz) quinoa, rinsed
1/8 tsp ground cinnamon
1/2 tsp brown sugar
1 cup (155 g/5 1/2 oz) fresh blueberries

01 Bring milk to a gentle simmer in a small saucepan. Add quinoa and return to the boil. Reduce heat to low, then cover and simmer for about 10–12 minutes, until three-quarters of the milk has been absorbed.
02 Stir in cinnamon, sugar and a pinch of sea salt. Cook for another 5–8 minutes, until almost all the milk has been absorbed. Stir in half the blueberries and cook for 30 seconds. Serve topped with remaining blueberries, and maybe some extra milk and a sprinkling of brown sugar, if desired. It's great with a big dollop of natural yoghurt too.
Makes 2 serves, or 1 really large one

APPLE MAPLE BIRCHER *

This creamy, uncooked breakfast is halfway between porridge and muesli (granola), and is perfect for those who like neither, or both. Start this the night before—it takes just a second before you nip off to bed. You'll thank yourself for being such an awesome planner the next day.

2 cups (200 g/7 oz) rolled (porridge) oats
2 tbsp whole almonds or hazelnuts, roughly chopped
2 apples, roughly grated
½ cup (125 ml/4 fl oz) milk or apple juice
yoghurt, to serve
maple syrup, for drizzling
pinch of ground cinnamon

01 The night before, combine oats, nuts and apple in a bowl with 1 cup (250 ml/9 fl oz) water. Mix together well, cover with plastic wrap and leave in the fridge overnight.
02 In the morning, mix again, add milk or apple juice, then spoon into two bowls.
03 Top each with a dollop of yoghurt, a drizzle of maple syrup and a sprinkling of cinnamon. Add some extra grated apple or chopped nuts, if you like.
Serves 2

CRUNCHY CHEWY MUESLI BARS *

This is the ultimate breakfast on the run. It's full of nuts and seeds and is too easy to make. The ingredients may read like a list of all things healthy, but the muesli bar is actually quite high in sugar. One piece—two max—is probably more than enough . . . any more and you'll feel a little buzzy and buttery. The super-healthy chia seeds can be expensive, but are good to have on hand for this sort of thing; you can add them to muffins and homemade muesli (see page 27) too. Experiment with macadamia nuts instead of walnuts, and pepitas (pumpkin seeds) in place of the flaked almonds, if you fancy. Store these in the fridge or freezer, they're lovely cold and chewy.

2 cups (200 g/7 oz) rolled (porridge) oats
⅓ cup (30 g/1 oz) desiccated coconut
⅓ cup (35 g/1¼ oz) flaked almonds
¼ cup (25 g/1 oz) ground almonds
1 cup (25 g/1 oz) puffed quinoa or rice
¼ cup (30 g/1 oz) walnuts, roughly chopped
⅓ cup (55 g/2 oz) dried cranberries
1 tbsp chia seeds (optional)
¾ cup (260 g/9¼ oz) honey
¼ cup (45 g/1½ oz) brown sugar
½ cup (125 ml/4 fl oz) vegetable oil or light olive oil

01 Preheat oven to 130°C (250°F). Lightly grease and line a 25 cm x 25 cm (10 inch x 10 inch) baking tin.
02 In a bowl, combine oats, coconut, flaked almonds, ground almonds, quinoa or rice, walnuts, cranberries and chia seeds (if using).
03 In a small saucepan, combine honey, sugar and oil and stir over low heat until the sugar has dissolved. Pour the liquid over the dry ingredients and stir until well combined, mixing with clean, dry hands if necessary.
04 Press mixture into baking tin so it's quite tightly packed. Bake for 50–55 minutes, until golden brown. Remove from oven and leave in tin for 5 minutes to cool slightly, then turn out onto a board.
05 Leave for another 5 minutes, then cut into squares while still warm. Store in an airtight container, or freeze in a snap-lock bag and remove one at a time for packed lunches or a morning snack.
Makes 16

BACON AND CORN MUFFINS **

These are great for breakfast—bacon and eggs in a handy little parcel—but I also love them as a snack, or at the end of any sort of day. The trick with muffins is to keep the raw batter only just mixed. Keep it really lumpy and light, or you'll end up with hard little bullets you won't want to eat.

6 slices free-range bacon, rind removed, diced
½ red onion, finely chopped
1 cup (150 g/5½ oz) plain (all-purpose) flour
1 cup (190 g/6¾ oz) fine polenta
2 tsp sugar
1 tbsp baking powder
1 tsp sea salt
1 egg
½ cup (125 ml/4 fl oz) milk
60 g (2¼ oz) butter, melted
300 g (10½ oz) creamed corn

01 Preheat oven to 220°C (425°F). Lightly grease a 12-hole muffin tin with butter, or line with paper cases.
02 Cook bacon and onion in a frying pan over medium–high heat until crispy.
03 Sift flour, polenta, sugar, baking powder and salt into a bowl. In another bowl, combine egg, milk, butter and creamed corn and mix well. Gently fold wet ingredients into dry ingredients—the batter should be lumpy. Add bacon mixture and fold it through.
04 Spoon batter into muffin holes and bake for 15–20 minutes until muffins have risen and are golden.
05 Remove from oven, leave to cool in tin for 5 minutes, then transfer to a wire rack to cool completely.
Makes 12

POTATO HASH BROWNS **

The thought of these frying in the morning is enough to prevent a weekend sleep-in. Get the oil hot and these will be crunchy and soft. One hash brown with a sliver of smoked salmon please. Or bacon.

550 g (1 lb 4 oz) desiree potatoes, peeled
1 onion
2 free-range eggs, lightly beaten
½ cup (125 ml/4 fl oz) rice bran oil or vegetable oil

01 Roughly grate potatoes and onion and place in a colander. Heat a large heavy-based frying pan over medium–high heat.
02 Squeeze all liquid out of potato mixture with your hands, to make it as dry as possible. Place the mixture in a bowl with the eggs, season with a few pinches of sea salt and freshly ground black pepper, then mix to combine.
03 Add oil to hot pan and let it heat for about 10 seconds. Drop heaped tablespoons of potato mixture into the pan and flatten each one down with a spatula to form patties. Don't overcrowd the pan—there should be a few centimetres (about an inch) of space between each hash brown.
04 Fry for 2–3 minutes on each side, until crisp and golden brown. Serve sizzling hot.
Serves 4–6

BAKED BEANS *

Homemade baked beans says 'check out my mad culinary skills'. It says 'I am a domestic superhero of the gastronomic kind'. Plus they taste awesome. (See pic page 16.)

1 tbsp olive oil
1 onion, finely chopped
3 slices bacon, rind removed, or about 80 g (2¾ oz) pancetta, finely chopped
1 garlic clove, finely chopped
1 small thyme sprig
2 tsp sweet paprika
2 tsp brown sugar
1 tbsp tomato paste (concentrated purée)
400 g (14 oz) tin chopped tomatoes
2 x 400 g (14 oz) tins borlotti beans, rinsed and drained

01 Heat oil in a deep heavy-based frying pan over medium heat. Add onion and cook until just translucent and soft, about 3 minutes.
02 Add bacon or pancetta and cook for 5 minutes, until crisp. Add garlic, thyme and paprika and cook, stirring, for 1 minute.
03 Stir in sugar, tomato paste, tomatoes and beans. Cook, stirring, until heated through—about 5 minutes. Season with sea salt and freshly ground black pepper.
Serves 4—make this with buttered toast and a poarched egg per person

WRAPPED-UP BREAKFAST BURRITOS **

The inspiration for this breakfast-in-a-wrap comes from a Sydney cafe called The Little Marionette, where they roll it up in baking paper, hand you a little rug and pack you off to the park opposite to eat. I'll often meet friends at the park with the express plan to order one when I get there. These ones are filled with creamy scrambled eggs, grated cheese and avocado, and you can add Tabasco or tomato sauce (ketchup) as you like. They're great for those summery mornings when the park or beach is calling and you want something breakfasty to go.

2 flour or corn tortillas
4 large free-range eggs
¼ tsp ground cumin
¼ cup (60 ml/2 fl oz) milk or cream
1 tbsp olive oil
¼ cup (25 g/1 oz) grated cheddar cheese
½ avocado, sliced
a dollop of tomato chutney

01 Heat a non-stick frying pan over medium heat, without any oil. Add tortillas one at a time to warm them through, flipping each one over once. Remove from pan and set aside.
02 Time to scramble the eggs. Combine eggs, cumin and milk or cream in a bowl, season with sea salt and freshly ground black pepper, and beat lightly.
03 Heat oil in same frying pan used to heat tortillas, over low heat. Pour in egg mixture and lightly scrape along the bottom of the pan using a silicone spatula or flat-tipped wooden spoon. Slowly drag the spatula along the bottom of the pan to lift the cooked egg from the bottom, making sure the egg doesn't catch. Repeat this gentle movement until eggs are almost cooked. Now remove the pan from heat—the eggs will continue to cook in the hot pan and you don't want them to go dry.
04 Divide the eggs between the tortillas, placing them in a strip in the middle, then top with cheese, avocado and chutney. Fold the bottom of the tortillas along a short edge of the mixture, then pull over the sides to create a wrap whose bottom won't fall out. Wrap in foil or baking paper to take away, or eat as is on a plate.
Serves 2

* try me

ZUCCHINI FRITTERS WITH MELTY CHEESE **

When fried, zucchini goes all sweet and juicy. These fritters are great matched with a runny fried egg at breakfast. OK fine, I'll admit it: I sometimes have these for dinner, topped with a slice of runny camembert cheese. Oh my goodness.

4 large zucchini (courgettes)
1 tsp sea salt, plus extra to taste
2 golden shallots, thinly sliced
2 large eggs, lightly beaten
½ cup (75 g/2½ oz) self-raising flour
rice bran oil, for frying
lemon wedges, to serve
a slice of gooey cheese, to serve (optional)

01 Wash zucchini and trim ends off. Grate each zucchini using the largest hole on your grater. In a colander, toss zucchini with salt, then set aside for 10 minutes.
02 Wring out zucchini to extract water. Return deflated zucchini shreds to a bowl, add another pinch of salt. Add shallots, eggs and a grinding of black pepper. Add flour, then fold mixture together lightly.
03 Heat a large frying pan over medium heat. Add 2 tbsp oil, then drop small bunches of zucchini mixture into pan, leaving plenty of space between each fritter so they don't become soggy. Press each fritter with a spatula, then cook until edges underneath are golden, about 3–4 minutes. Flip and fry on the other side for 2–3 minutes until golden.
04 Drain fritters on paper towels. Repeat with remaining mixture, adding more oil as needed. Serve.
Makes about 10

TIP: These fritters keep well, either chilled in the fridge for two days or frozen in a well-sealed package for a month. When you're ready to use them, simply spread them out on a baking tray and cook in a 180°C (350°F) oven until they're hot and crisp again.

MEGA TORTILLA ESPANOLA **

This is Mexican-style street food meets whatever's-in-the-fridge. A little bit throw-it-together and a little bit late-night cure. Go with your gut. (See pic page 38.)

2–3 tbsp olive oil
1 onion, finely chopped
1 large chorizo (or other) sausage, sliced
1 cup (about 200 g/7 oz) cooked potatoes (boiled, roasted, whatever), sliced
5 cherry tomatoes
½ bunch flat-leaf (Italian) parsley, roughly chopped
1 cup (100 g/3½ oz) cheese, grated, crumbled (whatever)
4–5 free-range eggs

01 Preheat grill (broiler) to medium–high.
02 Heat oil in a large ovenproof frying pan that has deep sides. Fry onion and sausage over medium heat, turning frequently until slightly crispy, for about 5 minutes. Add potatoes, cherry tomatoes and parsley, then finally the cheese.
03 Break eggs into pan. Season with sea salt and freshly ground black pepper. Cover with a lid or large plate and cook for about 5 minutes, until it has firmed up. Turn off heat.
04 Place pan under grill, with handle poking out. Wrap handle in foil if it's made of wood or plastic, and make sure handle stays outside oven door, which should stay open. Grill (broil) tortilla for about 5 minutes, until tomatoes cook a bit and things turn golden. Serve.
Serves 4–6

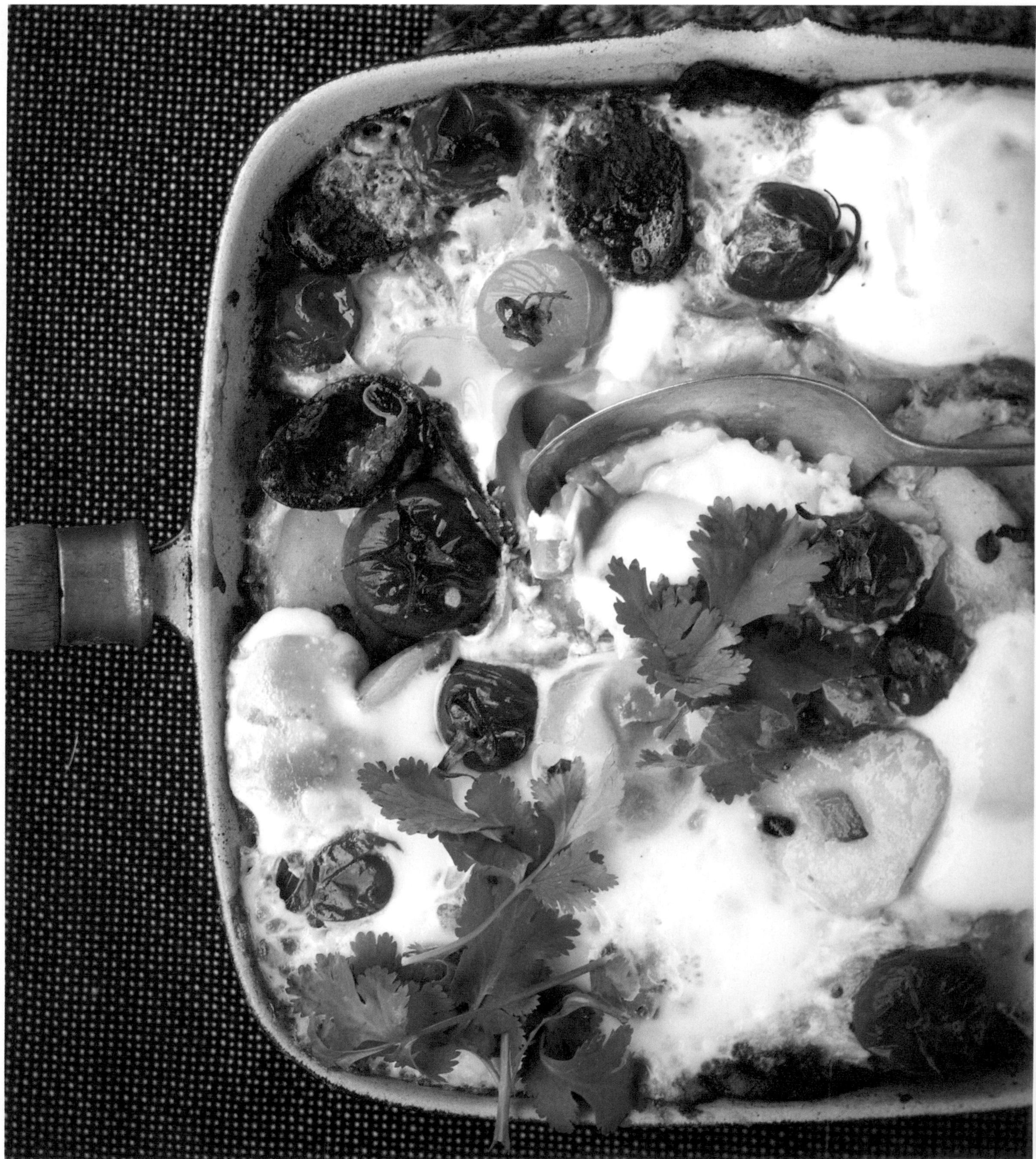

HOW TO DICE OR CHOP AN ONION

Hold an onion on its side on a chopping board. Use a sharp, small to medium-sized knife to cut about 1-2 cm (½-¾ inch) off the tip (the non-root end). Turn the onion so the root end is facing you, then cut the onion in half through the root end. Remove the dried outer layer of both halves, keeping the root attached.
Place one half on a chopping board, flat side down. With the point of the knife facing the root end, make slices along the grain of the onion close together for very fine dice, or for larger dice just make four or five slices across. Now slice all the way through to the board, but not through the root end, so the slices are still attached at the root end.
Holding onto the root end with your hand that isn't holding the knife, make slices from one side of the onion to the other, either very thinly, or about four or five slices for larger dice. The dice will fall away from the onion as you slice. Cut all the way to the root end, then discard the root.
Repeat with other onion half. Note: because an onion is made up of many layers, it does a lot of the cutting for you!

Left: Mega tortilla Española (page 36)
Right: Pizza topping eggs (page 22)

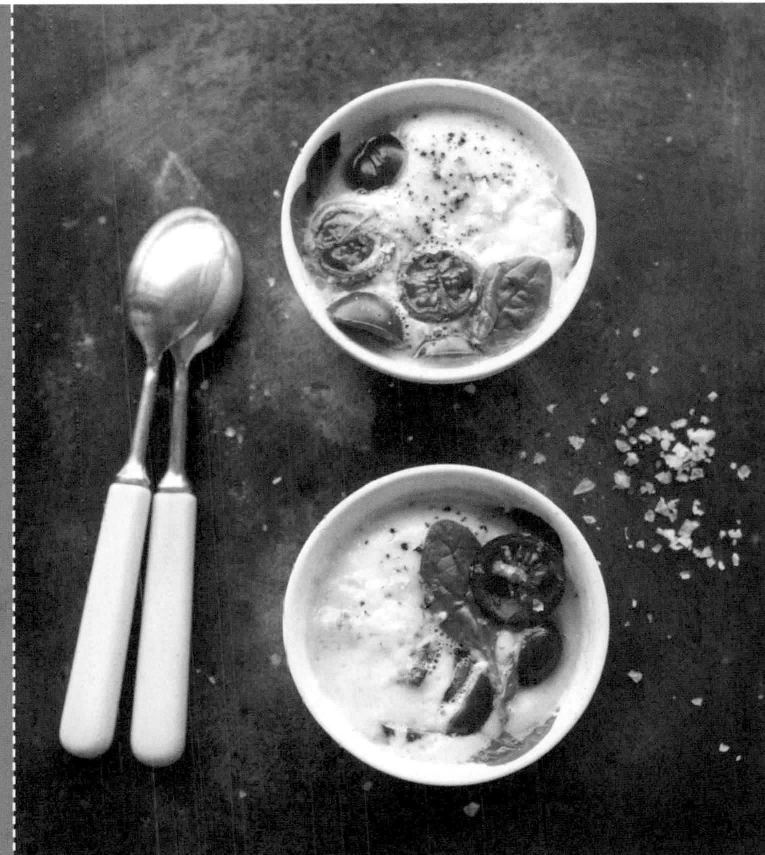

SLICING AN ONION OR GOLDEN SHALLOT

First, hold the onion or shallot on its side on a chopping board. Use a sharp, small to medium-sized knife to cut about 1 cm (½ inch) off the non-root end of the onion, or a bit less for a shallot. Now cut the onion or shallot in half through the root end. Remove the skin.
Lay the onion or shallot flat on chopping board and cut it into even slices–either acrossways or from root to tip. (Personally, I prefer them sliced from root to tip.) Then just discard the root end.

SPOONABLE FRENCH TOAST WITH MAPLE BERRIES **

I was the French Toast Queen as a teenager. That was actually what my family called me on the odd Friday night in the hope that I'd blossom Saturday morning all summery and fresh, and wake the house with the buttery, eggy smell that comes from something excellent frying. Mostly I didn't, I'm sorry to say, and my wonderful dad would often arise with the springy step dads just have, and make them for me instead. I've since discovered baked French toast. In this version, we have all the same ingredients, but the whole dish goes in the oven, and is spooned out in delicious bowlfuls to the sleepy-headed. It's breakfast for a lazy, floppy morning.

2 cups (500 ml/17 fl oz) milk
3 free-range eggs
zest of 1 lemon
1 tsp vanilla extract
10 g (1/4 oz) butter
6–8 slices yesterday's bread, crusts removed, cut in half into triangles
1 cup (125 g/4 1/2 oz) raspberries or other berries (frozen is OK)
1 tbsp maple syrup
yoghurt, to serve

01 Preheat oven to 180°C (350°F). In a bowl, whisk together milk, eggs, lemon zest and vanilla extract.
02 Butter a 20 cm (8 inch) baking dish. Arrange half the bread slices in the dish, scatter most of the raspberries over, then top with the remaining bread slices. Pour milk mixture over the top, then decorate with the remaining raspberries. Drizzle with maple syrup and let it all soak for 10 minutes.
03 Now bake for 45–50 minutes, or until golden brown on top but still soft inside. Serve with dollops of yoghurt.
Serves 4

RASPBERRY PIKELETS *

You could do far worse than make this for the people you love. It's a fruity twist on the classic pikelet—and it's totally possible to scoff them for dessert too.

1 cup (150 g/5 1/2 oz) self-raising flour
pinch of sea salt
1 1/2 tbsp sugar
1/4 tsp bicarbonate of soda (baking soda)
1 egg
1 cup (250 ml/9 fl oz) buttermilk (see note on buttermilk, page 42)
1/2 cup (70 g/2 1/2 oz) frozen raspberries
40 g (1 1/2 oz) butter, plus extra butter for pan-frying
honey, for drizzling

01 Sift flour, salt, sugar and bicarbonate of soda into a bowl. In another bowl, lightly beat egg with buttermilk using a fork.
02 Make a well in the centre of the flour mixture with a wooden spoon and add the egg mixture to the well, stirring gently and drawing in the flour from the sides to make a batter. Add raspberries and fold them through. Don't over-mix; the batter should be quite lumpy. If the batter thickens, add a little more milk.
03 In a large frying pan, melt the butter over low heat, then pour it into the batter and gently fold it through. Put large dollops of mixture back into the frying pan, about three at a time. Cook until bubbly on top and brown underneath—about 3 minutes. Turn to brown the other side, and don't worry if the raspberries stick a little.
04 Transfer pikelets to one half of a clean tea towel (dish towel), folding the other half over the top to keep them warm. Add a little more butter to the pan and repeat with the remaining batter.
05 Serve drizzled with honey—perhaps with a bowl of natural yoghurt for dolloping, if you like.
Serves 6

EYES CLOSED STRAWBERRY JAM *

Strawberry jam in 20 minutes. That's quicker than walking up to the shops and back. That's quicker than it takes to heat up croissants. That's about the same time it takes to heat the kettle, inform the flatmates or Mum and Dad they're having breakfast in bed, and then wait for the shock to subside.

2 punnets (500 g/1 lb 2 oz) strawberries
3 tbsp lemon juice
1½ cups (330 g/11½ oz) sugar
2–3 sterilised jars

01 Wash strawberries and remove green stalks using a small knife. Place strawberries in a large microwave-proof bowl with the lemon juice. Cook on high for 3 minutes.
02 Add sugar and stir mixture and cook for another 20 minutes on high. Watch the mixture to make sure it's not overflowing.
03 Test the jam by dropping a little onto a cold saucer—it should gel slightly. If it's not ready, cook for another 5 minutes. Give the jam a gentle stir, ensuring the sugar is fully dissolved at the bottom.
04 Being very careful ladle it into hot sterilised jars and seal. Label with your name, the date, and 'strawberry jam'!
Makes 2–3 jars

how to

MAKE YOUR OWN BUTTERMILK

Don't freak out if you don't have buttermilk but are dying for a batch of pikelets. It's easy to make your own. Add 1 tbsp white vinegar or lemon juice to 1 cup (250 ml/9 fl oz) milk and let it rest for 10 minutes to do its acidic magic on the milk. Don't worry if it looks curdled, it's perfect.

CINNAMON BERRY MUFFINS **

The secret behind muffins that are light and fluffy is not to over-mix the batter. You want to fold everything together so it barely looks mixed.

1½ cups (225 g/8 oz) self-raising flour
1 cup (150 g/5½ oz) wholemeal (whole-wheat) self-raising flour
1 tsp ground cinnamon
¾ cup (165 g/5¾ oz) tightly packed brown sugar
1 cup (250 ml/9 fl oz) buttermilk
½ cup (130 g/4½ oz) low-fat yoghurt
2 eggs, lightly beaten
2 tbsp vegetable oil
2 cups (250 g/9 oz) frozen mixed berries

01 Preheat oven to 180°C (350°F). Line a 12-hole muffin tin with paper cases.
02 Sift flours and cinnamon into a large mixing bowl, pour wholemeal husks into the bowl from the sieve. Add sugar, then make a well in the centre.
03 In another bowl, whisk buttermilk, yoghurt, eggs and oil with a fork until well combined. Pour mixture into the well in the flour mixture. Add berries, then very gently combine everything together. Don't over-mix at this stage—you want to draw all the ingredients together, but not beat or stir too much. It should be a lumpy mess.
04 Spoon mixture into muffin cases, filling them to the top. Bake for 20 minutes, until golden.
05 Remove from oven and leave to cool in tin for 10 minutes, before removing from tin and eating!
Makes 12

TIP: These muffins freeze well. Just pop them into snap-lock bags, freeze them, and take one out in the morning to stick in your lunchbox. It will be defrosted by lunch.

APPETIT

Crisp rosemary flatbreads * Flaky cheese straws * My kind of cheese biscuit * Popping edamame * Holy-moley guacamole * Smokin' eggplant dip * Mean green bruschetta * Hummus * Grilled corn salsa with corn chips * Mozzarella-stuffed croquettes * Green savoury pancakes with sesame drizzling sauce * Prawn and chestnut gyoza with black vinegar dipping sauce * Filo triangles (3 ways): Big fat Greek triangles; Spicy tomato salsa triangles; Walnut honey triangles * Prawn summer rolls * Satay dipping sauce * Rice cake teriyaki stacks * Apple cinnamon pop-tarts * Sweet crunchy nutty chewy couscous * Seeded orange scones * Strawberry straps * Peanut butter popcorn balls

SNACKS

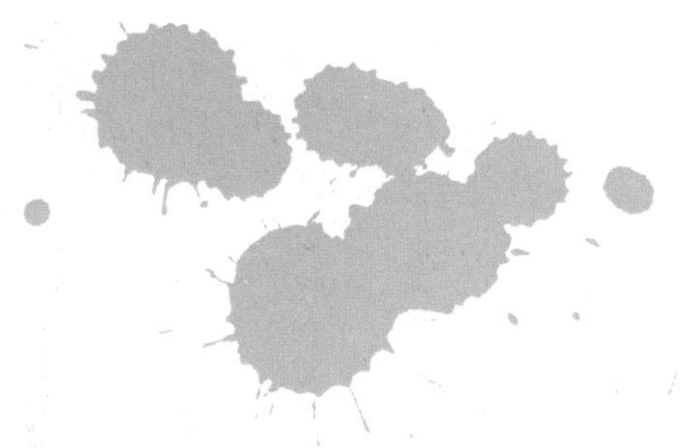

This book kind of demands a love of food. I don't believe it's possible to cook well unless you love to eat ...

... Unless you feel it in your bones that a slice of sourdough toast, charred a little and rubbed with raw garlic, topped with fresh tomato and drizzled with golden-green extra virgin olive oil, is a more amazing snack than a packet of bought biscuits, it's really much harder to be a good cook. Skills in the kitchen can be learned. But that is so much easier if you dream about what you'll snack on later while you're still eating breakfast.

A friend of mine once said the big difference between us is that she eats to *live*, while I live to *eat*. Food for her is only sustenance—it's about choosing the right foods to make her healthy and eating so that she doesn't collapse in a pile on the carpet from hunger. For me, food has always been one of the most interesting things to do. That involves finding good produce, traipsing to the markets, growing herbs and vegetables, learning how to make a sesame chicken salad, and then dreaming up what to cook and eat for the next meal.

Perhaps neither extreme is ideal; nobody loves an obsessive creature. But if you love food and can cook, you're not destined to a life of takeaway kebabs. By tasting food you become more interested in cooking it. In cooking it, you become more interested in tasting more, trying more, and so on until you're a genuine gastronome. So go ahead and taste it.

Snacking is where all this begins, if for no other reason than it's the time when most of us turn to convenience food—to packets of things. It's with that gnarling call of the stomach, between meals, that most of us will *neeeed* something sugary, crunchy, crispy, salty, creamy to snack on. Sugar, salt and fat are often the most appealing snacks because they give you an immediate hit. But then afterwards they make you feel really sluggish and tired and sometimes pretty grumpy.

And this is where this chapter comes to the rescue. Some of the snacks take a bit of time, but others are as simple as churning up some chickpeas, garlic, tahini and lemon juice for the best dip in town. Pick your favourites and start making stuff ahead so you have something decent to snack when hunger strikes. You'll look and feel a whole lot better for it—promise!

CRISP ROSEMARY FLATBREADS **

The Sardinian flatbread known as *carta musica*, or sheet music, is so named because it's almost impossibly thin. Perhaps it's also to do with the musical crunch they make when you eat them. The traditional version uses yeast, which I've omitted for expedience, and the result is literally a cracker.

1¾ cups (260 g/9¼ oz) plain (all-purpose) flour
1 tsp baking powder
1 tbsp rosemary leaves, roughly chopped
⅓ cup (80 ml/2½ fl oz) olive oil

01 Preheat oven to 210°C (415°F). Place a baking tray in the oven to heat up.
02 Whisk together flour, baking powder, ½ tsp sea salt and rosemary in a bowl. Make a well in the centre. Add oil and ½ cup (125 ml/4 fl oz) water and gradually stir into flour, slowly drawing more flour into the mixture, until a dough forms.
03 Gently knead dough on a lightly floured work surface for a few minutes. It will be very oily and soft.
04 Divide dough into six pieces. Then use a rolling pin to roll out one piece on a sheet of baking paper, into a longish irregular rustic shape, about 20 cm x 10 cm (8 inches x 4 inches). You roll it out on the baking paper because transferring something this thin and delicate is just not do-able. Sprinkle it with a little sea salt. Remove baking tray from oven, then slide dough and paper together onto the tray.
05 Bake for 6–8 minutes, or until the dough is just golden around the edges. Keep an eye on it—you don't want it too brown. Repeat with remaining dough. Serve immediately, or store in an airtight container for several days.
Makes 6 large flatbread, though you can crack these up to serve

TIP: You can add almost anything to the dough base: dried herbs, sesame seeds, spices, a pinch of curry powder, or finely grate a little parmesan cheese over the crispbread halfway through baking.

ANOTHER TIP: Make sure the oven is properly hot, and heat the baking tray too so the bread cooks properly underneath. When rolling the dough out the shapes can be irregular, but they should be so super-thin you can almost see through them.

FLAKY CHEESE STRAWS **

Pastry gilded with salty cheese—chewy and crispy and crumbling apart at a bite. These totally easy cheesy straws take little more than 30 minutes. You can experiment a bit: swap the cheese for roasted, crushed nuts and a sprinkling of sugar. They look a bit mad, but they taste great.

2 sheets frozen puff pastry, thawed
1 egg
½ cup (60 g/2¼ oz) grated parmesan cheese
1 cup (100 g/3½ oz) grated cheddar cheese

01 Preheat oven to 220°C (425°F). Line a baking tray with baking paper.
02 Roll out pastry on a lightly floured board until each sheet is about the thickness of a $1 coin.
03 In a small bowl, lightly beat egg with 1 tbsp water, then brush mixture over pastry. Sprinkle one sheet evenly with all the cheese, then lay the other sheet on top, with the egg-brushed side facing down. Press down lightly to close any bubbles. Cut the sheet lengthways into 8–10 slices, then twist each strip loosely to form a twist. Place on baking tray.
04 Bake for 15 minutes, or until golden and puffed. Turn each pastry straw and bake for another 2 minutes, being careful not to overcook. Set aside to cool before serving.
Makes about 8–10

MY KIND OF CHEESE BISCUIT **

These really simple cheese biscuits are good with a sprig of rosemary leaves finely chopped and bound in, or are good straight up.

1¼ cups (155 g/5⅝ oz) plain (all purpose) flour
¾ cup (75 g/2½ oz) grated parmesan cheese
½ cup (60 g/2¼ oz) grated cheddar cheese
½ tsp cayenne pepper
125 g (4½ oz) cold butter, cut into 1–2 cm (½–¾ inch) cubes
1 tbsp iced water

01 Add flour, cheeses, half the cayenne and a pinch of sea salt in a food processor and whiz for a few seconds. Add butter cubes and water and process, turning on and off frequently, until mixture starts to stick in a ball around the blade. Turn off machine.
02 Transfer dough to a floured surface and knead lightly. Halve and place each portion in a square of plastic wrap. Roll each half, with the help of the plastic wrap, into a 2.5 cm (1 inch) diameter cylinder. You should have two cylinders of dough wrapped.
03 Place in the refrigerator to chill for 30 minutes. You can keep these pastry rolls in the fridge for up to a week before baking, or in the freezer for 2 months before thawing, slicing and baking.
04 When ready to bake, preheat oven to 190°C (375°F). Lightly oil two baking trays.
05 Cut dough into 5 mm (¼ inch) thick slices and arrange on prepared trays. Sprinkle each with a little of the remaining cayenne. Bake for 12–15 minutes until light golden and crisp. Transfer to a wire rack to cool. Store in an airtight container for up to 1 week.
Makes about 48 biscuits

POPPING EDAMAME *

I can barely sit in a Japanese restaurant without getting a bowl of these little soy beans in skins. Don't eat the outer pod—you just hold it up to your mouth and pop the bean into your mouth.

450 g (1 lb) frozen edamame (soy beans)

Japanese dressing
1 tbsp lemon juice
2 tsp mirin (Japanese rice wine)
2 tsp rice vinegar
2 tbsp toasted sesame oil
1–2 tsp toasted sesame seeds
pinch of sea salt

01 Steam frozen soy beans in a steamer for 8–10 minutes. Alternatively, add to a large pot of salted, boiling water and cook for 5 minutes, until tender. Drain and transfer to a bowl.
02 Combine all the dressing ingredients in a medium bowl and whisk together with a fork. Toss soy beans through. Serve while still hot, with an empty bowl for discarded pods.
Serves 2–6, depending on how much you want to share

TIP: These are also great without the dressing—just sprinkled with sea salt and even a tiny pinch of dried chilli flakes if you like.

in my world

SALTY GRASSHOPPER TACOS

If you ever find yourself leaning at a tequila bar in Mexico looking for a snack (as you do), there's a good chance a couple of fresh corn tacos will arrive, filled with a little pile of insect bodies: heads, antennae, everything. The *tacos de chapulines* is a local delicacy of grasshopper tacos. The insects are salty and crunchy and a little bit meaty, and come with a smear of avocado, a scattering of coriander (cilantro) leaves and some chopped onion.

in my world

CRUNCHY TARANTULA SNACKS

Imagine a crunchy, deep-fried snack sold by the roadside--soft on the inside, and with chewy bits too. Sounds alright? In parts of Cambodia, hairy eight-legged tarantulas are eaten whole as a bit of a snack. Spiders about the size of a man's hand! They breed in holes, and locals dig them out with sticks. They're fried with garlic, sugar and salt until the legs go almost completely stiff and crispy. The taste is quite bland, with a crispy exterior and soft centre. The legs contain little flesh, but the head and body have a white meat inside. The abdomen is apparently horrible, and contains a brown paste consisting of organs, sometimes eggs, and excrement. Many recommend not eating it. A journalist for *The Times* newspaper in London described eating one like this: 'The legs are the size and colour of a Cadbury chocolate finger . . . They're cooked whole, which is particularly repellent--eyes, fangs, the lot. Pulling the legs off without squeezing the pus out of the abdomen is tricky.'

HOLY-MOLEY GUACAMOLE *

Guacamole from the supermarket is padded out with all sorts of weird ingredients—onion powder, acidic additive this and that . . . no thanks! Some ready-made guacamole can hardly be called guacamole at all. Resist the urge to over-mix guacamole: it should have lots of chunks in it—an unruly texture bound together with vibrant-green avocado flesh and herbs. It's not a purée, so *never* use a blender for it—a fork does just perfectly.

1 avocado, halved, stone removed
¼ bunch coriander (cilantro) leaves
¼ bunch flat-leaf (Italian) parsley leaves
juice of 1 lime
1 golden shallot, finely diced
1 tbsp extra virgin olive oil

01 Scoop flesh out of avocado, into a small bowl. Wash and roughly chop herbs, or just tear them apart with your hands. Add to bowl with lime juice.
02 Mash ingredients with a fork, squishing the avocado flesh between the tines to achieve a chunky but not puréed texture. Add shallot and oil, season to taste with sea salt and freshly ground black pepper, then stir to combine. Serve with plain corn chips or crackers for dipping.
Serves 2–4, depending on how much you want to share

TIP: For a fresh twist, you can top guacamole with some crumbled ricotta and fresh pomegranate seeds. If you're a health nut, you can sneak in 1 tbsp chia oil, which is full of omega-3 fatty acids and antioxidants, and even more vitamin-packed herbs.

SMOKIN' EGGPLANT DIP **

I remember a kid at school who hadn't the wildest dreamy idea what an eggplant was. He even tried to argue with me about whether eggs were plants! Even people who don't like eggplant—you know, those large, purple-skinned vegetables—do like this velvety, smoky dip.

2 medium-sized eggplants (aubergines)
½ cup (15 g/½ oz) chopped flat-leaf (Italian) parsley
2 garlic cloves, crushed
½ cup (130 g/4½ oz) natural yoghurt
2 tbsp tahini paste
squeeze of lemon juice
olive oil

01 Preheat oven to 180°C (350°F). Wash eggplants, place on a baking tray and bake for 1 hour, or until soft. Set aside to cool a little.
02 Cut eggplants in half, scoop flesh out into a bowl, then mash with a fork until quite smooth.
03 Add remaining ingredients and season with sea salt. Mix well, then leave to stand for 1 hour for all the flavours to mingle.
Makes 1 decent bowl, plus extra for snacks tomorrow

MEAN GREEN BRUSCHETTA *

The great thing about this super-powered green vegie mixture is its versatility. You can spread it on garlic-scratched toast—as it is here—or stir it through cooked pasta, or serve it as a perfect dip for tortilla chips. Make double quantities and store in an airtight container in the fridge for up to 3 days.

1 large head broccoli, cut into big chunks
2 cups (280 g/10 oz) frozen peas
½ bunch flat-leaf (Italian) parsley, roughly chopped
2 cups (90 g/3¼ oz) baby spinach, roughly chopped
¼ cup (40 g/1½ oz) toasted almonds, roughly chopped
2 tbsp extra virgin olive oil, plus extra for drizzling
4 thick slices sourdough bread
1 garlic clove, peeled

01 Add broccoli to boiling, salted water and cook for 4–6 minutes until it turns a bright green colour. Remove with a slotted spoon and refresh under cold running water for 10 seconds.
02 In the same boiling water, cook peas for 3 minutes, until just tender, then drain and refresh.
03 In a food processor, blend together broccoli, peas, parsley, spinach, toasted almonds and oil.
04 Meanwhile, toast the bread, then rub garlic clove over the toast, 'grating' it on the rough surface.
05 Spread broccoli mixture over toast, then cut into quarters. Season with sea salt and freshly ground black pepper, drizzle with a little more olive oil and serve.
Serves 2 people, 2 bruschetta each

TIP: Squeeze a little lime juice over bruschetta to serve, if desired.

HUMMUS *

This is the perfect after-exercise food because it's healthy, really tasty and packed with protein. Always keep a tin or two of chickpeas in the pantry for ready access to this dip. It's a cinch to whiz together.

400 g (14 oz) tin organic chickpeas, rinsed and drained
1 tbsp tahini paste
1 garlic clove, roughly chopped
juice of 1 lemon
¼ cup (60 ml/2 fl oz) extra virgin olive oil
crackers or vegetable sticks, to serve

01 Put chickpeas in a food processor with tahini, garlic and lemon juice. Blend on high for 30 seconds.
02 Turn machine off at the power point. Open lid, then use a wooden spoon to scrape the sides of the food processor. Add the oil. Turn power on and whiz again for 1–2 minutes, repeating the side-scraping if chickpeas stick again. Add more lemon juice, and sea salt and freshly ground black pepper to taste.
03 Serve scattered with chopped fresh herbs if you like, with crackers or vegetable sticks for dipping.
Serves 2–4, depending on how much you want to share

TIP: Try replacing the chickpeas with other tinned pulses and beans.

GRILLED CORN SALSA WITH CORN CHIPS *

This salsa is sweet and crunchy and totally easy. Omit the jalapeño chilli if you like things mild, and consider a splash of Tabasco sauce instead.

3 corn cobs, husks removed
2 tbsp olive oil
¼ red onion, finely diced
1 fresh jalapeño chilli, seeds removed, chopped
1 garlic clove, finely chopped
2 tomatoes, diced
1 cup (120 g/4¼ oz) tinned black beans, rinsed and drained
juice of 1 lime
plain corn chips, to serve

01 Preheat grill (broiler) to medium–high. Line a baking tray with baking paper.
02 Drizzle corn with olive oil and sprinkle with sea salt and freshly ground black pepper.
03 Place under grill and cook for 8–10 minutes, turning once or twice, until golden brown and starting to char a little. Remove from heat to cool.
04 Meanwhile, in a medium bowl, combine remaining ingredients. Carefully cut kernels off cob using a sharp knife, then add to bowl with other ingredients. Season with salt and pepper, drizzle with a little more oil, if it needs it.
05 Serve with corn chips for scooping.

Serves 2–4, depending on how much you want to share

MOZZARELLA-STUFFED CROQUETTES **

When I was really little I'd always get awestruck in the supermarket by the array of microwavable, just-throw-in-oven-then-eat foods on offer in the frozen food aisles. I was only allowed frozen berries, but it was those croquette potato balls I really wanted. Since then, I've read the ingredients lists on these things and even ventured to taste them—and I realise now why they were banned in our house! So I make these instead, and they are so, so much better.

6 medium desiree potatoes, peeled and quartered
200 g (7 oz) mozzarella cheese, roughly chopped
¼ cup (30 g/1 oz) grated parmesan cheese
3 large free-range eggs
1 cup (110 g/3¾ oz) dry breadcrumbs
1 cup (250 ml/9 fl oz) olive oil
1 cup (250 ml/9 fl oz) rice bran oil
½ bunch flat-leaf (Italian) parsley leaves, roughly chopped

01 Put potatoes in a large saucepan, cover with cold water and add salt. Cook until tender, about 15–20 minutes. Drain and leave to cool.
02 Mash potatoes then stir in cheeses, a few pinches of sea salt and freshly ground black pepper, and 1 egg. In a shallow bowl, lightly beat other 2 eggs with a fork. Pour breadcrumbs into another shallow bowl beside it. Line a baking tray with baking paper.
03 Form potato mixture into about 24 balls, measuring out with a ¼ cup (60 ml/2 fl oz) measure. Roll into slightly oblong shapes.
04 One at a time, dip croquettes into beaten egg, letting excess drip off, then roll in breadcrumbs to coat. Place on baking tray as you make them.
05 Heat ¼ cup (60 ml/2 fl oz) of each oil in a large frying pan over medium–high heat. Fry croquettes in batches, turning until golden brown on all sides—about 5 minutes per batch. Add and heat a little more of each oil between each batch.
06 Transfer each batch to paper towels, sprinkle with chopped parsley and serve immediately.

Makes 24

GREEN SAVOURY PANCAKES WITH SESAME DRIZZLING SAUCE **

Grab a few things from the cupboard, throw them together, cook them, eat them. (See pic page 44.)

3/4 cup (110 g/3 3/4 oz) plain (all-purpose) flour
1/4 cup (45 g/1 1/2 oz) rice flour
3 spring onions (scallions), cut diagonally into 3 cm (1 1/4 inch) lengths
1/2 carrot, coarsely grated, or cut into thin julienne strips about 3 cm (1 1/4 inches) long
rice bran oil or vegetable oil, for pan-frying

Sesame drizzling sauce
3 tbsp soy sauce
2 tsp sesame oil
1 spring onion (scallion), finely chopped
1 tsp sesame seeds
1/2 red chilli, seeds removed, finely chopped

01 Combine all the sesame drizzling sauce ingredients in a small bowl. Set aside.
02 To make pancakes, combine flours in a bowl and add 1 cup (250 ml/9 fl oz) cold water. Stir to combine, and add more water if needed to make a thin pancake batter. Add spring onion and carrot.
03 Heat a frying pan—one about 15 cm (6 inches) in diameter—over medium–high heat. Add about 2 tsp oil and once it's hot, ladle a spoonful of batter into the pan. Move pan around so pancake spreads out. You want it thin, so use a little pair of tongs to spread things out rather than add more batter.
04 Cook until golden brown (lift the edge with a spatula to check), then flip pancake over. Repeat with remaining batter, and add more oil as needed. Serve pancakes flat on a plate, cut into quarters and drizzled with sesame dressing.
Makes about 4

PRAWN AND CHESTNUT GYOZA WITH BLACK VINEGAR DIPPING SAUCE ***

There's something really cool about making dumplings. Not so much fun when you're terribly hungry, to be sure, but it's the hard-earned prize at the end that makes it all worthwhile. The water chestnuts give these an excellent crunch. You can make these ahead, freeze them in little snap-lock bags, and then cook when you need a snack.

300 g (10 1/2 oz) cooked local prawns (shrimp), chopped
2/3 cup (50 g/1 3/4 oz) finely shredded cabbage
1 tsp sesame oil
1 tbsp soy sauce
2 cm (3/4 inch) piece of ginger, peeled and grated
100 g (3 1/2 oz) tinned water chestnuts, rinsed and drained
2 spring onions (scallions), thinly sliced
20 gow gee wrappers
1 tbsp vegetable oil

Black vinegar dipping sauce
1/4 cup (60 ml/2 fl oz) soy sauce
1 tsp sesame oil
2 tsp black rice vinegar (optional)
2 tsp water

01 Combine prawns, cabbage, sesame oil, soy sauce, ginger, water chestnuts and spring onion in a bowl.
02 Lay wrappers on a work surface. Spoon 1 heaped tsp of prawn mixture on one side of a wrapper. Brush edges with cold water, then fold other half of wrapper over the filling. Press edges to seal and push out any air. Turn wrapper on its side, then turn it slightly into a half-moon shape. Repeat with remaining wrappers.
03 Heat oil in a large frying pan that has a lid. Arrange gyoza in pan and cook for 1–2 minutes, until bases are golden brown. Add 1/2 cup (125 ml/4 fl oz) hot water to pan, cover and cook for another 3–5 minutes, adding more water if it runs dry.

04 Remove from heat, remove lid and leave to rest for 1–2 minutes, so gyoza come away from pan easily.
05 Whisk dipping sauce ingredients together in a bowl. Serve with gyoza.
Makes 20

FILO TRIANGLES {3 WAYS}

Filo, or phyllo, is Greek for 'leaf', and it's no wonder this papery pastry is named such. Filo pastry is made of flour and water. Don't feel restricted by these fillings—experiment with leftovers (such as bolognese: messy but yum!), or jam and cream cheese. You can freeze some of them after you've rolled them—then, when you need a snack, just pop a few in the oven, bake and devour.

Big fat Greek triangles **

These are the original Greek spinach and cheese triangles, also called tiropita. They'll be a hit all round. (See pic page 61.)

½ cup (115 g/4 oz) ricotta cheese
½ cup (65 g/2¼ oz) feta cheese
2 handfuls baby spinach leaves, roughly chopped
2 eggs, lightly beaten
generous pinch of freshly grated nutmeg
8 sheets filo pastry
100 g (3½ oz) butter, melted

01 Preheat oven to 180°C (350°F). Line two baking trays with baking paper if making all triangles now.
02 Mix together cheeses, spinach, eggs and nutmeg.
03 Place filo sheets on a work surface and cut each into three rectangles. Take one rectangle and gently brush with melted butter. Spoon 1 tbsp of cheese mixture in one corner. Fold the rectangle from that corner diagonally to make a point, then fold over again in the opposite direction. Continue to fold pastry over itself, until the entire sheet is wrapped around the filling in a triangle shape. Repeat with remaining pastry and filling.
04 Place on baking trays, then brush tops with a little more butter. Bake for 15–20 minutes until golden.
Makes 24

Spicy tomato salsa triangles **

If one were to host a Mexican-themed party, wouldn't these be the best starter? Wouldn't they make the best starter, too, for the long day you still have ahead?

1 cup (125 g/4½ oz) tinned red kidney beans or black beans, rinsed and drained
2 large tomatoes, diced
1 handful flat-leaf (Italian) parsley or coriander (cilantro), roughly chopped
1 golden shallot, thinly sliced
pinch or two of paprika
8 sheets filo pastry
100 g (3½ oz) butter, melted

01 Preheat oven to 180°C (350°F). Line two baking trays with baking paper if making all triangles now.
02 In a bowl, mix together beans, tomato, herbs, shallot and paprika. Season with sea salt and freshly ground black pepper.
03 Place filo sheets on a work surface and cut each into three rectangles. Take one rectangle and brush with melted butter. Spoon 1 tbsp of bean mixture in one corner. Fold the rectangle from that corner diagonally to make a point, then fold over again in the opposite direction. Continue to fold pastry over itself, until the entire sheet is wrapped around the filling in a triangle shape. Repeat.
04 Place on baking trays and brush tops with a little butter. Bake for 15–20 minutes until golden.
Makes 24

Walnut honey triangles **

Dripping and oozing honey, these nutty crunchy nibbles are the perfect snack for a party. Or for you.

2 cups (115 g/4 oz) walnuts
1 tbsp caster (superfine) sugar
1 tsp ground cinnamon
8 sheets filo pastry
100 g (3½ oz) butter, melted

Honey syrup
⅓ cup (115 g/4 oz) honey
¼ cup (55 g/2 oz) sugar

01 Preheat oven to 180°C (350°F). Line two baking trays with baking paper if making all triangles now.
02 Put walnuts, sugar and cinnamon in a food processor and pulse until coarse crumbs form.
03 Place filo sheets on a work surface and cut each into three rectangles. Take one rectangle and gently brush with melted butter. Spoon 1 tbsp of nut mixture in one corner. Fold the rectangle from that corner diagonally to make a point, then fold over again in the opposite direction. Continue to fold pastry over itself, until the entire sheet is wrapped around the filling in a triangle shape. Repeat.
04 Place on baking trays, then brush tops with a little more butter. Bake for 15–20 minutes until golden. Remove from oven and set on a wire rack to cool.
05 Meanwhile, make honey syrup. Combine honey and sugar in a small saucepan with ¼ cup (60 ml/2 fl oz) water. Bring to a simmer and stir until sugar dissolves. Pour over triangles and serve.
Makes 24

Right: Big fat Greek triangles (page 59)

PRAWN SUMMER ROLLS **

Vietnamese mint is the secret ingredient here, but plain mint is fine if you can't get it. These neat and highly tasty little packages take some practice to roll, but after a bit you'll have it figured.

100 g (3½ oz) dried vermicelli noodles
juice of ½ lemon
2 tsp fish sauce
1 tbsp sesame oil
½ bunch mint, roughly chopped
½ bunch coriander (cilantro), chopped
150 g (5½ oz) packet of rice paper, 22 cm (8½ inches) round
1 cup (115 g/4 oz) bean sprouts
¼ Chinese cabbage (wong bok), finely shredded
15 Vietnamese mint leaves
15 large local prawns (shrimp), cooked, peeled and halved lengthways

01 Put noodles in a bowl, cover with boiling water and soak for 5–10 minutes, or until tender. Rinse with cold water, then drain well.
02 Toss noodles in a bowl with lemon juice, fish sauce and sesame oil. Mix in chopped mint and coriander and set aside.
03 Dip one rice paper round in hot water for 10 seconds, until soft. Place on a work surface. Arrange a small handful of noodles—a little bigger than a walnut—in the middle of the round. Top with a few bean sprouts, a little cabbage, 1 Vietnamese mint leaf and 2 prawn halves.
04 Fold the rice paper round in half over the filling, then fold in outer edges. Now roll the whole thing to form a small, tightly packed parcel, like a spring roll.
05 Repeat with remaining rice paper rounds and ingredients. Serve on a large platter with a yummy sauce, such as the Satay dipping sauce (see page 63).
Makes 15

HEY THERE GORGEOUS!

You've heard it all before . . . but honestly, hear it here again. The things you eat and put into your body have just as much impact on the condition of your skin, hair and nails as any product or cream. Forget lotions and potions--just eat really well and give yourself that gorgie glow.

First thing in the morning, before you eat a thing, boil the kettle and squeeze half a lemon into a cup (no sugar or honey!). Top with ½ cup (125 ml/4 fl oz) of boiling water and ½ cup of cold tap water, so it's sort of lukewarm. Sip the whole thing. This flushes your system with nutritious vitamins and antioxidants. It's acidic and sour but you'll get used to it! Do this every morning when you wake up and your skin will thank you for it.

Avocados are packed with healthy fats and oils, which make your hair glossy and your skin soft. Have ¼ avocado on a slice of toast (no butter, just salt and pepper) for breakfast or a snack. Add a squeeze of lemon or even some Tabasco sauce.

Fruit smoothies, with or without milk, are great for your skin. For an easy skin-saver, try blending together a cup or two of frozen mixed berries, a few drops of honey and ½ cup (125 ml/4 fl oz) sugar-free juice or milk. Add a few dollops of yoghurt if you're acne prone--the good bacteria in yoghurt helps you digest properly and eliminate toxins.

Your skin needs zinc. Teenage guys, in particular, can be deficient in this very important mineral. Without enough zinc, everyone is prone to breakouts, and spots don't heal as quickly when you do get them. Oysters contain more zinc per serve than any other food. Failing that, also good are red meats like beef, lamb and liver, baked beans, spinach, yoghurt, chickpeas, dry roasted almonds, red kidney beans, peas, milk, pepitas (pumpkin seeds) and sunflower seeds.

Oily fish like salmon, trout and tuna are amazing for your skin. It's all those omega-3 fatty acids that make you look all glowy and smooth. Their anti-inflammatory properties also help prevent breakouts.

Remember to drink your 2 litres (8 cups/70 fl oz) of water a day. OK, so you'll be popping off to the bathroom more often--but your skin will sparkle.

try me *

SATAY DIPPING SAUCE **

Need something peanutty for dipping? Throw these ingredients together and the ultimate dipping sauce is yours. This is the perfect dipping sauce for fresh spring rolls.

1 tbsp vegetable oil or rice bran oil
½ onion, finely chopped
1 garlic clove, finely chopped
1 small red chilli, finely chopped
¼ cup (70 g/2½ oz) crunchy peanut butter
juice of ½ lemon
1 tsp red wine vinegar
½ tsp maple syrup or brown sugar

01 Heat oil in a small saucepan, add onion and cook over medium-low heat until soft and translucent. Add garlic and chilli and stir until softened, about 1 minute.
02 Add peanut butter, lemon juice, vinegar, maple syrup or sugar and ½ cup (125 ml/4 fl oz) water. Stir to combine, then cook for 2 minutes, until sauce thickens. Serve in a little bowl, with a spoon for scooping.
Makes a small bowl of sauce

how to

KNIFE SCRAPING

If you've ever seen a chef scrape food from a board into a bowl or pan, you'll notice they never use the sharp side of the knife. Turn it upside down and use the blunt edge for scraping so you don't blunt the sharp edge.

RICE CAKE TERIYAKI STACKS ***

Leftovers. Whenever you have them, it's usually impossible to find a spot for them, or conjure the energy to want to eat them. And when you don't have them, you complain there's nothing in the fridge. Well, here is something you can do with leftover cooked sushi rice. I've even gone to the shops and bought a small container of sushi rice just to make these when I need something reliably snacky. I first found a version of this recipe in an old issue of *Gourmet*, an American magazine that sadly no longer exists.

2 cups (185 g/6½ oz) cooked sushi rice
2 tbsp teriyaki sauce
2 tbsp unsalted butter
1 tsp rice bran oil or vegetable oil
1 spring onion (scallion), thinly sliced diagonally

01 Line a tray that fits in your freezer with baking paper.
02 Place an egg ring or round cookie cutter—one about 8 cm (3¼ inches) in diameter—on the tray. Spoon one-quarter of the rice into the ring and press it down quite firmly so it's tightly packed. Lift ring up, leaving the rice disc on the tray. Repeat with remaining rice, to make four rice patties. Chill tray in the freezer for at least 10 minutes.
03 Remove rice cakes from freezer and drizzle with teriyaki sauce. Heat butter and oil in a large heavy-based frying pan over low heat, then add rice cakes, teriyaki side up.
04 Cook, rotating to ensure even browning, until golden brown underneath, about 8–10 minutes.
05 Turn rice cakes over, adding a little more oil if needed, and cook until golden on the other side, about 5 minutes. Transfer to plates.
06 In the same pan, cook spring onion until just wilted, about 1–2 minutes. Scatter over rice cakes and serve.
Makes 4

* try me

APPLE CINNAMON POP-TARTS **

Growing up in Australia, I didn't know what a Pop-Tart was until John Travolta got shot. In the movie *Pulp Fiction*, Bruce Willis basically shoots him because he gets a fright when a Pop-Tart pops up in the toaster. So I was determined to find a way to make them myself and discover what all the fuss is about. It turns out, filled with homemade strawberry jam (see page 42), they're pretty wicked.

1 sheet pre-rolled puff pastry
1 egg, beaten
3/4 cup (205 g/7 1/4 oz) apple sauce
1 tsp ground cinnamon

01 Preheat oven to 180°C (350°F). Line a baking tray with baking paper.
02 On a well-floured bench, roll out puff pastry. (It's already pre-rolled, but you want it rolled again for this recipe so it doesn't puff too much.) Make sure pastry isn't sticking to the bench by running a metal spatula underneath. Slice pastry in half, into two almost-square shapes. Turn each sheet around 90 degrees if needed and roll each one again—the pastry needs to be quite thin.
03 Trim each sheet to about 30 cm x 22 cm (12 inches x 8 1/2 inches). Cut each piece into nine 10 cm x 7.5 cm (4 inch x 3 inch) rectangles—to do this, cut each piece acrossways three times, and lengthways three times. You will have 18 small rectangles in total.
04 Brush beaten egg over one sheet. On the middle of sheet place 1/2 tbsp apple sauce and a sprinkle of cinnamon, keeping a 1 cm (1/2 inch) gap bare around the edge. Repeat with another seven pastry sheets.
05 Place a second rectangle of pastry on top of each, using your fingertips to press firmly around the pocket of filling to remove air and seal sides together.
06 Press the tines of a fork all around the edge of each parcel. Place on baking tray and prick each one with a fork a couple of times. Bake for 30 minutes until golden.
07 Remove from oven and cool.
Makes 9

TIP: Instead of apple and cinnamon, try a small dollop of jam, or peanut butter with a smidge of jam. For a no-sugar version, very thinly slice about 5 strawberries lengthways and place a piece or two in each pop-tart, with a tiny dollop of cream cheese.

SWEET CRUNCHY NUTTY CHEWY COUSCOUS *

This is *really* fast food. Couscous has to be the easiest hearty thing in the world to make. It's like an instant grain, and you can pretty much add any nutty, dried and fresh fruit topping you like.

2/3 cup (130 g/4 1/2 oz) instant couscous
1/4 cup (45 g/1 1/2 oz) sultanas (golden raisins), roughly chopped
30 g (1 oz) butter
1 tbsp brown sugar
1 tsp ground cinnamon
1 orange, peeled and cut into segments
4 fresh dates, pitted and sliced
2 tbsp pistachio nuts, cut into slivers
honey, for drizzling

01 Place couscous and sultanas in a heatproof bowl. Pour 1 1/4 cups (310 ml/10 3/4 fl oz) boiling water over and stir gently with a fork. Cover and set aside for 5 minutes, until all the liquid is absorbed.
02 Use a fork to separate the couscous grains, then stir in butter, sugar and cinnamon while couscous is still hot.
03 Divide mixture between four small bowls. Top with orange segments, scatter with dates and pistachios and drizzle with honey.
Serves 4

LOVE, HATE, TRY ANYWAY

Here are some things to try before sticking your nose up. You may hate them--but then again, you might not. Be adventurous, go on.

CANNED SARDINES. But only good-quality ones: it really matters with these. Try the spicy ones; the ones in tomato sauce are pretty good too. Have them on buttered toast, with a squeeze of lemon. Fresh sardines are also lovely seasoned with salt and pepper and done on the barbecue so they're properly charred. Squeeze lemon and a dash of Tabasco over the top. They're bony but you can remove them in one single manoeuvre. Or, find pre-filleted ones.

QUAIL EGGS. Teeny little eggs, how cute are they? Maybe don't bother frying them, but soft-boiled, peeled and added to salads, or dipped into dukkah or celery salt as a snack, they're pretty mighty.

SALTED ANCHOVIES. OK, so maybe not straight from the jar (well you may as well try that too), but fry up one or two, mix with steamed broccoli and garlic, then stir through cooked pasta. Or smudge one anchovy fillet into a leg of lamb with the garlic before roasting. Not too fishy after all.

BRUSSELS SPROUTS. But not boiled! They should be steamed so they're only just cooked through, then sautéed in butter with hazelnuts and a good sprinkling of salt.

SMELLY CHEESE. Smells bad, tastes great. Try it on crusty French bread. Block your nose to begin with if you have to.

DARK GREEN VEG. Broccoli, spinach, bok choy (pak choy), Chinese broccoli (gai larn) . . . all those dark green leafy vegies that are almost a bit bitter are totally good for you. But they can take some getting used to. Try frying up steamed broccoli and adding it to your favourite pasta with loads of crushed garlic and onion, so it all goes mushy like a dry-ish sauce. Add a big drizzle of olive oil. Like.

SEEDED ORANGE SCONES **

True scones are not overly sweet. Add a bit of crunch and texture by mixing in some healthy seeds. A spoonful of chopped chocolate wouldn't go astray either.

3 cups (450 g/1 lb) self-raising flour
1 tsp sea salt
60 g (2¼ oz) cold unsalted butter
4 tbsp mixed seeds, such as sunflower, pepitas (pumpkin seeds), sesame and poppy seeds
grated zest of 1 orange
1¼ cups (310 ml/10¾ fl oz) buttermilk
splash of milk, for brushing

01 Preheat oven to 210°C (425°F). Line a baking tray with baking paper.
02 Sift flour and salt, place in a food processor with butter and mix until crumbly. Add seeds and orange zest and blend again. Add most of the buttermilk, then fold together until just combined.
03 Tip out onto a floured work surface and pull dough together with your hands. Add the rest of the buttermilk if it isn't holding together.
04 Knead lightly by turning and pressing mixture with the heel of your hand a few times. Pat out into a round about 4 cm (1½ inches) thick. Use a round 4–5 cm (1½–2 inch) diameter cutter or glass tumbler to cut out scone shapes. Gather scraps together, knead lightly, then cut out more scone rounds.
05 Place scones on baking tray, about 3 cm (1¼ inches) apart. Brush with milk and bake for 10–15 minutes, or until scones have risen and are golden. Serve with butter and honey.
Serves 8

TIP: If you don't have a food processor, just sift the flour and salt into a bowl, rub in the butter with your fingertips until the mixture resembles crumbs, then add the seeds and orange zest. (Don't let the butter melt from the heat of your hands.) Continue as above.

STRAWBERRY STRAPS **

Chewy, blood coloured and completely sweet, the only thing wrong with this recipe is that you need a non-stick or silicone baking tray liner, which is worth investing in as a totally non-stick alternative to baking paper. There's a long waiting time before you'll actually be eating these. But the wait will be worth it. They keep for up to a month.

4½ cups (675 g/1 lb 7 oz) halved strawberries
¾ cup (165 g/5¾ oz) sugar

01 Preheat oven to 100°C (200°F). In a food processor, blend strawberries and sugar until smooth. Strain through a fine-mesh sieve into a heavy-based saucepan.
02 Gently bring to the boil, then simmer gently over medium–low heat for about 45 minutes, stirring occasionally. Reduce to just over 1 cup (250 ml/9 fl oz). The mixture will thicken to the point where a little plop of it onto the bench doesn't spread much—cook for another 10 minutes if needed.
03 Line a large baking tray with a non-stick baking tray liner. Pour mixture onto liner, being careful not to touch it—it will burn! (If you do burn yourself, run your skin continuously under cold water.) Use a spatula to spread the purée out as thinly and evenly as possible, so it's almost transparent.
04 Bake for about 2½ hours. Test mixture with your finger: it shouldn't stick to it, but should feel tacky.
05 Remove from oven. Keeping mixture on non-stick liner, place on a wire rack to cool for at least 3 hours.
07 Place a sheet of baking paper over the mixture, then peel off non-stick liner. Use scissors to cut mixture into about 8–10 straps, cutting paper as well. Roll up, keeping paper on, and store in a sealed container for up to 1 month.
Makes 8–10

make me *

PEANUT BUTTER POPCORN BALLS ***

These are 'sometimes food', not 'every day food'. That's not because they're gloriously difficult to make, but because they're basically fat and sugar. Having said that, one ball will give you enough energy to run around the block twice, and will have every friend in town running over to get their paws on one.

- 6 cups popcorn, made with 1 cup (220 g/7¾ oz) popping kernels
- 1½ cups (225 g/8 oz) dry roasted peanuts, roughly chopped
- ⅔ cup (140 g/5 oz) sugar
- ⅔ cup (170 ml/5½ fl oz) light corn syrup
- 2 tbsp honey
- ⅔ cup (180 g/6 oz) smooth peanut butter
- 2 tsp vanilla extract

01 Combine popcorn and peanuts in a large mixing bowl. Line a tray with baking paper.

02 In a heavy-based saucepan, bring sugar and corn syrup to the boil. Let it bubble for about 5 minutes—you need it very very hot. Be careful not to touch the liquid. It needs to reach the soft-ball stage (115°C/230°F), but if you don't have a candy thermometer just let it bubble away for 5–8 minutes.

03 Turn off heat, then add honey, peanut butter and vanilla—be careful, it will spit. Stir mixture, then pour it over popcorn and nuts and combine well. Set aside to cool slightly, to the point where you can handle it.

04 Once cool, lightly grease your hands, then roll walnut-sized balls of the mixture.

05 Place on baking tray for about 30 minutes, to set and cool completely before serving.

Makes 35

TIP: If you're serving these at a party, it's cute to wrap them individually in paper and pile them on a plate.

ANOTHER TIP: You can use glucose syrup derived from corn in place of the light corn syrup.

POTATO CHIPS

in my world

Potato chips were invented in the summer of 1853, when a native American chef called George Crum had a fussy customer who complained that his French fries were too soggy. He promptly sent them back to the kitchen. The chef cut up and fried a new batch, but the customer didn't like those either. Vexed and frustrated, the chef tried to annoy his customer by cutting the fries so thin the guy couldn't even pierce them with a fork without snapping them. But the plan backfired. The customer loved them, and potato crisps were soon one of the most popular items on the menu. It wasn't long before potato chips were packaged in bags and sold all over the United States—and then the world!

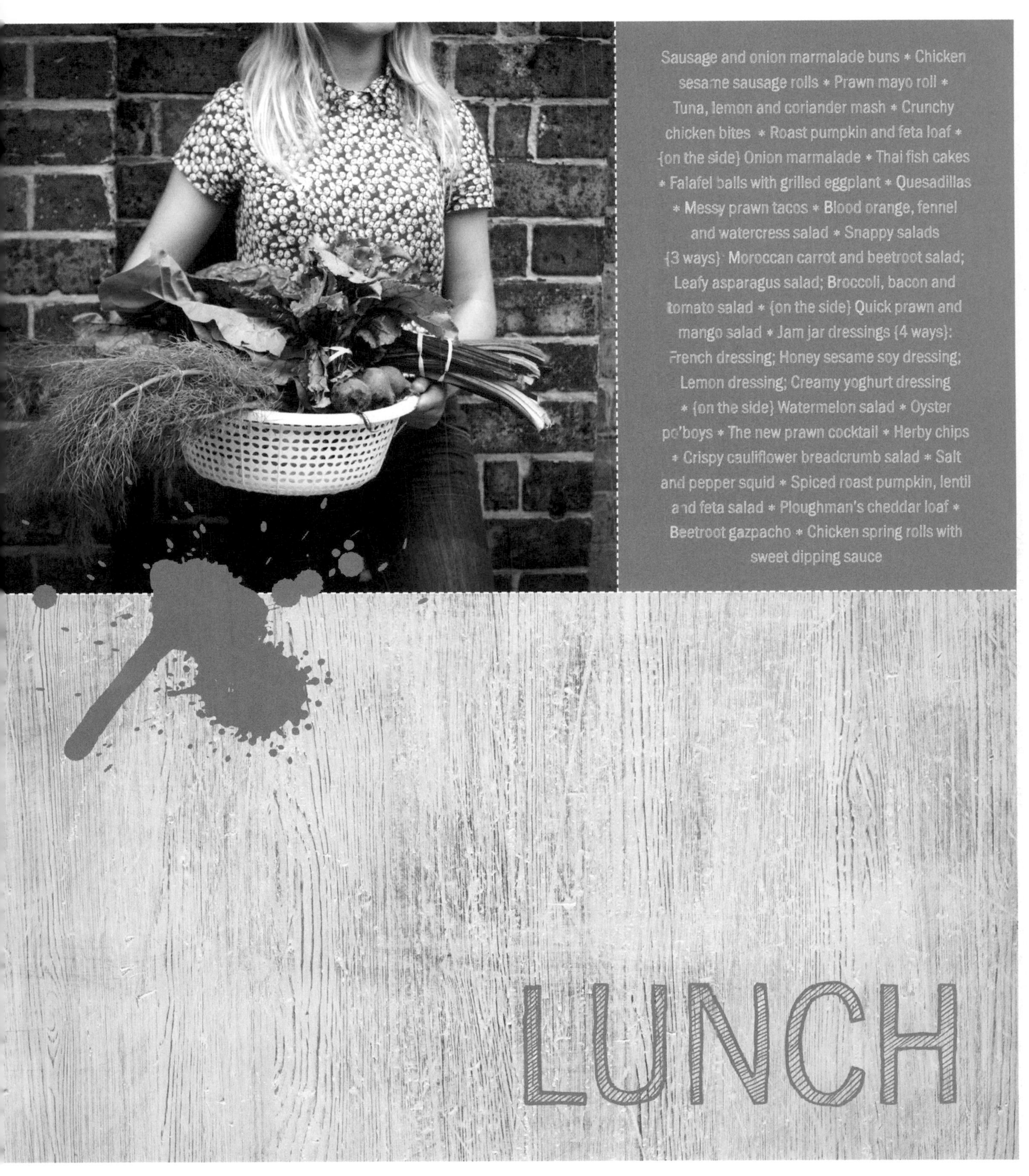

Sausage and onion marmalade buns * Chicken sesame sausage rolls * Prawn mayo roll * Tuna, lemon and coriander mash * Crunchy chicken bites * Roast pumpkin and feta loaf * {on the side} Onion marmalade * Thai fish cakes * Falafel balls with grilled eggplant * Quesadillas * Messy prawn tacos * Blood orange, fennel and watercress salad * Snappy salads {3 ways}: Moroccan carrot and beetroot salad; Leafy asparagus salad; Broccoli, bacon and tomato salad * {on the side} Quick prawn and mango salad * Jam jar dressings {4 ways}: French dressing; Honey sesame soy dressing; Lemon dressing; Creamy yoghurt dressing * {on the side} Watermelon salad * Oyster po'boys * The new prawn cocktail * Herby chips * Crispy cauliflower breadcrumb salad * Salt and pepper squid * Spiced roast pumpkin, lentil and feta salad * Ploughman's cheddar loaf * Beetroot gazpacho * Chicken spring rolls with sweet dipping sauce

LUNCH

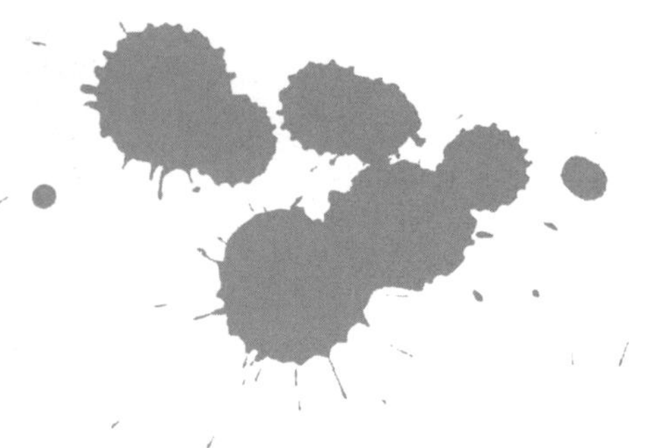

We've all seen the dodgy sanger: two slices of white bread bleeding a single soggy slice of tomato ...

... In Australia we have the squashed Vegemite sandwich, too, which some try to elevate by introducing a slice of rubbery cheese. OMG. But those lunchtime horror stories don't have to be yours.

It's OK turning to bought food now and then, but eat unhealthy takeaway or canteen food every day and you'll start looking like a bit of a meat pie yourself. Eating fresh food for lunch makes you feel fresh through the afternoon—and of course healthier in the long run.

This chapter is a bit of a lunchtime free-for-all, offering possibilities to turn to during the week. It's all about not being a square, and thinking outside the (lunch) box. And then of course there's the weekend lunch. Ahhh the blissful sunny lunch on the back lawn, had between throwing the ball to the dog and trying to distract him from your food. Make something for yourself, for everyone, on the weekend. Just because it's the weekend doesn't mean you should leave it to someone else to look after lunch. Get up and get cooking.

OK, so a few words on the mind-boggling potential of weekend lunches. My favourite lunch is one with a friend on the balcony, with my legs crossed in the sun, a plate balancing on my lap, loving that it's finally the weekend. What's on that plate depends entirely on my mood, the weather, my friends, how late I went to bed. There are stacks of newspapers and magazines, and I've probably just finished my morning coffee, frankly. There's music playing, but not drowning out everything so we can't chat.

There are, of course, days we want something quick before we head out and actually be a bit active, too. A quesadilla, a chopped salad, some grilled vegetables or shredded chicken and mayonnaise thrown between two slices of rye . . . all excellent options for food-on-the-run. Flick through this chapter and you may think I've gone a bit mad. Beetroot gazpacho? Oyster po'boy? Are these things that people really eat? *Mais oui,* as the French would say. We are upping the ante on the potential of lunch. And life.

SAUSAGE AND ONION MARMALADE BUNS *

I like to think the sausage sandwich is very Australiana. I want to draw a kangaroo on your brown paper lunch bag. I want to give you a souvenir fluffy koala and a postcard of Santa Claus riding on a surfboard, and then pack you off. Let's hope the old-fashioned sausage sandwich continues to stand the test of time. And let's hope the crocodile-foot key ring does not.

½ tbsp olive oil
2 free-range pork sausages
4 soft round bread rolls
1 tsp Dijon mustard
2 tbsp Onion marmalade (see recipe page 81)

01 Heat oil in a frying pan over medium heat. Cook sausages for 5–8 minutes, turning frequently to brown evenly, until cooked through.
02 Slice sausages lengthways, then acrossways. Open buns and spread a little mustard on one side of each. Divide sausages between them, then dollop some onion marmalade on each.
03 Close buns, wrap in plastic wrap and place in your lunchbox with an icepack or a frozen bottle of water.
Serves 2

TIP: Add a few sticks of cucumber, some crunchy lettuce, or anything that won't sog up your buns.

ANOTHER TIP: Don't have any onion marmalade? Tomato ketchup is a no-brainer, a trustworthy option for those about to miss the bus.

CHICKEN SESAME SAUSAGE ROLLS **

You know exactly what's in these homemade chicken sausage rolls, and they can be frozen to boot. They're great cold, so are perfect for packed lunches. Everyone will be so jealous. You *made these?* Wow.

700 g (1 lb 9 oz) free-range or organic minced (ground) chicken
½ bunch flat-leaf (Italian) parsley, finely chopped
1 tsp chopped thyme leaves
½ bunch spring onions (scallions), thinly sliced
2 sheets frozen puff pastry, thawed, halved
1 egg, lightly beaten
2 tbsp sesame seeds

01 Preheat oven to 200°C (400°F). Line a baking tray with baking paper.
02 In a bowl, combine chicken, herbs and spring onion. Season with sea salt and freshly ground black pepper and mix together well. Use your hands, if necessary, to squish everything together properly.
03 Place one-quarter of the mixture on a long edge of each pastry strip, pressing mixture together well to form a long sausage. Lightly brush the pastry edges with water. Fold pastry over filling to form a long roll, which will be open at the ends.
04 Cut each roll into four. Place on baking tray, brush with beaten egg and sprinkle with sesame seeds. Bake for 25–30 minutes until golden and puffed.
Makes 16 small rolls

TIP: These rolls aren't brilliant reheated in the microwave; the pastry just doesn't make it. If you want to reheat a few at home though, just warm them in a preheated 180°C (350°F) oven for 5 minutes, watching they don't burn. Only reheat them once: you can't reheat anything more than once or you risk food poisoning.

SANDWICH
BOX

DO NOT LITTER
POKKA
POKKA

PRAWN MAYO ROLL **

There's this place in downtown New York called the Pearl Oyster Bar, which does the most darling lobster rolls. Lobster doused in mayo, in a soft brioche roll, with shoestring fries on the side. Ah sigh. This is my cheaper version, which I do when I'm dreaming of the Big Apple. If you're taking this for school or office lunch, have all the different components ready the night before, as you'll probably be in a rush in the morning. Then simply fill the rolls, pack and go.

400 g (14 oz) cooked large local prawns (shrimp), in shells
3 tbsp homemade Mayonnaise (see recipe page 180)
1 celery stalk, finely chopped
juice of ½ lemon
2 soft hot-dog or split-top rolls, split
few watercress sprigs

01 Peel prawns and chop into 2 cm (¾ inch) pieces. Combine in a bowl with mayo, celery and lemon juice. Season with sea salt and freshly ground black pepper to taste.
02 Divide mixture between two rolls and top with some watercress. Wrap well and pack with an icepack.
Makes 2

TIP: If you don't have your own homemade mayo try Japanese mayonnaise. I've heard a top chef say the Kewpie brand (the one in the plastic bottle and red lid) is often as good as the one we can make at home. I have to agree: I use it on sushi, in tacos, and definitely in this prawn and mayo roll. It lasts forever in the fridge too.

ANOTHER TIP: A spike of chilli is great in these. Add a few drops of Tabasco to the mayo, or try one of those mega hot sauces you can buy. Or, there's the ever reliable sprinkle of cayenne pepper.

TUNA, LEMON AND CORIANDER MASH *

If you're not a sandwich person (welcome to the club), this might be your lunchbox saviour. Whip it up the night before, dollop into an airtight container and refrigerate, then pack some crackers, bread or grissini for dipping. If I'm having friends over for lunch I often whip up a bowl of this, and serve alongside the Crisp rosemary flatbreads (see page 49), maybe omitting the rosemary and adding a sprinkle of ground black pepper instead. This mash is also great in a sandwich—just slathered on thick, with some sliced cucumber or grated carrot.

1 egg yolk
1 tsp Dijon mustard
½ cup (125 ml/4 fl oz) olive oil
2 x 185 g (6½ oz) tins dolphin-safe tuna in brine
2 golden shallots, finely chopped
4 tablespoons chopped coriander (cilantro)
grated zest of ½ lemon
juice of 1 lemon

01 Whisk egg yolk and mustard in a small bowl until well combined. Gradually add oil in a slow stream, whisking constantly, until mixture thickens.
02 Drain tuna and mash with a fork, then add to a bowl with shallot, coriander, lemon zest and lemon juice. Season with sea salt and freshly ground black pepper. Spoon into a serving bowl, cover and chill until ready to serve. Serve with crackers or grissini, or use to fill sandwiches or baguette rolls.
Serves 2

CRUNCHY CHICKEN BITES **

Tuck these into pitta bread with some cucumber sticks, or have on their own. Thank heavens it's not just a sandwich for lunch today. I just about lived on these at uni. A girl needs something crunchy and good to get her through a three-hour tutorial on Emily Dickinson.

500 g (1 lb 2 oz) free-range or organic minced (ground) chicken
2 tsp sesame oil
1/4 cup (30 g/1 oz) dry breadcrumbs
grated zest of 1 lemon
2–3 spring onions (scallions), roughly chopped
1/4 cup (45 g/1 1/2 oz) water chestnuts, roughly chopped
1/3 bunch coriander (cilantro), stalks finely chopped, leaves whole
3 tbsp olive oil
soy sauce, for drizzling

01 In a bowl, combine all ingredients except oil and soy sauce. Season with freshly ground black pepper. With clean hands, squish the mixture together until it's well combined. Divide it into four balls, then divide each of these into six small balls, to make 24 balls. Wet your hands while you're making balls if the mixture sticks to you.
02 Place balls in a bowl and drizzle with 1 tbsp oil. Gently roll them around to coat them. Cover and place in the fridge until you're ready to cook (up to 1 day).
03 In a large frying pan, heat the remaining oil over medium-high heat. Cook balls in two or three batches, turning them with tongs until golden brown all over—about 8–10 minutes for each batch. Drizzle with soy sauce (or pack with some of those little fish-shaped soy bottles and an icepack).
Makes 24

TIP: After cooking, you can freeze the chicken bites in little snap-lock bags; they thaw just fine.

ROAST PUMPKIN AND FETA LOAF **

Sweet pumpkin and salty feta cheese make this a lunchy option that also soothes the afternoon sweet cravings. A spread of butter on a few slices of this is an easily packed option for everyday living.

400 g (14 oz) pumpkin (winter squash), peeled and cut into 3–4 cm (1 1/4–1 1/2 inch) chunks
3 tbsp olive oil
1 tbsp balsamic vinegar
1 onion, roughly chopped
1/3 cup (55 g/2 oz) pepitas (pumpkin seeds)
3/4 cup (185 ml/6 fl oz) buttermilk
2 eggs, lightly beaten
1 tsp brown sugar
3 cups (450 g/1 lb) self-raising flour
1/2 tsp paprika
150 g (5 1/2 oz) Danish feta cheese, broken into 1 cm (1/2 inch) chunks

01 Preheat oven to 180°C (350°F). Butter and line a 23 cm x 8 cm (9 inch x 3 1/4 inch) loaf (bar) tin.
02 Toss pumpkin, oil and vinegar together on a baking tray and season with sea salt and freshly ground black pepper. Roast for 12–15 minutes until pumpkin is golden brown and soft when pierced with a skewer. Remove from oven, let cool a little, then smash each pumpkin piece once with a fork. Set aside.
03 In a bowl, mix the onion, pepitas, buttermilk, eggs and sugar until smooth. Fold in the flour and paprika, then gently fold in the feta and pumpkin.
04 Pour mixture into tin. Reduce oven temperature to 160°C (315°F). Bake for 55–60 minutes until a skewer inserted into loaf comes out clean.
05 Allow to cool in tin, before turning out onto a wire rack. Slice and pack for lunch.
Makes 10–12 slices

by the way

THE MULTI-LAYERED TEAR-JERKER: THE ONION

Here's a word of wisdom on onions from Margaret Fulton:

'As I write, my granddaughters are busily chopping onions for a party we're having. One is making dolmades, rice-stuffed vine leaves, the other is making our family favourite, piroshki, little savoury yeast buns with an onion and cabbage filling. One granddaughter is wearing sunglasses to cope with the tear-inducing onion juices (Kate), the other is entirely unaffected (Louise). The tear-promoting properties vary from onion to onion and person to person. One consistent fact is that no developed cuisine can do without them. They are an absolute necessity no matter if we're doing an Indian banquet or a Chinese stir-fry, a British roast dinner or an Italian ragu. We all love onions. A great way to appreciate onions on their own is to simply cut into thick wedges, roll in olive oil and slow oven-roast until very tender. Remove from oven and drizzle with a little balsamic vinegar. Yum! Great served with crusty bread or as part of an antipasto platter. By the way, if you are particularly prone to crying during onion cutting, try first skinning the onion under a cold tap, or sit well back from the onion, so that your face isn't right in the firing line. Otherwise, give the sunglasses a go.'

ONION MARMALADE **

A dollop with a sausage, a plop with roast potatoes, a smear on a ham sandwich, a scratching with cheese and crackers, a spoonful in my mouth.

3 tbsp olive oil
2 red onions, thinly sliced
2 brown onions, thinly sliced
3 tbsp red wine vinegar

01 Heat oil in a large heavy-based frying pan and add onions. Cover and cook over low heat for 5–8 minutes, stirring now and then to prevent sticking or browning.

02 Remove lid and cook, stirring, for another 10–15 minutes until onion is very soft. Stir in vinegar and cook, uncovered, for another 5–8 minutes until vinegar has reduced and onion has caramelised. Season with sea salt and freshly ground black pepper; cool and store in a jar in the fridge.

Makes 1 medium jar, about 2 cups (500 ml/17 fl oz) in volume

WORLD TOUR

THAI FISH CAKES **

If that lunchtime hunger comes with a craving for something more exotic than a peanut butter sandwich, this one works. Pack these up with an iceblock or a frozen bottle of water, so they stay fresh and cold. These are great for dinner, too—just pack up leftovers as a lunchtime morsel.

600 g (1 lb 5 oz) white fish fillets, skinned, boned, cubed
2 tbsp red curry paste
1 tbsp fish sauce
1 tsp sugar
250 g (9 oz) green beans, cut into 5 mm (1/4 inch) lengths
coriander (cilantro) leaves, to garnish

Cucumber pickle

2 Lebanese (short) cucumbers, halved lengthways, then thinly sliced
1 spring onion (scallion), finely chopped
1/3 cup (80 ml/2 1/2 fl oz) white vinegar
2 tbsp caster (superfine) sugar
1 bird's eye chilli, seeds removed, sliced

01 Mince fish, in batches, in a food processor. Transfer to a large bowl and add 1 1/2 tbsp water, curry paste, fish sauce, sugar and a good pinch of sea salt. Mix well. Add beans and mix again with your hands.
02 With wetted hands, form the mixture into 20 small cakes, about 5 cm (2 inches) round and 1 cm (1/2 inch) thick. Refrigerate for 10 minutes.
03 Meanwhile, combine all cucumber pickle ingredients in a bowl.
04 Lightly spray a non-stick frying pan with cooking oil spray and heat over high heat. Cook fish cakes in batches for 3 minutes each, turning halfway through. Arrange on a serving plate and serve with cucumber pickle.
Makes about 20

TIP: You can freeze the cooked fish cakes, then heat them up as you want them.

FALAFEL BALLS WITH GRILLED EGGPLANT **

Packets of pocket or pitta bread make a nice change from the ordinary sandwich. Easy-to-make falafel balls can be prepared ahead of time and kept in the freezer, and they're great cold for lunch. Take three or four out the night before and put them in the fridge, ready for the next day's lunch.

1 eggplant (aubergine), cut into 1 cm (1/2 inch) rounds
3 tbsp olive oil, for brushing
400 g (14 oz) tin chickpeas, rinsed and drained
1 egg, lightly beaten
1/2 tsp ground cumin
1/2 tsp cayenne pepper
1/2 tsp ground turmeric
1 tbsp coriander (cilantro) leaves, chopped
1 tbsp flat-leaf (Italian) parsley, chopped
1 garlic clove, finely chopped
1 tbsp tahini paste or olive oil
1/2 cup (55 g/2 oz) dry breadcrumbs
1/3 cup (50 g/1 3/4 oz) plain (all-purpose) flour
rice bran oil, olive oil or vegetable oil, for pan-frying
5 small pitta breads

To serve

lettuce leaves
sliced tomato
hummus or natural yoghurt
lemon wedge

* try me

01 Brush eggplant slices with olive oil and fry in a pan on both sides until golden and tender. Set aside.
02 Blend chickpeas in a food processor until finely chopped, then transfer to a bowl. Add the egg, spices, herbs, garlic, tahini and breadcrumbs, then combine to make a soft, firm mixture—add 1–2 tbsp water if needed to help bind together.
03 Form mixture into small oval balls, about 2 cm (3/4 inch) in diameter. Spread the flour on a plate, then roll balls in the flour.
04 Heat a 5 mm (1/4 inch) depth of oil in a large frying pan over medium heat. When oil is hot but not smoking, fry the falafel balls, in batches, for 3–4 minutes, or until golden brown. Remove and drain on paper towels.
05 Let them cool, then pack for lunch, or store them in the freezer in snap-lock bags—they will keep for up to 1 month.
06 Pack with a few pieces of eggplant, which you can use to wrap up the balls. Otherwise, just pop the eggplant and falafel in a half-slice of pitta bread, with lettuce, tomato and hummus to make a wrap. Pack a wedge of lemon for squeezing too.
Makes about 16 falafel balls

QUESADILLAS **

There were days in the creation of this book where I didn't leave the house until about 5 p.m. I'd grab a morning coffee and the papers, sit at my desk and tap tap tap until something niggled away. About midday I'd call a hunger break (or its other name for the freelance journalist: procrastination). So there I am, head in the pantry, wondering what I can eat that's not a jar of jam. Ladies and gentlemen, I can now declare, this book was built on that great Mexican staple, the quesadilla. Here's how.

1 large corn or wheat tortilla
2 slices prosciutto
jalapeño chillies, from a jar
2 tbsp grated cheese
1 golden shallot, finely sliced
few coriander (cilantro) sprigs
1 tsp olive oil

01 Heat a chargrill pan or griddle—one of those frying pans with the grooves on it—over high heat.
02 Meanwhile, place tortilla on bench in front of you and cover with prosciutto, all laid out flat.
03 Over one half of the tortilla, scatter jalapeño, cheese, shallot and coriander. Fold the other half of the tortilla over the filling-topped half, to create a half-moon.
04 Brush top with oil, then carefully flip over and oil other side. Carefully move tortilla to pan, which will now be very hot. Press down with a heatproof spatula and really flatten tortilla. Cook for 1–2 minutes each side until golden brown and nicely striped.
05 Remove to a chopping board and cut into thirds. Arriba Arriba!
Serves 1

HENNY CO.
BASCO
BRAND
ER SAUCE

MESSY PRAWN TACOS **

It's times like this I'm so glad I live in Australia. The sun's beating down, there's salt on my skin from the surf, I have too many freckles despite the hat and sun cream, and my friends are around for a long and very lazy lunch. Last thing I want to do is spend the whole time in the kitchen, so I do these tacos. Messy and glorious.

1 kg (2 lb 4 oz) raw local prawns (shrimp)
¼ Chinese cabbage (wong bok), very finely shredded
juice of 1 lime
2 tbsp olive oil
1 onion, finely chopped
1 tsp ground cumin
1 tsp ground paprika
1 tsp ground allspice
1 bunch coriander (cilantro), stalks and leaves roughly chopped
1 ripe avocado
jalapeño peppers, from a jar
mayonnaise, to serve
2 limes, cut into wedges
12 mini tortillas

01 Peel prawns by pulling off head, then tail, then legs and shell in one swift movement. Set prawns aside; discard shells.
02 Marinate cabbage in a bowl with half the lime juice and a few big pinches of sea salt. Toss together and set aside for 30 minutes to soften.
03 Heat oil in a large frying pan and fry onion over medium–low heat, stirring gently until soft and translucent but not browned. Turn heat to high. Add prawns to pan and cook for 3–5 minutes, turning with tongs so they turn golden brown on both sides—be careful not to overcook them.
04 Add spices and toss to coat prawns. Season, add half the coriander, then remove from heat. Place in a serving dish and decorate with a few coriander leaves.
05 Halve avocado, remove stone, then scoop flesh out into a little bowl. Mix in the remaining lime juice and coriander to make a guacamole.
06 Place cabbage in a colander and squeeze out the juices, then place in a serving bowl (the cabbage will be soft, with a tender bite).
07 Take prawns, guacamole and cabbage to the table, with separate little dishes of jalapeño, mayonnaise and lime wedges. Serve tortillas on a little plate and let everyone help themselves. Things will get messy, but so so good.
Serves 4–6

BLOOD ORANGE, FENNEL AND WATERCRESS SALAD **

Here's a sweet and peppery little accompaniment for just about any lunch. Or have it on its own: just a fork, a plate and you.

2 blood oranges
1 fennel bulb, very thinly sliced
1 large bunch watercress, thick stalks removed
1 golden shallot, thinly sliced lengthways
2 tsp raspberry vinegar
2 tbsp olive oil

01 Peel oranges with a small, sharp serrated knife, balancing oranges on a board, and removing the bitter white pith along with the peel. Cut oranges acrossways into slices 1 cm (½ inch) thick. Arrange on a serving platter in a single layer.
02 In a bowl, combine the fennel, watercress and shallot. In a small bowl, whisk together vinegar and oil until combined; season with sea salt and freshly ground black pepper to taste. Pour dressing over fennel and watercress, then toss together.
03 Arrange watercress salad over orange slices. Pour any remaining dressing over the top.
Serves 4 as a side salad

SNAPPY SALADS {3 WAYS}

Be it a leafy herby French salad tossed with a simple vinaigrette, a spiced Moroccan pile of grated vegetables or a thrown-together salad of room-temperature roast vegetables tossed with mint leaves and a splash of white balsamic vinegar, I love a salad. Experiment with herbs from the garden and different types of lettuce in one salad, or add some crumbled feta or toasted nuts. Salads, to my mind, are one of the great culinary inventions.

Moroccan carrot and beetroot salad *

Morocco, that North African country that gives us tagines and preserved lemon, couscous and some of the most intricate and gorgeous design, architecture and people, invented this brilliant salad. I had it on my travels there, and now make it all the time.

01 Peel 2 raw beetroot (beets) and 2 carrots, then grate them into a bowl. Sprinkle with a pinch of ground cumin and season well with sea salt and freshly ground black pepper. Drizzle with Lemon dressing (see page 90), or just the juice from ½ lemon and extra virgin olive oil, then toss together lightly.

Serves 2–4, depending on whether it's a side dish or a main

Leafy asparagus salad *

Just because it's a salad doesn't mean it's predictable. Asparagus is lovely tossed together with salad leaves, and the creamy dressing just seals the whole marvellous deal.

01 Trim woody hard ends from 1 bunch (175 g/6 oz) asparagus. Using a vegetable peeler, slice asparagus lengthways into a bowl. Add a few handfuls of lovely crunchy mixed lettuce leaves (such as watercress, radicchio, cos (romaine), even iceberg torn up a little), then drizzle the lot with Creamy yoghurt dressing (see page 90) or your favourite dressing. Toss together using very clean hands (not at the table!), or some salad servers.

Serves 2–4, depending on whether it's a side dish or a main

Broccoli, bacon and tomato salad **

Crunchy, salty, bacony and healthy. Dude . . . Try this.

01 Cut 1 head of broccoli into florets, then blanch in boiling, salted water until just cooked—about 2–5 minutes. Drain and refresh under cold running water; drain well and place in a bowl. Fry 3 bacon slices in a frying pan over medium–high heat until crispy, then break up into bite-sized pieces. Add bacon to broccoli with about 8 halved cherry tomatoes. Snip over ½ bunch chives, sprinkle with French dressing (see page 90), toss together and serve.

Serves 2–4, depending on whether it's a side dish or a main

by the way

FLOWER POWER

Flowers are not just for Valentine's Day. Some little petals scattered fresh on a sweet or savoury dish can add a lovely flavour and make it totally pretty.

Dandelion flowers have a slightly bitter taste but are great in green salads.

Marigold flowers taste slightly peppery. Use the petals scattered in mixed salads.

Rocket flowers are pretty and peppery. Throw them over a salad or rich pasta dish.

Nasturtiums are peppery numbers, and the flowers add a pretty bright orange or yellow to salads or even a Beef carpaccio (see page 119). You can eat the leaves and the flowers, and they grow in the garden like crazy.

on the side

QUICK PRAWN AND MANGO SALAD **

In Sydney there's something uniquely summery about both prawns and mangoes. Together they're a pleasing perfect match for a backyard lawn, kick-the-ball-around, barbecue-is-fired-up afternoon. Remember your hat and sunscreen.

1 mango
400 g (14 oz) large cooked local prawns (shrimp), peeled, deveined and sliced in half lengthways
1–2 handfuls watercress sprigs, or crunchy green cos (romaine) lettuce leaves
olive oil, for drizzling
juice of ½ lime
flat-leaf (Italian) parsley or coriander (cilantro), torn

01 Peel mango using a vegetable peeler. Thinly slice the flesh, discarding the stone. Place mango in a bowl with prawns and watercress or cos lettuce, then gently toss.
02 Mix together oil, lime juice and herbs. Season with sea salt and freshly ground black pepper and drizzle over salad. **Serves 2**

JAM JAR DRESSINGS {4 WAYS}

Throw the ingredients in a clean, empty jar, screw the lid on tight, shake shake shake, then pour. These four dressings can be used on just about any salad or even steamed vegetables. As a general guide, dressings should be three parts oil to one part acid (lemon juice or vinegar), and should taste a little bit too acidic. Once it's on the salad it will be perfect.

French dressing *

Every self-respecting home cook, chef and burgeoning gastronome has this on their need-to-know repertoire. Add a little to your salad, toss it together, then add a little more if really needed. Nobody loves a soggy salad.

01 In a jar, combine ½ finely chopped garlic clove, 1 tsp Dijon mustard, 2 tbsp red or white wine vinegar, a pinch of sea salt and freshly ground black pepper and 6 tbsp extra virgin olive oil. Put the lid on and shake vigorously until it's properly creamy. Drizzle sparingly over a salad and store any leftovers in the fridge.

Makes ½ small jar of dressing

Honey sesame soy dressing *

Perfect for any Asian-style salad, or even cold leftover noodles.

01 In a jar, combine 1 tsp honey, 2 tsp soy sauce, juice of ½ lemon, 1 tbsp mirin (Japanese rice wine), 1 teaspoon sesame seeds, 2 tsp sesame oil and 5 tbsp extra virgin olive oil. Put the lid on, shake and drizzle.

Makes ½ small jar of dressing

Lemon dressing *

Simple and elegant—perfect for blanched vegetables or a perfect green salad.

01 In a jar, combine juice of ½ lemon, 6 tbsp extra virgin olive oil and a pinch of sea salt and freshly ground black pepper. Put the lid on, shake and drizzle.

Makes ½ small jar of dressing

Creamy yoghurt dressing **

Creamy and so good, this goes with vegetable salads or plain leafy greens with maybe some leftover roast chicken torn into bite-sized pieces and thrown in.

01 In a jar, combine 6 tbsp natural yoghurt, 1 tbsp extra virgin olive oil, 2 tbsp white or red wine vinegar, 1–2 tbsp chopped herbs (like mint or parsley), and a pinch of sea salt and freshly ground black pepper. Put the lid on, shake and drizzle.

Makes ½ small jar of dressing

in my world

SALAD DRESSING

When my mother trained at London's Le Cordon Bleu cookery school in the 1960s, an important test for salads was whether they were dressed properly. A teacher would walk around the class and literally lift the entire salad out of the bowl with their hands, then look into the serving bowl. The bowl was not to have any puddle, pool or lake of dressing in the bottom. There could be a light film of dressing, and that's all.

how to

DRESS A SALAD

- # Too often people overdress salads, thinking it makes salads better, instead of the mushy, cloying, acidic chaos they really are. Every leaf should be very lightly coated, but there should be nothing in the bottom of the bowl.
- # If you've overdressed your salad, lift it out of the bowl with tongs or clean hands, let the drips fall off, and place it in another bowl.
- # Use half the dressing you think you'll need, toss it together, then add a little more if the salad still looks underdressed.

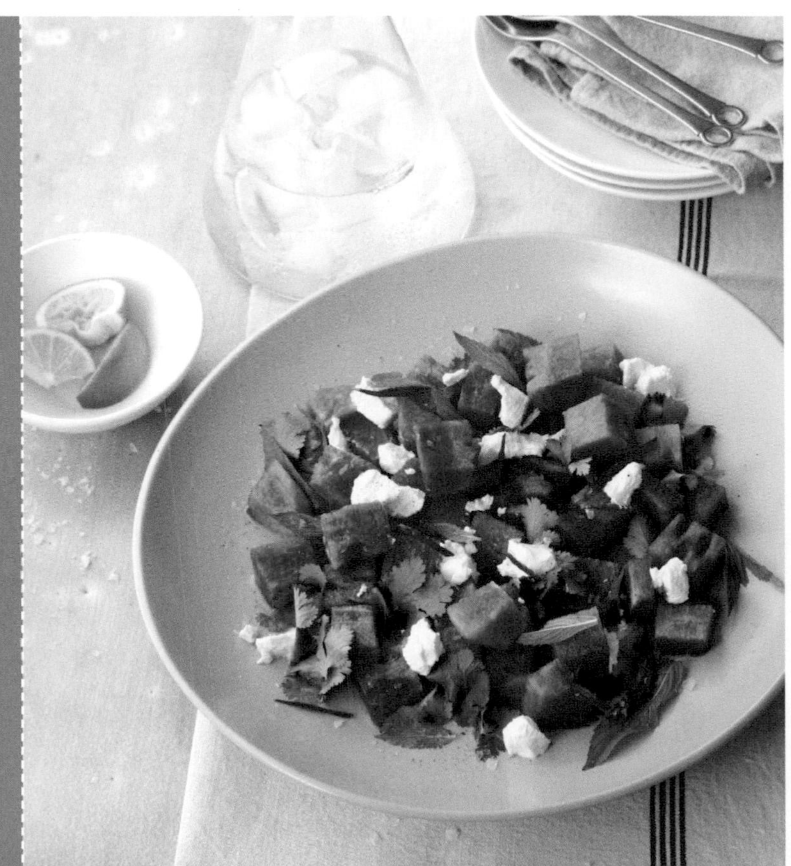

WATERMELON SALAD *

Watermelon in summer is like a massive glass of cold juice, but with a crispy, messy, fresh edge. Tossed together with sea salt, coriander (cilantro) leaves and mild Danish feta cheese, it's just the best salad side for a weekend barbecue. Serve really cold, with a cold drink for extra measure. This is a perfect addition to a barbecue.

850 g (1 lb 14 oz) watermelon, seeds removed, flesh cut into 3 cm (1¼ inch) cubes
juice of 1 lime
½ small red chilli, seeds removed, thinly sliced
180 g (6 oz) Danish feta cheese, or a little more or less if you prefer
½ bunch coriander (cilantro) leaves

01 Put watermelon in a serving bowl. Sprinkle with lime juice and chilli, then crumble feta over. Toss lightly, cover and store in the fridge until ready to serve. Sprinkle with coriander and a good pinch of sea salt just before serving.

Serves 4–6 as a side

by the way

SQUID!

Whenever possible, buy whole baby local squid (sometimes called baby calamari) rather than the imported skinned and gutted variety. And never buy those calamari rings. The light purple mottling on baby squids' exterior is so thin it can be eaten as is, so you don't need to peel the squid first.

how to

PEELING PRAWNS

Prawny hands. Ewwww. It's time you got over that 'food-is-gross' thing. I only ever buy whole prawns, and then I peel them myself. Call me crazy but I'm not mad on the idea that someone else–or worse, a machine–has fiddled with my crustaceans. It's easy, don't be squeamish: just pull off the head, then the tail, then roll your finger under the shell and pull it off with the legs in one swift move.

If you're peeling raw prawns, put your thumb under the prawn between the head and the body and lift the head up and off–as you do, grab hold of the long dark inner tract that runs through the prawn, pinch tightly and then gently pull it out in one piece as you remove the head.

OYSTER PO'BOYS **

A New Orleans signature sandwich, piled with either fried prawns, chips or fried oysters, and slathered with mayonnaise, sliced pickles and a slab of tomato, then wrapped in butcher's paper. Instead of oysters you can use little peeled local raw prawns (shrimp)—just cook them a tad longer.

1–2 cups (250 ml–500 ml/9 fl oz–17 fl oz) rice bran oil or peanut oil
1 egg
2/3 cup (170 ml/5 1/2 fl oz) milk
1/3 cup (50 g/1 3/4 oz) plain (all-purpose) flour
1–2 tsp smoked paprika
1/3 cup (65 g/2 1/4 oz) fine semolina
20 Sydney rock oysters, shucked
4 small soft white rolls, split
mayonnaise, to serve
1 baby cos (romaine) lettuce, leaves separated, each halved lengthways
4 cherry tomatoes, thinly sliced

01 Preheat oil in a wok or large heavy-based saucepan over medium heat.
02 Meanwhile, in a small bowl, whisk together egg and milk. Season with sea salt and freshly ground black pepper and set aside.
03 Spread flour on a plate and sprinkle with paprika. Sprinkle semolina over another plate. Lightly dust oysters in flour, then dip in egg mixture, then semolina.
04 Use tongs to carefully drop oysters, in batches of about five, into hot oil—be very careful as the hot oil may spit. Cook oysters until golden, 2–3 minutes per batch. Drain on paper towels, season with salt and pepper and keep warm.
05 Spread rolls generously with mayonnaise; top with lettuce and tomato, then the oysters. Serve while oysters are still hot.
Makes 4 good-sized po'boys

TIP: You can buy jars of raw (not marinated) oysters from most good fish markets or providores, which are excellent value. Otherwise, ask your fishmonger to shuck about 20 for you.

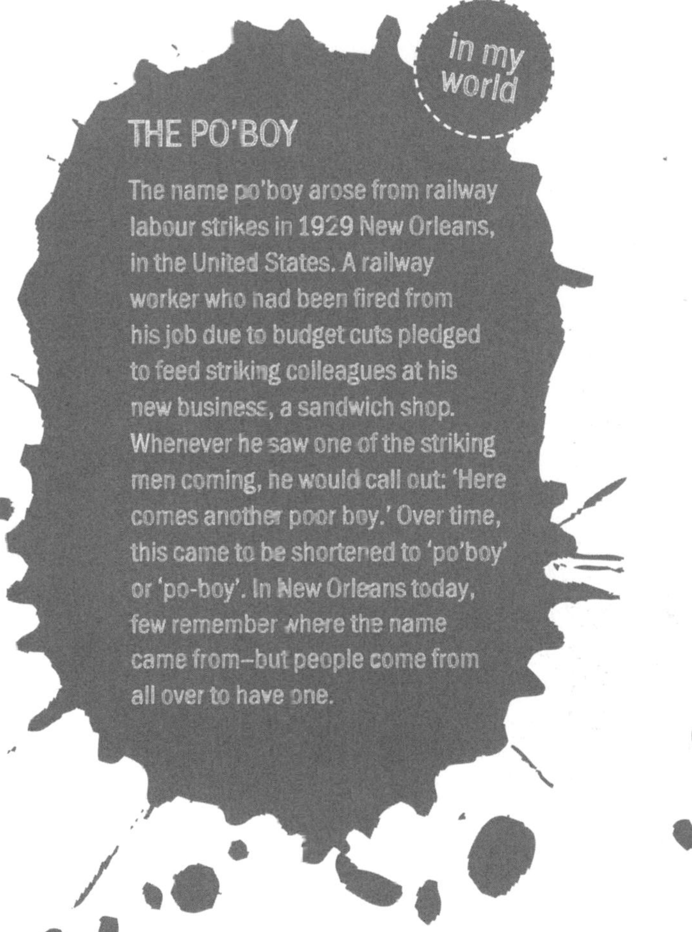

THE PO'BOY

The name po'boy arose from railway labour strikes in 1929 New Orleans, in the United States. A railway worker who had been fired from his job due to budget cuts pledged to feed striking colleagues at his new business, a sandwich shop. Whenever he saw one of the striking men coming, he would call out: 'Here comes another poor boy.' Over time, this came to be shortened to 'po'boy' or 'po-boy'. In New Orleans today, few remember where the name came from—but people come from all over to have one.

* try me

THE NEW PRAWN COCKTAIL **

You may not believe this, but the prawn cocktail was once the height of dinner-party sophistication. Now, it's just lunch. And to add insult to injury, we've improved on it greatly. This is a cool crunchy thing, packed with flavour. You'll show everyone how it's done now.

1 tbsp olive oil
1 garlic clove, finely chopped
1 tbsp smoked paprika
20 large raw local prawns (shrimp), heads and shells discarded, tails kept on
juice of 1/2 lime
1/2 iceberg lettuce, cut into 4 wedges
1 cup (about 30 g/1 oz) fresh greens, such as watercress, rocket (arugula), coriander (cilantro), mint or flat-leaf (Italian) parsley, or a mixture
1 lime, cut into wedges

Cocktail sauce

2/3 cup (165 g/5 3/4 oz) mayonnaise
1 tbsp tomato ketchup
1 tsp Worcestershire sauce
juice of 1/4 lemon
dash of Tabasco sauce

01 Prepare cocktail sauce. Place all ingredients in a bowl and whisk together with a fork. Season to taste.
02 In a bowl, mix together oil, garlic, paprika, prawns and lime juice. Season well.
03 Heat a large heavy-based frying pan. Add half the prawns and cook, turning frequently, until golden brown on both sides, about 2–3 minutes. Remove with tongs and set aside; repeat with remaining prawns.
04 Arrange lettuce wedges and prawns on a large platter. Scatter fresh greens and drizzle with cocktail sauce. Serve with lime wedges and Tabasco to spice things up even more.
Serves 4

HERBY CHIPS ***

Hot chips wrapped in paper: is there anything more divinely shareable? Take these to the lawn, dear friends, on a scattered, summery, relaxed afternoon. (See pic on page 96.)

750 g (1 lb 10 oz) kipfler (fingerling) potatoes
vegetable oil or rice bran oil, for deep-frying
8 garlic cloves, unpeeled
1/2 bunch rosemary
1/2 bunch flat-leaf (Italian) parsley
2 tsp dried chilli flakes (optional)
good-quality malt vinegar, for drizzling

01 Place potatoes in a large saucepan of cold water. Bring to the boil and cook for 15–20 minutes until just cooked and still firm in the centre. Drain well, then allow to cool on paper towels. Crush cooled potatoes a little by pressing down on them with the palm of your hand.
02 Meanwhile, heat about 2 cups (500 ml/17 fl oz) oil in a wok or heavy-based saucepan. Test the heat by gently dropping a small cube of bread into the oil—it should turn golden in about 10 seconds.
03 Carefully add potatoes to hot oil in about five batches. Cook each batch for about 2 minutes, turning using tongs until golden brown and crispy. Remove with tongs or a slotted spoon onto paper towels.
04 Add garlic to oil and fry for 30 seconds, until soft—be careful of hot oil, as the garlic may pop open and splash. Scoop garlic out onto paper towels with potatoes. Drop herbs into hot oil and remove immediately.
05 Break up herbs over the potatoes. Sprinkle with chilli flakes, toss everything together, and transfer the whole lot to a sheet of butcher's paper on a large wooden board. Season with sea salt and offer vinegar for sprinkling.
Serves 4

DON'T BURN, BABY, BURN

I'm sitting here worrying about you and hot oil. I'm thinking, 'Goodness dear me, I do hope they use great care and undying precautions while heating the hot oil—or I'll be in hot oil myself!' Here's how to make sure I don't get into trouble, you don't hurt yourself, and you still get to enjoy sizzling hot food.

First, find some longish tongs; make sure they're clean and totally dry.
Second, put some shoes on. Not sandals—go and get some proper lace-ups or boots, so if that hot oil spits, your toes don't blister and hop.
Now, find a long apron that's easy to take off, long enough to cover your legs, and high enough to cover your top. Wrap the apron strings around you, so you tie it up at the front. If disaster strikes and you get splattered with hot oil, that oil-drenched apron will be quick and easy to take off.
Finally, clean up the benches, empty the sink of dishes and make sure you're working in a clean and clear space. You need easy access to the cold tap in case you get a splash of oil on you. If that does happen, and I hope it doesn't, gently run the affected part under cold water for 10–20 minutes, then get some ice wrapped in clean paper towel and hold it on the burn for the rest of the day. Don't cover it with cream or anything until a lot of the heat has come out of it. Even if it feels OK, just keep the ice on it anyway. If the burn is really bad, obviously get it properly looked at, in case you need to call the doctor.

Yes, this hot oil malarky is serious stuff. So the best thing to do is take ridiculously good care not to burn yourself in the first place.

Left: Herby chips (page 94)

CRISPY CAULIFLOWER BREADCRUMB SALAD **

Judge not the cauliflower by name. This is not the cream-soaked, watery thing you had at Aunt Mildred's house last winter. Sicily, as in Italy, has inspired this crunchy dish. Italy is the source of some of the best food in the world. It's to do with the climate, and the Italian zest for food and life and more food. If we could learn more from the Italians, we'd be better cooks, and better eaters.

1 large cauliflower, cut into small 4 cm (1½ inch) florets, stalks chopped to same size
6 tbsp olive oil
3 garlic cloves, thinly sliced
¾ cup (85 g/3 oz) dry breadcrumbs
1 handful flat-leaf (Italian) parsley leaves
40 g (1½ oz) pecorino cheese, finely grated
juice of ½ lemon

01 Preheat oven to 210°C (415°F). Line two baking trays with baking paper.
02 Put cauliflower florets and stalks in a large bowl. Add half the oil, season with sea salt and freshly ground black pepper and toss to coat. Spread cauliflower in a single layer over baking trays. Roast, turning occasionally, for about 50 minutes until golden. Remove from oven and allow to cool to room temperature.
03 Meanwhile, heat the remaining oil in a small saucepan over low heat. Add garlic and cook until soft, about 5 minutes. Add breadcrumbs, increase the heat to medium–low and cook for another 3 minutes, or until crumbs are golden and crispy.
04 Tip breadcrumb mixture into a large bowl. Add cauliflower and gently toss. Transfer to a serving platter, if desired. Scatter with parsley and cheese, sprinkle with lemon juice and serve.
Serves 4–6

SALT AND PEPPER SQUID ***

I've ruined many clothes with oil trying to cook this dish. Here's what I've learned: all squid splatters, but wet squid splatters more. Lots of squid splatters more than small portions. Now this is brave work, cleaning squid. I've done it and, truly, so can you. (See pic on page 72.)

500 g (1 lb 2 oz) baby local squid
1 tsp Sichuan peppercorns
2 tbsp sea salt
6 tbsp tapioca flour (also called arrowroot flour)
4 cups (1 litre/35 fl oz) rice bran oil or peanut oil
1 large red chilli, sliced
4 spring onions (scallions), sliced
1 lime, cut into wedges

01 To prepare and clean the squid, gently pull tentacles and insides from body. Feel inside the squid and pull out hard, transparent backbone and discard it. Cut off tentacles just below the eye and set aside; discard eye and insides. Slice body into 1 cm (½ inch) thick rings, then dry with paper towels and set aside with tentacles.
02 Roughly grind Sichuan peppercorns and salt, using a mortar and pestle or clean coffee grinder. Combine tapioca flour and pepper mixture on a plate.
03 Heat oil in a small heavy-based saucepan or wok until very hot—it should sizzle when tested with a piece of chilli. Add chilli and spring onion and fry until crispy, about 20–30 seconds, then remove with tongs or a slotted spoon and set aside.
04 Working in four batches, coat squid in flour mixture, shaking off excess flour before gently dropping squid into the oil. Cook until golden, about 2–3 minutes, then remove with tongs or a slotted spoon and drain on paper towels. Toss together with chilli and spring onion, sprinkle with more sea salt and serve at once, with lime wedges.
Serves 4

TIP: The trick here is to cook the squid quickly at a high temperature to keep it tender, as there's no thick batter for the oil to get through. The light flour dredging gives the coating a light, crisp edge. If you don't have tapioca flour, the more common cornflour (cornstarch) has a similar effect when frying as well. And be sure to read the must-dos on page 97 for tips on deep-frying.

TO BLANCH OR BOIL?

When cooking vegetables, should you boil the water first, then add the vegetables, or put them in cold water and turn the heat up? Here's a great general rule to remember.

If the vegetable grows above ground–like green beans, broccoli, peas, zucchini (courgette) and so many vegies do–they should be added to a saucepan full of boiling (usually salted) water. It means these vegies, which need very little cooking, are done in a flash.

If the vegetable grows underground–like potatoes and carrots–they go into cold water, then onto the heat. This stops them getting too cooked on the outside before their insides are even warm.

SPICED ROAST PUMPKIN, LENTIL AND FETA SALAD **

Roast pumpkin will jazz up any leafy greens. Not a salad fan? Here's your man. It's all nutty lentils, salty cheese and sweet—almost sticky—pumpkin, tossed together and outlandishly labelling itself a salad.

½ butternut pumpkin (squash), peeled, seeds removed, then cut into 2–3 cm (¾–1¼ inch) cubes
3 tbsp olive oil
1 tsp ground cumin
1 tsp smoked paprika
400 g (14 oz) tin green lentils, rinsed and drained
4 cups (200 g/7 oz) baby spinach leaves
1 cup (130 g/4½ oz) crumbled Danish feta cheese
3 tbsp roughly torn mint leaves
1 tbsp red wine vinegar

01 Preheat oven to 190°C (375°F). Place pumpkin on a baking tray, drizzle with 2 tbsp oil and season with sea salt and freshly ground black pepper. Roast for 15 minutes.
02 Remove from oven. Sprinkle the pumpkin with cumin and paprika. Toss together well, turning pumpkin over, then roast for another 10–15 minutes until soft and easily pierced with a knife. Set aside to cool to room temperature.
03 Place pumpkin and 1–2 tbsp of its cooking oil in a large serving bowl. Add remaining ingredients and toss together well. Season to taste with salt and pepper and serve.
Serves 4

TIP: Instead of lentils you can use extra green leaves like rocket (arugula) or cos (romaine) lettuce.

PLOUGHMAN'S CHEDDAR LOAF *

Excellent things stuffed into a large loaf of bread. This is perfect picnic food.

1 large round loaf wholemeal (whole-wheat) or seeded bread
1/3 cup (115 g/4 oz) onion marmalade (see recipe page 81)
200 g (7 oz) cheddar cheese
10 baby cornichons (small crisp gherkin pickles)
6–8 slices free-range ham
1 handful baby spinach leaves

01 Using a small, serrated knife, cut a circle out of top of loaf, about 1 cm (1/2 inch) in from top outside edge of loaf. Use your hands to pull out as much of the fluffy inside bread as you can; reserve top of the loaf and insides.
02 Spread a little onion marmalade on inside bottom of loaf, then layer a few slices of cheese, 3 or 4 cornichons and 2 slices of ham inside. Sprinkle over half the spinach leaves, then some of the insides of the bread.
03 Repeat layers again until loaf is quite full. Replace top of the loaf.
04 Wrap the whole loaf tightly in plastic wrap, then place in the fridge until ready to serve—overnight if you like. Cut into thick slices or wedges to serve.
Serves 6–8

BEETROOT GAZPACHO **

I'm obsessed with beetroot, that bloody-red root vegetable. Whenever I see the glorious grubby bunches of baby beetroot at the greengrocer, I buy buy buy, like some crazed beetroot monopolist. Its sheer versatility has it roasted, or shredded and mixed with chocolate in cakes, hidden in burgers, tucked into ravioli . . . and pounded into this cold, creamy soup. Sure, cold beetroot soup sounds a bit weird, but this soup is summery and fragrant, acidic and sweet, and is everything you'll want one hot summer afternoon. A variation of this recipe appears in my dear friend Kristin Hove's cookbook, *Collected.*

750 g (1 lb 12 oz) baby beetroot (beets), leaves and stalks discarded
1 small onion, finely chopped
1 garlic clove, finely chopped
1 tbsp capers
1/2 cup (55 g/2 oz) dry breadcrumbs
3 cups (750 ml/26 fl oz) vegetable stock
1 tbsp red wine vinegar
1 cup (260 g/9 1/4 oz) natural yoghurt, plus extra to serve
2 tsp brown sugar
1/2 bunch chives

01 Wash beetroot and place in a large saucepan. Cover with cold water and cook over medium–high heat for 35–40 minutes, until easily pierced with a knife. Remove from heat, drain well and leave to cool. Once cool, slip off the skins with your hands and discard them.
02 Roughly chop beetroot and place in a blender. Add onion, garlic, capers and breadcrumbs, then pulse a few times until you get a chunky paste. Add stock, vinegar, yoghurt and sugar and blend to form a soup. Season to taste with sea salt and freshly ground black pepper.
03 Chill in the fridge for at least 2 hours, or until ready to serve.
04 Pour into little glasses and top with a small dollop of yoghurt. Use scissors to snip chives over the top, then serve.
Serves 6–8 as a light lunch, or more if served in little glasses as a starter for a longer, larger meal

TIP: This is also great made using roasted beetroot, which makes things even sweeter.

CHICKEN SPRING ROLLS WITH SWEET DIPPING SAUCE ***

This is the most snackable snack there is. Odd perhaps, that it's in the lunch chapter. But I just know you'll be hankering for these early one Saturday afternoon after the beach, and everyone will just call it lunch. I say to use between 20–25 wrappers here—it just depends how big your carrots are (and how much mixture you snack on before you finish rolling them!).

100 g (3½ oz) dried vermicelli noodles
1 tbsp vegetable oil or rice bran oil
2 garlic cloves, finely chopped
250 g (9 oz) free-range or organic minced (ground) chicken
½ bunch coriander (cilantro), stalks finely chopped, leaves left whole
2 carrots, coarsely grated
3 cups (225 g/8 oz) finely shredded cabbage
¼ cup (45 g/1½ oz) water chestnuts, roughly chopped
2 tbsp soy sauce
20–25 frozen spring roll wrappers, thawed
rice bran oil, for deep frying

Sweet dipping sauce
¼ cup (55 g/2 oz) white sugar
¼ cup (60 ml/2 fl oz) white vinegar
3 tsp fish sauce

01 Soak noodles in warm water for 10 minutes until soft. Drain and rinse, then use scissors to cut the noodle bundle in half once or twice.
02 To make the filling, heat oil in a large heavy-based frying pan over medium–high heat. Add garlic, chicken, coriander stalks and a good grind of black pepper. Stir-fry until chicken is light brown and almost cooked, about 2 minutes. Use a wooden spoon to break up chicken as it cooks.
03 Add carrot (reserving 1 tbsp for the sauce) and cabbage. Stir-fry until vegetables soften a little, about 4–5 minutes. Remove from heat and stir in coriander leaves, water chestnuts and soy sauce. Add the noodles and fold together to combine.
04 Put the sweet dipping sauce ingredients in a small saucepan with 2 tbsp water. Bring to a gentle simmer for 3 minutes, until sugar has dissolved. Turn off heat, add the reserved carrot and set aside.
05 Before you roll spring rolls, fill a little bowl with water. Place a wrapper on a work surface with one corner pointing towards you. Place 1 heaped tbsp of the chicken noodle mixture on the corner closest to you. Roll corner over filling until you can't see the filling, then fold in the two sides. Now roll up quite firmly, like a cigar with tucked-in sides. Just before you finish rolling, dip your finger in the bowl of water and dab a little on the top corner of wrapper. Now roll it up and seal, then place it on a plate. Repeat with remaining wrappers and mixture.
06 To cook spring rolls, heat a wok or large, heavy-based saucepan and pour in enough oil to go 6–7 cm (2½–2¾ inches) up the sides. Test the oil is hot enough by dropping a small piece of bread into the oil. If the oil bubbles crazily, it is hot enough.
07 Using tongs, place one-quarter of the spring rolls into the oil, turning to coat. Cook until golden all over, about 3–4 minutes. Remove with tongs and place on a paper towel to drain. Repeat with remaining spring rolls. Serve on a big platter with sweet dipping sauce.
Makes 20–25

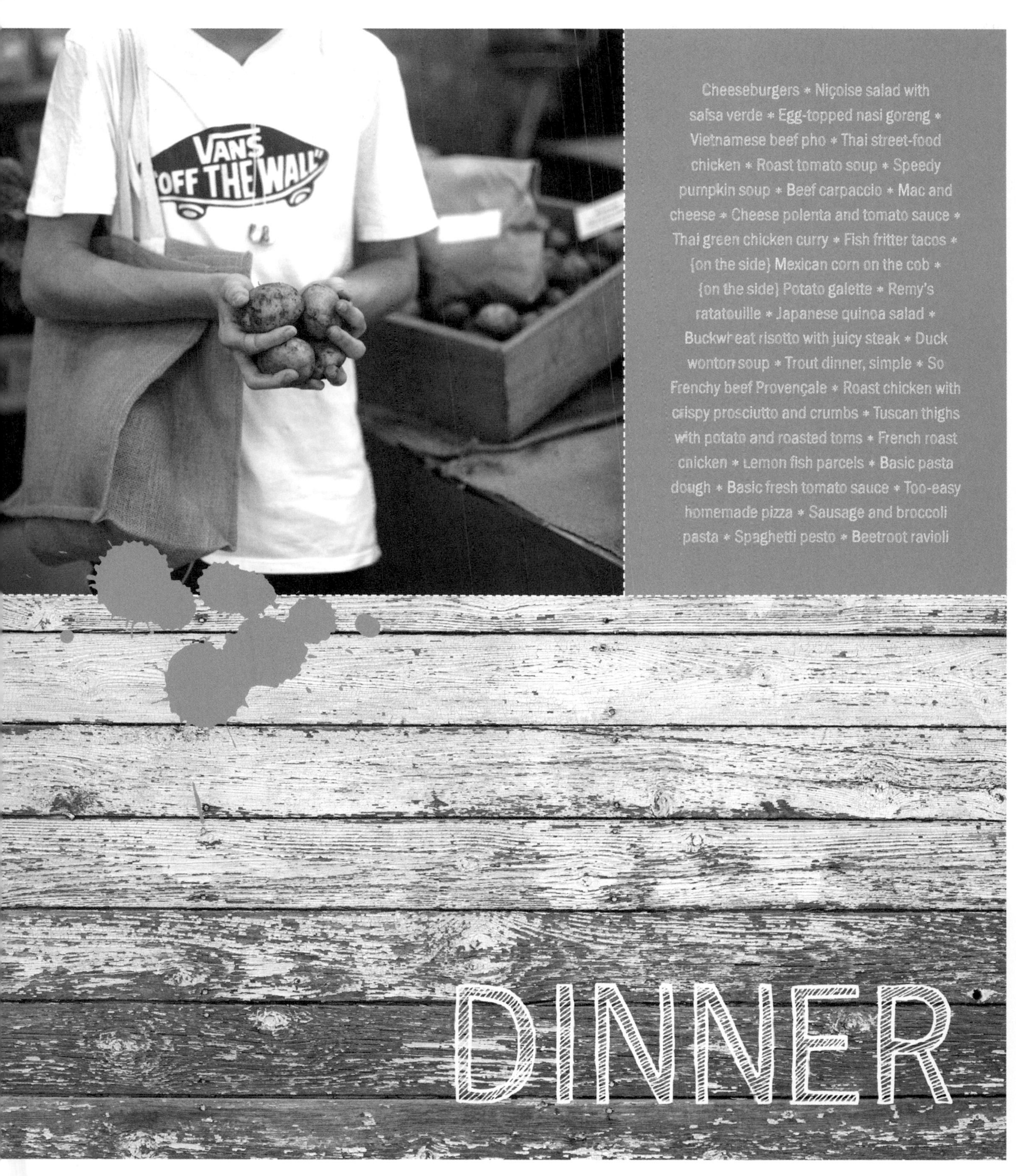

VANS
"OFF THE WALL"
Cheeseburgers * Niçoise salad with salsa verde * Egg-topped nasi goreng * Vietnamese beef pho * Thai street-food chicken * Roast tomato soup * Speedy pumpkin soup * Beef carpaccio * Mac and cheese * Cheese polenta and tomato sauce * Thai green chicken curry * Fish fritter tacos * {on the side} Mexican corn on the cob * {on the side} Potato galette * Remy's ratatouille * Japanese quinoa salad * Buckwheat risotto with juicy steak * Duck wonton soup * Trout dinner, simple * So Frenchy beef Provençale * Roast chicken with crispy prosciutto and crumbs * Tuscan thighs with potato and roasted toms * French roast chicken * Lemon fish parcels * Basic pasta dough * Basic fresh tomato sauce * Too-easy homemade pizza * Sausage and broccoli pasta * Spaghetti pesto * Beetroot ravioli
DINNER

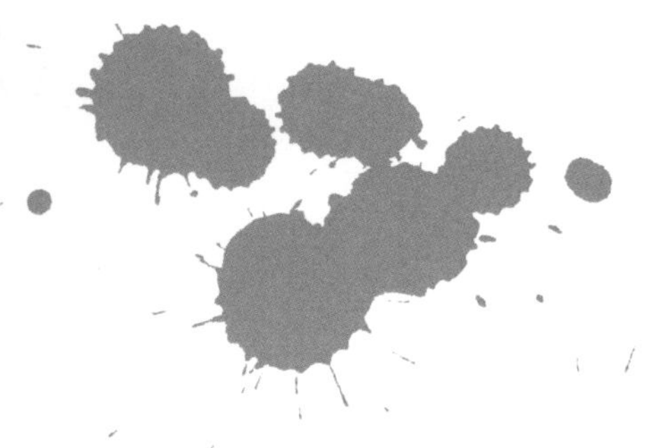

Set the table nicely, and slip on an apron that fits ...

... Cooking something for the entire family or a group of friends can be fraught. Who's vegetarian, vegan, gluten intolerant, broccoli averse, soy mad, and who is not? So-and-so doesn't eat fish, and Aunty Whatsit hates potatoes.

Now that you've started on your culinary journey, don't worry too much about such things—just carry right on. Forge ahead with whatever dinner you had planned, and they'll pick and work around you. You'll love the meal you dish up . . . and I suspect Aunty Whatsit secretly will too. Rest assured there are recipes in this chapter to suit all tastes. First up we have . . . cheeseburgers. But there are splendid offerings from around the world too, like Niçoise salad with salsa verde, or a steaming bowl of Vietnamese beef pho. There's Thai green chicken curry, Beetroot ravioli and crispy fish tacos too.

In some recipes the process is explained in 200-odd words; in others as few as 140. Not quite Twitter, but close. Some recipes may have loads of ingredients, so the shopping is more hefty, but then they'll be easy to make. Others need lots of chopping and dicing and prep work, but then everything is cooked in a flash. Others just need a long slow cooking time, so they'll take a while to finish, but meanwhile you can get on with other things. Yay.

So, remember to read the entire recipe through and make sure you have everything. Find the right pans, saucepans, serving platters. Measure the main ingredients out, and do feel free to experiment with the ingredients a bit—these recipes are just a base for your own individual flair. It's time to become a true dinner adventurer.

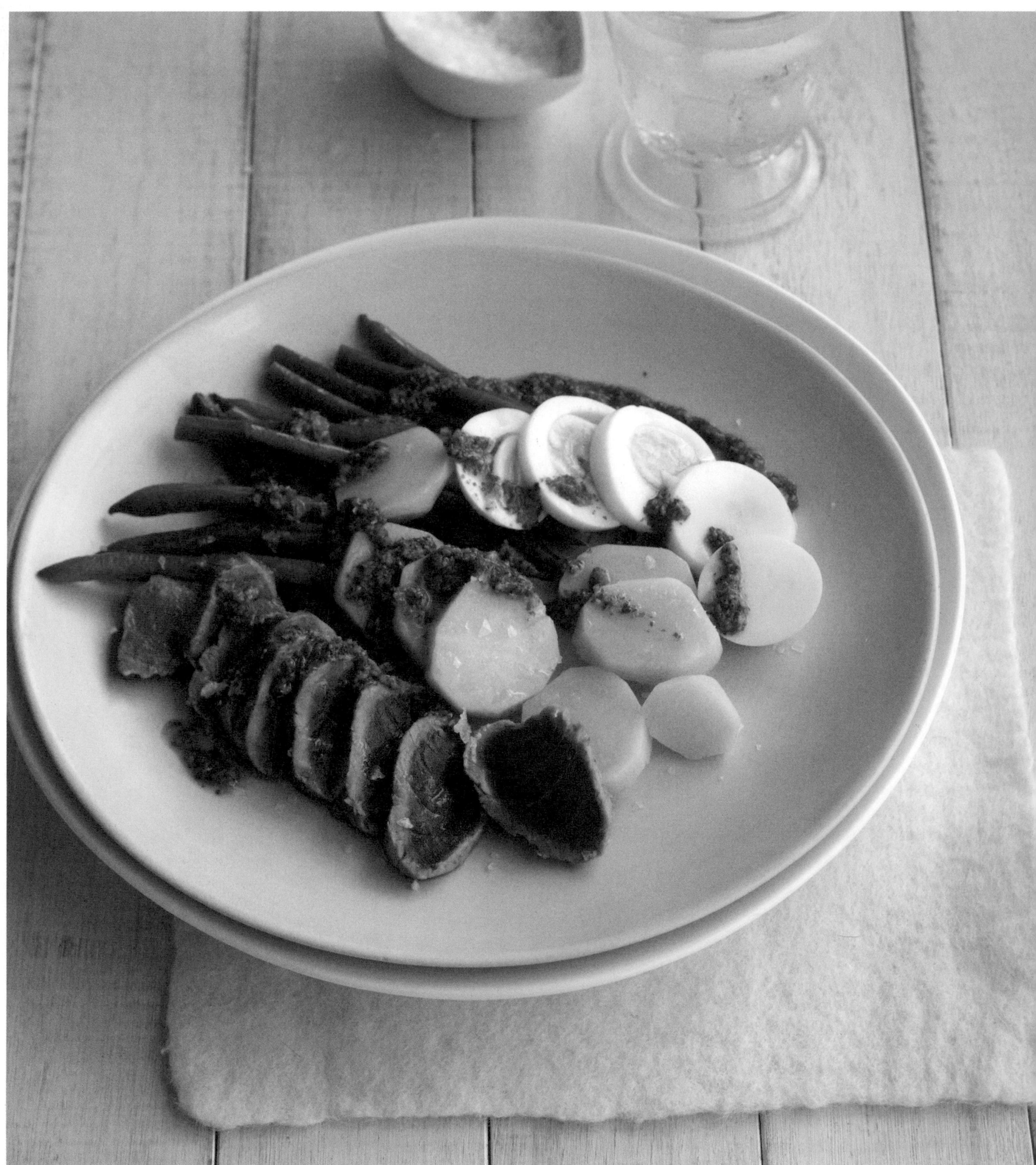

CHEESEBURGERS *

These are mini and hand-sized, so you're not tackling some ridiculous beast that your mouth can't get around. Honestly, you can make these quicker than it takes to get your shoes on and go up to McDonald's. And the taste is something else.

250 g (9 oz) good-quality minced (ground) beef
1 tsp dried oregano
2 tsp crushed garlic
1/4 tsp sea salt
1 tbsp rice bran oil
2 soft burger buns
2 slices Swiss or other cheese
4 baby cornichons (small crisp gherkin pickles), thinly sliced
tomato ketchup, to serve
mustard, to serve (optional)

01 In a bowl, combine beef, oregano, garlic and salt. Using your hands, squish it all together to get flavours mixed. Shape beef into two flattish patties, about 9–10 cm (3½–4 inches) in diameter (or the same width as your buns, if they're small).
02 Heat oil in a frying pan over high heat and seal burgers on one side so they brown quickly. Reduce heat and cook for 4 minutes, then turn them over and cook for another 2 minutes. Remove patties to a plate, cover with foil and let rest for 5 minutes.
03 Split burger buns, then fry cut sides in the meaty, garlicky oil left behind in same frying pan for 1 minute.
04 Arrange burger so you have bottom bun topped by a pattie, then cheese, then cornichon slices. Drizzle with ketchup and mustard, if using, then top with top bun and serve.
Serves 2

TIP: Feel free to go nuts and double or even triple the quantities, if you like. This makes 2 burgers, but you could just cook dinner for everyone.

NICOISE SALAD WITH SALSA VERDE **

This is a sort of 'deconstructed' Niçoise salad that looks awesome on a plate and lets you nibble on the various parts in any order. If you can't get a piece of fresh tuna, use a drained tin of dolphin-safe tuna in brine. If you do buy fresh tuna, get a fillet instead of a cutlet, and make sure it's yellowfin tuna. This version of the classic French Niçoise salad is drizzled with salsa verde, a super-easy herby sauce that is packed with vitamins and flavour. Store any leftover salsa verde in a sealed container in the fridge. It will keep for about 2 days and is really great for breakfast, drizzled over sliced avocado and tomato on toasted Turkish bread.

450 g (1 lb) yellowfin tuna fillet
1 tbsp olive oil
400 g (14 oz) kipfler (fingerling) potatoes, scrubbed clean
3 eggs, at room temperature
250 g (9 oz) green beans, tailed

Salsa verde
½ cup (30 g/1 oz) flat-leaf (Italian) parsley, finely chopped
½ cup (30 g/1 oz) basil, finely chopped
½ cup (15 g/½ oz) watercress, finely chopped
¼ cup (15 g/½ oz) mint, finely chopped
1 garlic clove, finely chopped
1 tsp capers, finely chopped
1–2 anchovy fillets, finely chopped (optional)
1 tbsp white wine vinegar
100 ml (3½ fl oz) extra virgin olive oil
squeeze of lemon juice, or to taste

01 Heat a frying pan over high heat. Coat entire tuna fillet in freshly ground black pepper and drizzle and coat with olive oil. Sear tuna for 10 seconds on each side, so outside is slightly brown, but inside is still very pink and rare. Remove from heat and set aside.

02 Put potatoes in a saucepan and cover with cold water. Cook, uncovered, over high heat for about 15 minutes, until potatoes are tender when pierced with a skewer. Drain well.
03 Lower eggs into a saucepan of warm water and bring to the boil, stirring to centre the yolks. Once simmering, allow eggs to cook for 4 minutes. Remove from water, then leave to cool in cold water.
04 Drop beans into a pan of boiling, salted water, then cover and cook for 3–5 minutes, or until crisp but still tender. Drain immediately and refresh in iced water; drain again.
05 To make the salsa verde, place all ingredients in a large bowl and whisk until well combined. Season to taste with salt and pepper, adding more lemon juice if desired.
06 To assemble the salad, slice potatoes into rounds about 1 cm (3/4 inch) thick; arrange on a serving plate with beans. Peel eggs, then slice each one acrossways into four and arrange on plate. Thinly slice tuna and arrange over salad. Drizzle with about 3 tbsp salsa verde and serve.
Serves 4 as a light meal

EGG-TOPPED NASI GORENG **

Everything ended in mushed-up spicy catastrophe for my dad when he made this in his early 20s with flatmates in London. So bad was it that he labelled the dish 'nasty gone wrong'. It's been known by this name by my family ever since. But two words of Indonesian will help stave off hunger anywhere in that scattered nation of islands: *nasi goreng.*

3 tbsp rice bran oil or peanut oil
3 spring onions (scallions), thinly sliced diagonally
4 garlic cloves, finely chopped
3 small green chillies, thinly sliced
2 tbsp kecap manis
2 tbsp soy sauce or tamari
3 cups (550 g/1 lb 4 oz) cooked, cold rice
4 eggs

To serve
prawn (shrimp) crackers (optional)
1 Lebanese (short) cucumber, halved and thickly sliced
1 handful cherry tomatoes, halved
2 iceberg lettuce leaves, roughly chopped
lemon or lime wedges
sambal chilli sauce (optional)

01 Heat a wok over high heat for 30 seconds. Add 2 tbsp oil and when a wisp of smoke appears, add spring onion and fry quickly. Add garlic and chilli, then kecap manis and soy sauce or tamari, and stir-fry for 10 seconds.
02 Add rice and stir-fry, moving everything around continuously with a spatula or spoon until lightly coloured and hot, about 2–3 minutes. Turn off heat and transfer to individual bowls.
03 Wipe down wok immediately and fry prawn crackers according to packet instructions, if using.
04 In a large frying pan, heat remaining 1 tbsp oil and fry eggs, sunny-side up. When done, place them on top of rice, 1 egg per serving. Serve with cucumber, tomatoes, lettuce and citrus wedges. Top with prawn crackers and chilli sauce.
Serves 4

in my world

ROGUE DINNERS FROM ALL OVER

Do you think people who suck the insides out of prawn heads are taking the whole gastronomy thing a bit far? Ever said 'ewww gross' at some kid's lunch at school because it had roasted eggplant (aubergine) in it? Man, you need to get out more.

- A popular Cantonese dish in China is braised chicken feet, which you nibble on whole to pick off the skin and meat. And then there's jellyfish–cold and often served with a vinegar dipping sauce.
- In parts of the United States it's not hard to get a meal of alligator, and in Mexico a bit of a roadside delicacy is cow's-eye tacos (apparently it's quite wobbly, with a bit of crunch in parts).
- In Scotland, a dish called haggis contains sheep's heart, liver and lungs, along with oats. It's traditionally cooked in a sheep's stomach.
- Black pudding, or blood pudding, is a type of sausage made all over the world using either pig, cow, sheep, duck or goat blood, and mixed with fillers like bread, fat, chestnuts, barley or rice.
- We all know the French love their frogs' legs and their *escargot*, or snails, which they do with a lovely herby butter. And you can get sea slug for lunch in lots of different countries.
- In the Basque region of Spain, an expensive delicacy is baby eels, which look like spaghetti. Spain is also known for pricey and delicate sea snails found on seaside cliffs.

All over the world, people are eating more curious things than you can probably imagine. Suddenly that steamed broccoli is starting to look like a pretty safe option, hey.

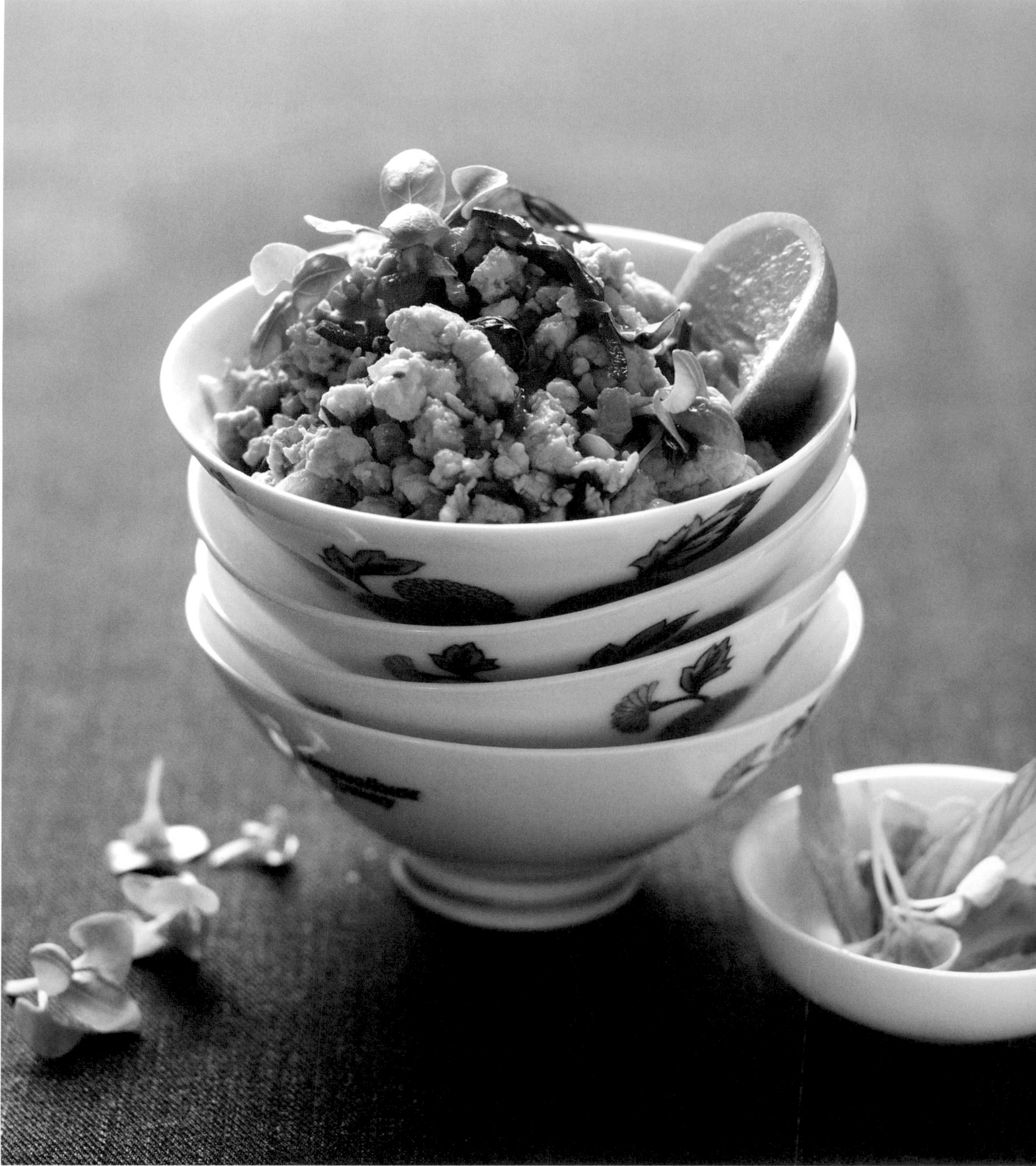

VIETNAMESE BEEF PHO **

This totally slurpable, gently flavoured beef noodle soup is a staple all over Vietnam, where it's cooked in massive pots and slurped at tiny plastic roadside tables. Add more or less chilli and spice. Be flexible, too, on the amount of noodles—and don't worry about the inevitable spillage from all that slurping. Get everything sliced and ready to go, then just throw it all together: this is the ultimate one-dish meal.

4 cups (1 litre/35 fl oz) good-quality beef stock
1 tsp black peppercorns
1 knob of fresh ginger
1 cinnamon stick
250 g (9 oz) rice vermicelli noodles
200 g (7 oz) fresh bean sprouts, tails trimmed
500 g (1 lb 2 oz) beef fillet or rump, very thinly sliced
2 white onions, thinly sliced
1 carrot, cut into julienne strips
½ bunch mint or Vietnamese mint, leaves picked
½ bunch coriander (cilantro), roughly chopped
1 chilli, thinly sliced (optional)
lime or lemon wedges, to serve

01 Get four bowls ready for assembling the pho.
02 Pour stock into a large saucepan. Add 2 cups (500 ml/17 fl oz) water, along with peppercorns, ginger and cinnamon stick. Simmer for 10 minutes.
03 Put noodles in a medium-sized bowl, then pour boiling water over to cover them. Let them soak for 5 minutes, or until tender. Drain and rinse noodles, then divide them among bowls. Top each with bean sprouts, beef, onion slices and carrot.
04 Pour hot stock over noodles; sprinkle soup with mint and coriander, and chilli if using. Serve immediately, with citrus wedges.
Serves 4

THAI STREET-FOOD CHICKEN **

This chunky Thai fry-up is my fail-safe tasty dish. A friend had this street-side in Thailand and brought back a variation on the recipe, clever man, and we made it a couple of times a week for months, truly. I mince the chicken breast myself because it's a healthy option—it's premium meat with no fat on it, instead of the fatty odds and ends often hidden in bought minced (ground) chicken. But feel free to use free-range chicken mince instead, and skip the first step. This easy stir-fry is also very versatile, so feel free to mess around with the flavours a bit. Add some chopped chilli with the garlic, more fish sauce and Vietnamese mint leaves—taste it and see what you like best.

500 g (1 lb 2 oz) boneless, skinless free-range or organic chicken breasts
½ bunch basil
2 tbsp rice bran oil or vegetable oil
1 white or brown onion, finely chopped
2 garlic cloves, chopped
½ tbsp fish sauce
1 tbsp lime juice
1 tbsp soy sauce or tamari
1 cup (30 g/1 oz) coriander (cilantro) leaves
1 cup (20 g/¾ oz) mint leaves
lettuce cups or steamed rice, to serve

01 Chop chicken into large pieces and place half in a food processor. Process on 'pulse' setting a few times, until a rough and chunky mince is formed (you don't want a purée). Remove chicken from food processor and mince remaining chicken.
02 Remove and discard woody ends of basil, but keep softer stalks. Pluck off leaves, then tear them roughly with your hands. Finely chop softer stalks, keeping them separate.
03 Make sure you have all the other ingredients chopped and measured and ready to go.

04 Heat a wok or large frying pan over high heat and add oil. Add onion and toss lightly until it is translucent (about 1–2 minutes), being careful not to burn it.
05 Reduce heat to medium, add chicken, garlic and chopped basil stalks. Stir-fry, breaking up chicken with a wooden spoon, until chicken is lightly browned and mostly cooked through.
06 Add torn basil leaves, then fish sauce, lime juice and soy sauce or tamari. Toss for 10–20 seconds, then turn off heat. Add coriander and mint leaves and toss one more time.
07 Serve in individual lettuce cups, or with steamed brown rice or jasmine rice.
Serves 4

TIP: This is a great way to use up chicken you've had in the freezer; just remember to first thaw it completely, overnight in the fridge. You can also use boneless, skinless chicken thighs, well trimmed of fat, if that is what you have on hand.

ANOTHER TIP: This dish is also great cold. Pack it up with an ice pack to keep it cool and some pitta bread to stuff it into, and some mint leaves or cucumber sticks for a fresh crunch.

in my world

ABOUT TOMATOES

- Spanish explorers and colonists introduced tomatoes to Europe in the early 1500s.
- Italians call tomatoes *pomodoro*, or 'apples of gold'.
- Tomatoes were originally used by the Italians as a repellent for ants and mosquitoes.

ROAST TOMATO SOUP **

You'll almost laugh when you try this. How is something so definitely savoury so sweet? This soup is perfect for the sweet-toothed. It's a great way to use up those mushy tomatoes that are so ripe nobody will eat them whole. Use only larger tomatoes, if that's all you have on hand, and just cut them in quarters before roasting.

800 g (1 lb 12 oz) ripe cherry tomatoes
3–4 large tomatoes, quartered
4 garlic cloves, unpeeled
100 ml (3½ fl oz) olive oil, plus extra for drizzling
1 red onion, chopped
¼ cup (60 ml/2 fl oz) red wine vinegar
½ bunch basil, leaves torn
crème fraîche, to serve (optional)

01 Preheat oven to 200°C (400°F). Pick green tops off the tomatoes. Put tomatoes in a roasting tin with garlic cloves. Drizzle with 2–3 tbsp oil, sprinkle with sea salt and toss everything together. Roast on top shelf of oven for 15 minutes.
02 Meanwhile, heat the remaining oil in a large saucepan over low heat and cook onion for 10 minutes, or until soft and translucent. Stir in the vinegar, then let vinegar reduce down for 5 minutes.
03 Take tomatoes and garlic out of oven. Carefully remove skins from garlic, using two forks to pull flesh out of skin. Add tomatoes and garlic to pan of onion. Scoop mixture into a food processor and blend—doing it in two batches if machine is small.
04 Add basil and whiz quickly, leaving soup chunky. Pour soup into individual bowls and drizzle with a little more oil. Add a swirl of crème fraîche, if you like, and serve.
Serves 4

TIP: Spice things up by adding a finely chopped chilli to the food processor with the tomatoes.

SPEEDY PUMPKIN SOUP **

Roasted pumpkin goes all sweet and caramelly. Blended into soup it's a gorgeous easy meal. Mop up with crusty bread.

1 butternut pumpkin (squash), seeds removed, peeled, cut into 6 cm (2½ inch) pieces
1 onion, peeled and cut into quarters
8 garlic cloves, peeled
2 tbsp olive oil
300 ml (10½ fl oz) pouring (whipping) cream
300 ml (10½ fl oz) chicken or vegetable stock
crusty bread, to serve
crème fraîche, to serve (optional)

01 Preheat oven to 200°C (400°F). Combine pumpkin, onion and garlic in a roasting tin. Drizzle with oil, toss together, then roast for about 25 minutes until pumpkin is tender and caramelised.
02 Remove tin from oven. Using tongs, transfer everything to a blender, then pour in cream and stock. Blend until mixture is smooth, then taste to see if it needs a little sea salt and freshly ground black pepper. Heat soup in a saucepan and serve hot with crusty bread and a dollop of crème fraîche, if desired.
Serves 4–6

BEEF CARPACCIO **

Okay yes I know, this is pretty adventurous . . . but I refuse to box you in as supremely fussy eaters who won't try anything new. Before you turn the page in disgust, hear me out. Beef carpaccio—which is essentially transparently thin slices of perfect-quality beef drizzled with olive oil, and spiked with a squeeze of lemon and parmesan cheese—is not, by any stretch of the imagination, underdone steak. It's not bloody and meaty and chewy, as underdone steak can be. It's soft and you'll love it. Heard of sashimi? Well this is beef sashimi. This is the perfect amount for two, so double the recipe if you (you clever chef, you!) are cooking for four.

250 g (9 oz) beef fillet, cut from the centre
1 tbsp extra virgin olive oil, plus extra for drizzling
1 handful baby rocket (arugula) leaves
shaved parmesan cheese, sliced using a vegetable peeler, to serve
1 lemon, cut in half, to serve

Dressing
2 tbsp Mayonnaise (see page 180)
1–2 tsp lemon juice
2 tsp Worcestershire sauce
1 tbsp milk

01 Use a very sharp knife to trim beef of all fat, or ask your butcher to do this for you. Now, thinly slice beef, cutting it acrossways.
02 Lay pieces on a large sheet of plastic wrap, spreading them out across the sheet. Place another sheet of plastic wrap over the top. Gently bash beef using a rolling pin, to make pieces as thin as possible —almost transparent.
03 Remove top sheet of plastic and transfer beef to a serving platter by flipping the second sheet over on to the platter, then drizzle with oil.
04 Mix together dressing ingredients and season to taste with sea salt and freshly ground black pepper.
05 When you're ready to eat, drizzle dressing over beef. Scatter rocket and parmesan over and season with salt and pepper. Finally, drizzle the lot with a little more oil and serve with lemon halves.
Serves 2

* like me

MAC AND CHEESE **

Here's an easy version of everyone's favourite. This one is studded with yummy peas and is topped with buttery breadcrumbs. If you have dry breadcrumbs, you can use them instead of making buttered ones. Just add 25 g (1 oz) butter to dot over the breadcrumbs before you pop the macaroni cheese in the oven. Serve up large spoonfuls of this gooey and crunchy pasta at the table, with a green salad on the side. You can also make this dish in advance up to a day ahead. Don't bake it, just keep it in the fridge, then pop it in a preheated oven when you're ready.

375 g (13 oz) macaroni
1 cup (140 g/5 oz) frozen peas
200 g (7 oz) mascarpone cheese
1 cup (100 g/3½ oz) grated cheddar cheese
100 g (3½ oz) grated parmesan cheese, plus extra for topping
pinch of freshly grated nutmeg
½ cup (125 ml/4 fl oz) milk
1 medium-sized (approximately 200 g/7 oz) ball mozzarella cheese

Buttered breadcrumbs
3 thick slices bread
20 g (¾ oz) butter, or 1 tbsp olive oil

01 Preheat oven to 200°C (400°F).
02 Drop macaroni into a large saucepan of boiling, salted water. Cook for 8–10 minutes, or until tender but still with a firm bite (a couple of minutes less than it says on the packet). During last 2 minutes of cooking, drop peas into water to blanch. Drain pasta and peas together.
03 Heat a medium-sized saucepan over medium heat. Add mascarpone and grated cheeses as well as nutmeg. Stir until cheese melts, about 2 minutes.
04 Stir in milk, season with freshly ground black pepper, then remove from heat. Add macaroni and peas and stir to combine.
05 Pour macaroni into a large baking dish, or individual ovenproof dishes if you prefer. Break up mozzarella ball into small pieces, and scatter over macaroni. Top with extra parmesan cheese.
06 To make the buttered breadcrumbs, blend bread in a food processor into crumbs. Heat butter or oil in a frying pan and toss crumbs over medium heat for 5 minutes, or until golden.
07 Sprinkle breadcrumbs over macaroni and bake for 15 minutes, or until golden on top.
Serves 4

TIP: You can make a traditional macaroni cheese by making a more challenging roux, if you like (see page 121). Add the cooked pasta, peas, cheese and nutmeg to the sauce once it's nice and thick. Place in a buttered baking dish, top with breadcrumbs and cook for 15 minutes, or until golden.

CHEESE POLENTA AND TOMATO SAUCE **

This is like an elegant cheesy gruel. Not quite pasta, not quite mashed potato, but as tasty as both, with extra ooze and awesomeness. Topped with tomato sauce and served with a leafy green salad, this is a really warming, wintery weeknight meal. Or have as a side to a main meal.

1 cup (180 g/6 oz) coarse polenta
⅓ cup (50 g/1¾ oz) finely grated parmesan cheese, or other favourite cheese, plus extra for sprinkling
50 g (1¾ oz) butter
1½ cups (375 ml/13 fl oz) Basic fresh tomato sauce (see page 138)

01 Bring 3 cups (750 ml/26 fl oz) water to the boil in a large heavy-based saucepan over high heat. Slowly add polenta in a thin stream, whisking constantly until all polenta has been added, so that lumps don't form.

A ROUX FOR YOU

Traditionally used to make macaroni and cheese, a roux (pronounced 'roo') is a butter and flour concoction used to thicken soups and sauces.

To make a roux, melt 30 g (1 oz) butter in a saucepan over low heat. Slowly stir in 2 tbsp plain (all-purpose) flour and cook for 1 minute, stirring constantly. You need to stir gently and continuously until the flour absorbs the fat, to produce an evenly textured paste. (The longer a roux is cooked, the less you will be able to taste the flour, and the darker your sauce will be.) Slowly add 2 cups (500 ml/17 fl oz) milk, stirring it into the butter and flour mixture, and cook until the sauce thickens, about 5–8 minutes.

TIP: when blending roux with stock to make a soup, gravy or sauce, gradually add the hot stock to the roux (not the other way around), and whisk continuously so you don't get lumps.

02 Reduce heat to low and simmer, stirring constantly with a wooden spoon, until mixture thickens slightly and water is absorbed—about 10 minutes. Check polenta is cooked by tasting a little: it should be soft, with a gentle bite. Cook for another 2 minutes, adding 1 tbsp water, if needed.
03 Once cooked, stir in cheese and butter. Set aside and cover with a lid to keep polenta warm until you're ready to serve.
04 Meanwhile, heat tomato sauce in a small saucepan over medium heat.
05 Spoon polenta onto plates or into shallow bowls. Make a depression in the middle, then spoon tomato sauce into depression. Sprinkle with extra cheese and a good grinding of black pepper. Serve with a crunchy green salad to have afterwards.
Serves 4 as a simple meal with a salad, or 4–6 as a hearty side

THAI GREEN CHICKEN CURRY **

If you're anything like me, this will become the staple of late nights and quick meals and what-should-me-and-my-flatmate-have-for-dinner queries. I'm sharing it with you now, thinking you can probably handle the heat and won't run screaming out of the kitchen. Of course, if it's not quite hot enough for you, add a little more green curry paste next time.

600 g (1 lb 5 oz) boneless, skinless chicken thighs
270 ml (9½ fl oz) tin coconut milk (don't shake the tin)
1 tbsp green curry paste
1 cup (140 g/5 oz) frozen peas
½ cup (125 ml/4 fl oz) chicken or vegetable stock, or water
1 tbsp fish sauce
10–12 basil or Thai basil leaves
steamed jasmine rice, to serve
lime or lemon wedges, to serve

01 Cut chicken into bite-sized pieces, about 3 cm (1¼ inches), removing as much fat as you can. (You can use chicken breasts if you're squeamish or don't fancy dealing with fat.)
02 Scoop creamy top from tin of coconut milk into a medium-sized, heavy-based saucepan. Add curry paste and cook, stirring with a wooden spoon over medium–low heat for 1–2 minutes.
03 Increase heat to medium–high. Add chicken and stir-fry for 2 minutes to seal and lightly brown meat.
04 Add the rest of the coconut milk, the peas and stock and simmer gently for 10 minutes. Add fish sauce and whole basil leaves in the last minute of cooking. Serve with steamed rice, and citrus wedges for squeezing.
Serves 4

TIP: I also love those walnut-sized Thai eggplants in this dish; just cut them in half or quarters and add after the chicken. Stir and let them brown a little, then add the liquid and cook the curry for an extra 10 minutes, until the eggplant is soft and done.

how to
CHICKEN BREASTS OR THIGHS?
Both are great, depending on what you're making. Thigh is more fatty, it's a brown meat, while breast is very lean with almost no fat. Breast is more likely to dry out, and needs less cooking. I like chicken thighs for curries and stews, anything that demands long, slow cooking. For stir-fries, breast does well, though be careful not to overcook it.

FISH FRITTER TACOS ***

There's possibly nothing more welcoming of summer than deep-fried, battered fish. But this takes the salt-and-vinegar staple up a notch, wrapped with Mexican flavours. This is my all-time favourite dinner, most of the time. Make all the parts and pop everything on the table. Sit back and watch the flurry of hungry activity. Smile smugly, then dig in yourself.

Guacamole

1 avocado, roughly chopped
1/4 bunch coriander (cilantro), roughly chopped
1/2 tsp smoked paprika
juice of 1 lime

Pico de gallo

200 g (7 oz) cherry tomatoes, roughly chopped
2 golden shallots, finely chopped
juice of 1 lime
1 chilli, seeds removed, finely chopped (optional)

To serve

4–5 tbsp Japanese or homemade Mayonnaise (see page 180)
1/2 bunch coriander (cilantro), roughly chopped
1 lime, cut into wedges
12–20 mini tortilla wraps

Fish fritters

550 g (1 lb 4 oz) skinless flathead fillets
2/3 cup (100 g/3 1/2 oz) self-raising flour
50 g (1 3/4 oz) tapioca or rice flour
1 cup (250 ml/9 fl oz) cold beer
2 cups (500 ml/17 fl oz) rice bran oil, safflower oil or vegetable oil

01 First make the guacamole. Combine ingredients in a small bowl and mash roughly. Season to taste with sea salt and freshly ground black pepper.

02 Combine pico de gallo ingredients in a bowl, and season with a tiny pinch of sea salt and freshly ground black pepper.

03 Now get everything else ready before cooking the fish. Put guacamole and pico de gallo on the table, with separate little bowls of mayonnaise, chopped coriander and lime wedges, and a small plate of tortilla wraps.

04 To make the fish fritters, cut fish into slightly larger than bite-sized pieces, about 4 cm (1 1/2 inches) long. Combine flours, beer and a pinch of sea salt and black pepper in a large bowl, then mix well with a whisk—the batter should be quite runny.

05 Meanwhile, heat oil in a wok or large saucepan until a tiny drop of batter in the oil spits and sizzles.

06 Using tongs, gently drop each piece into the hot oil, cooking fish in batches—be careful not to crowd pan. Fry each batch for about 4 minutes until golden brown, turning once or twice. Use tongs to remove fish to a plate lined with paper towels. Sprinkle with a pinch of sea salt. Repeat with remaining fish.

07 Pile fish fritters onto a serving platter. Take to the table piping hot, ready to be rolled up in tacos with other ingredients.

Serves 4–6

TIP: Make the fish fritters without all the other hullabaloo if you fancy. Just sprinkle with sea salt and proper malt vinegar to take it back to the old classic.

MEXICAN CORN ON THE COB *

These luscious cobs go really well with grilled lamb cutlets or Fish fritter tacos (see page 124).

4 corn cobs
4 tbsp homemade Mayonnaise (see page 180)
juice of 1 lime
¼ tsp chilli powder (optional)
½ cup (60 g/2¼ oz) grated parmesan cheese (or a Mexican cheese like quesa fresco)

01 Break or cut corn cobs in half acrossways to make 8 mini cobs.
02 Put a steamer basket in a large wide pot (one that has a lid), then pour in about 5–8 cm (2–3¼ inches) of water. Arrange corn in steamer basket so it's not overcrowded. Cover and steam over medium–high heat for 15 minutes, or until bright yellow and tender.
03 Meanwhile, put mayonnaise and lime juice in a small bowl, with chilli powder if using. Mix together with a fork to make a dressing, then season to taste with sea salt and freshly ground black pepper.
04 Once corn is cooked, arrange it on a platter. Drizzle with dressing, then sprinkle with cheese. Serve and eat with your fingers.
Makes 8

on the side

POTATO GALETTE **

This is a crisp-exteriored kingly pancake of a side dish. Just cut straight into quarters at the table. Then fight your friends for the rest.

5 large desiree potatoes, very thinly sliced
2 tbsp rice bran oil
1 garlic clove, thinly sliced
25 g (1 oz) butter

01 Toss potato slices, oil and garlic together in a bowl. Season with sea salt and freshly ground black pepper and set aside for 10–15 minutes. Drain off juices.
02 Heat a large heavy-based deep-sided frying pan over medium–high heat. Add butter and immediately start layering potato slices in pan, so they sit flat. Create a spiral pattern if you like. Add remaining potato slices and arrange them so they sit evenly in the pan.
03 Place a plate that will fit just inside frying pan over potatoes, to press them down. Cook for 8–10 minutes, taking a peek underneath every now and then to check the galette is not burning.
04 When galette is golden and crispy underneath, turn it out onto a large plate. To do this, remove smaller plate, then place a large plate over pan. Carefully turn galette out onto plate by turning frying pan upside down—watch out for oil drips!
05 Return frying pan to heat and carefully transfer galette back into pan, crispy side up. Cook for another 8–10 minutes, covered with a lid or plate.
06 Turn galette out onto a plate or board, and serve in big wedges.
Serves 4 as a side dish

TIP: There's no need to peel the potatoes here—the skin gives it all definition. And use a mandolin (my favourite kitchen gadget) if you have one, but be sure to use the safety shield.

make me *

REMY'S RATATOUILLE **

Remy is the star of the animated movie *Ratatouille*. He is a charming, food-obsessed rat who teams up with a clueless garbage boy called Linguini, who works at a restaurant in Paris that's been unable to keep its customers. So Remy teaches Linguini how to cook, and makes up a fancy version of ratatouille that impresses the most powerful food critic in Paris. Ratatouille is a French dish packed with vegetables and flavour. It's great with a simple steak but I also love leftovers packed into a bread roll with a wedge of cheddar cheese, served at room temperature. Or just have it on its own.

In Remy the rat's layered ratatouille, everything is thinly sliced acrossways, fanned out in a baking dish, drenched in fresh tomato sauce, then baked. All the fun is in the vegetable slicing—you need to get those slim Japanese or Lebanese eggplants that are shaped more like zucchini, so the vegetables are almost the same width as each other. When serving, drizzle the lot with vinaigrette, raise a glass to Remy the rat, and declare, '*Bon appetit!*'

2 large zucchini (courgettes)
2 Japanese eggplants (aubergines)
2 yellow baby (pattypan) squash
4 roma (plum) tomatoes
1 garlic clove, finely chopped
1 tbsp olive oil

Tomato sauce
2 tbsp extra virgin olive oil
1 garlic clove, finely chopped
1 onion, finely chopped
400 g (14 oz) tin chopped tomatoes
1 thyme sprig
1 small handful flat-leaf (Italian) parsley

Vinaigrette
1 tbsp extra virgin olive oil
1 tsp red wine vinegar
mixed fresh herbs (such as thyme, chervil, parsley), roughly chopped

01 Preheat oven to 170°C (325°F).
02 First, make the tomato sauce. Heat oil in a heavy-based saucepan over low heat. Cook garlic and onion for 8–10 minutes, or until soft and translucent (but not brown). Add tomatoes, thyme and parsley. Simmer for 10 minutes until sauce has reduced. Season with sea salt and freshly ground black pepper, then remove and discard herbs.
03 Meanwhile, thinly slice zucchini, eggplants and squash, cutting them acrossways into 3 mm (1/8 inch) rounds. Cut tomatoes just as thinly.
04 Reserve 1 tbsp tomato sauce; spread rest in bottom of a 20 cm (8 inch) diameter, straight-sided baking dish or roasting tin.
05 Arrange the four thinly sliced vegetables in an alternating strip down the centre of the dish. Then overlap remaining vegetables in a close spiral around centre strip. Repeat until the dish is filled. Scatter with garlic and drizzle with oil.
06 Cover dish with foil and seal well around edges. Bake for 1 hour, or until vegetables are tender when tested with a small knife. Remove foil and bake for another 20 minutes.
07 Combine vinaigrette ingredients in a small bowl and mix in reserved tomato sauce. Season to taste. To serve, drizzle vinaigrette around spoonfulls of ratatouille on plates.
Serves 4

JAPANESE QUINOA SALAD *

Although it's a relative newcomer to kitchen pantries, quinoa (pronounced 'keen-wah') is an ancient grain. It's protein-packed, gluten free, full of vitamins and minerals—yep, another superfood. Quinoa cooks in 15 minutes, and you can tell when it's done because the seeds show a little white thread curling up inside.

1 cup (200 g/7 oz) quinoa
2 cups (500 ml/17 fl oz) chicken or vegetable stock
1 large carrot, peeled
½ red capsicum (pepper) (optional)
½ bunch coriander (cilantro), stalks and leaves roughly chopped
¼ cup (40 g/1½ oz) cashew nuts (or other favourite nut), toasted and roughly chopped
1 tbsp sesame seeds, toasted, plus extra to serve
1 toasted nori (seaweed) sheet, roughly chopped

Dressing
juice of 1 lemon
2 tsp sesame oil
1 tsp finely grated fresh ginger
1 tsp tamari or soy sauce
1 tsp honey (optional)

01 Rinse quinoa in cold water, then drain well.
02 Heat stock in a medium-sized saucepan and add quinoa. Cook for 15 minutes, or until quinoa is soft. The liquid should run almost dry in bottom of the saucepan, but be careful not to burn it—add a little more stock or water as needed. Remove from heat and set aside.
03 Meanwhile, cut carrot and capsicum (if using) into julienne strips and place in a serving bowl. Add coriander, cashews and sesame seeds.
04 Combine dressing ingredients in a bowl and mix lightly with a fork. Add cooked quinoa to salad, then drizzle with dressing and toss lightly. Serve sprinkled with nori and extra sesame seeds.
Serves 2, or 4 as a side dish

BUCKWHEAT RISOTTO WITH JUICY STEAK **

OK, so this isn't really a risotto. But it's still a soft, tasty grain fed by lovely stock, that pairs beautifully with the earthy, pan-fried mushrooms. I love going to the weekend markets and filling a brown paper bag with whatever mushrooms are on special . . . portobello, wood-ear mushooms, nameko, shiitake, oyster, Swiss brown, wild pine and little button mushrooms. Topped with a perfectly done steak, sliced so the juices run all over the 'risotto', this is a dish to impress. Double the quantities if you're cooking for four.

1 cup (195 g/6¾ oz) buckwheat
1 thick grass-fed steak (scotch fillet or porterhouse both work well)
150 g (5½ oz) wild mushrooms
1 brown onion, finely chopped
2 garlic cloves, finely chopped
2 tbsp olive oil
40 g (1½ oz) butter
¼ cup (60 ml/2 fl oz) white wine or verjuice

01 Add buckwheat to a large saucepan of boiling, salted water. Leave to simmer for 30 minutes, until soft but with a bite. Drain and set aside.
02 Meanwhile, take steak out of the fridge and let it reach room temperature. Slice mushrooms so they are all about the same size (leave small ones whole).
03 To cook the steak, heat a frying pan over high heat. Season steak on both sides with sea salt and freshly ground black pepper, and rub with 1 tsp oil. When pan is very hot, gently place steak in middle of the frying pan. Leave the steak alone, so it can develop a proper crust. Cook for 3 minutes, then turn once only, and cook the other side for about 2 minutes. Press the steak in the pan with your finger—it should be soft, with some resistance. Remove steak to a board, cover with foil and leave to rest for at least 5 minutes.

how to

DON'T BOIL STOCK

Boiling a stock can make it cloudy, because boiling recirculates impurities. Instead, keep stock at a gentle simmer, and then use a large spoon to scrape off any froth and impurities from the top as it cooks.

by the way

DELICIOUS IDEAS FOR COOKED DUCK BREAST

- Make a duck pho soup. Thinly slice the duck and use it instead of the beef in the pho recipe on page 115.
- Thinly slice it and use instead of the steak in the buckwheat risotto recipe on page 128.
- Thinly slice it and add to a salad of mango, crunchy cos (romaine) lettuce and watercress, with some coriander (cilantro) leaves, thinly sliced golden shallots and a small splash of the Honey sesame soy dressing (page 90).
- Get a packet or two of Peking duck pancakes from a Chinese grocer. Warm them up, then place in a pile on the table with the thinly sliced duck breast, seasoned with Chinese five-spice salt instead of normal salt. You'll need a little bowl of hoisin sauce, thin sticks of cucumber, and about 3 spring onions (scallions) that have been sliced very finely on the diagonal. Let everyone help themselves to the duck, sauce, spring onion and cucumber, which are wrapped up in the pancakes to eat over and over.

try me *

04 Meanwhile, heat half the butter and another 1 tbsp oil in a heavy-based saucepan over low heat. Add onion and cook for 2 minutes, or until onion is tender and translucent. Add garlic and mushrooms and toss in pan for 1–2 minutes, or until softened. Add buckwheat, wine or verjuice and remaining oil and butter. Stir gently, then cover and cook over low heat for 5 minutes, or until juices are mostly absorbed. Leave covered until you're ready to serve.

05 Take foil off the steak. Use a sharp knife to slice steak acrossways, into 1 cm (½ inch) slices across grain of meat. Divide buckwheat risotto between plates and arrange steak slices on top. Pour juices from board over top and serve.

Serves 2

DUCK WONTON SOUP **

Get a whole bought duck from one of those awesome Chinese BBQ King–style shops with the hanging ducks and chickens in the window. Ask them to debone the duck for you. I ask for a beheading, too—I don't need to be dealing with beaks! But do keep the bones to make the soup these little dumplings will be served in. You'll only need half a duck to serve four, but by all means double the quantities to make double the wontons and freeze half (before cooking them) for another time.

½ Chinese roast duck, boned (keep bones for stock)
4 dried or 6 fresh shiitake mushrooms, stalks and caps separated
6–8 spring onions (scallions), trimmed
1 star anise
1 cinnamon stick
½ bunch coriander (cilantro), roughly chopped
small knob of fresh ginger, about 25 g (1 oz)
2 tbsp oyster sauce
2 tsp sesame oil
30 egg wonton wrappers

01 Shred duck by pulling meat apart into small, stringy pieces using two forks or your fingers. Chop larger duck pieces with a knife. Discard skin and fat. If using dried shiitake mushrooms, place them in a small bowl, cover with boiling water and let them soften completely.

02 To make the stock, place duck bones in a large pot with 3 spring onions, the star anise, cinnamon, half the coriander, the ginger and shiitake mushroom stalks. Cover with 6 cups (1.5 litres/52 fl oz) water. Bring to the boil, then reduce heat and simmer for about 1½ hours with lid on. Remove from heat, scoop away and discard any foam, then set aside.

03 Meanwhile, finely chop mushrooms and remaining spring onions; reserve a few spring onions to serve. Add mushrooms and spring onions to a mixing bowl with duck meat, oyster sauce and sesame oil. Season with freshly ground black pepper and mix to combine.

04 Lay about 8 wonton wrappers on a work surface, then place 1 heaped tsp duck mixture in the centre of each. Brush or dab edges of wrappers with water, then bring up sides and pinch into money-bag shapes. Repeat with remaining wrappers and duck mixture.

05 Strain stock through a sieve into another clean saucepan. Discard all solids and spices.

06 Heat broth, then add wontons in batches and cook each batch for about 5 minutes. Using a slotted spoon, remove wontons to serving bowls, then top with hot broth. Scatter with remaining coriander and reserved spring onion and serve.

Serves 4

TROUT DINNER, SIMPLE **

Pan-frying is one of the simplest ways to cook. And it's especially easy with fish: you can see the heat creeping up the side of the fish, and it visibly changes colour and texture as it cooks. You want your pan really hot for this dish, so the trout skin is crispy, like bacon. You don't have to eat the skin, but do give it a try. If you can't get trout, just use your favourite fish. It's really good with lemony spinach.

2 thick ocean trout fillets, about 200 g (7 oz) each, skin on, scales and bones removed
olive oil, for drizzling

Lemony spinach
25 g (1 oz) knob of butter
3 cups (150 g/5½ oz) baby spinach leaves, washed
1 lemon, cut into wedges

01 Season trout with sea salt and freshly ground black pepper by rubbing it all over both sides of fish. Drizzle with a little oil.
02 Heat a non-stick frying pan over high heat. When pan is hot, add both trout fillets, skin side down. Cook for 3 minutes, and shake pan now and then to make sure fish doesn't stick. Don't press fish with a spoon or spatula—all the lovely juices will come out and the fish will go dry.
03 Use tongs to flip fish over. Cook for another 30 seconds (a little more if you like it well done), then remove from heat. Transfer trout to a serving platter or individual plates, skin side up.
04 Put pan back over heat. Add butter and spinach, season with salt and pepper, and cook for 1 minute, or until spinach has wilted. Quickly transfer to platter or plates and serve with lemon wedges, for squeezing over.
Serves 2

TIP: A good serving of fish for one person is about 200 g (7 oz), so if you're making this for the whole family, get 1 piece of fish for each person. Younger brothers or sisters may like to share one piece.

SO FRENCHY BEEF PROVENCALE **

Salut! Put on your stripy T-shirt and grab a baguette for mopping up sauces, this totally Frenchy hot-pot of beef and carrots will have you joyously singing "*allez les bleu*" on repeat. This classic dish is all do-ahead, and then just leave it to simmer for a couple of hours while you practice your vowels. *Je suis, tu es, il est . . .*

750g (1 lb 10 oz) chuck steak, cut into 4 cm (1½ inch) cubes, large pieces of fat discarded
2 garlic cloves, roughly chopped
4 tbsp olive oil
1½ cups (375 ml/13 fl oz) red wine
100 g (3½ oz) pancetta or free-range bacon, roughly chopped (optional)
2 brown onions, chopped
3 carrots, thickly sliced acrossways
400 g (14 oz) tin chopped tomatoes
about 8 cherry tomatoes, cut in half
½ cup (125 ml/4 fl oz) beef or free-range chicken stock
2 strips orange rind
½ bunch flat leaf (Italian) parsley, finely chopped, to serve

01 Place beef, garlic, 1 tbsp olive oil and the wine in a large bowl and let marinate in the fridge for at least 1 hour.
02 When beef is marinated, heat a heavy-based casserole dish (that has a well-fitting lid) over medium-high heat. Add remaining oil and pancetta or bacon (if using), and sauté for 3 minutes, until a little brown.

03 Using a sieve, drain beef and collect marinade in a small saucepan. Boil marinade until reduced by half, about 10 minutes.
04 Meanwhile, add onion to pancetta or bacon. Cook, stirring gently, until onion is soft and translucent. Turn heat to high, add beef and let it brown, turning pieces every now and then with tongs, about 5–8 minutes. Don't move meat around too much or juices will come out and make the meat dry.
05 Add carrot, tomatoes, stock, orange rind and reduced marinade from saucepan. Mix together gently, then cover and simmer for 2-2½ hours, until meat is tender. Serve at the table in big spoonfuls into bowls. Offer crusty baguette for mopping up juices, or serve with creamy mash potatoes. Sprinkle the lot with finely chopped parsley.
Serves 6

TIP: Wine? Moi? Yes, it's OK, the alcohol will totally burn off while cooking.

ANOTHER TIP: To create the orange rind, grab one orange and one vegetable peeler. Wash the orange and then peel two long slices of rind from the orange to add to the pot.

YET ANOTHER TIP: Wine can be expensive stuff, but get your hands on what Australians call a cleanskin bottle. They are a fraction of the price because they don't have the winery's name on the label. Ask your wine seller what is the best full-bodied wine for this—cleanskins can vary a lot in quality and you want something good for about a fiver.

ROAST CHICKEN WITH CRISPY PROSCIUTTO AND CRUMBS **

This is the roast to make when you don't have a whole bird, or don't fancy tackling the carving. You can change the portions depending on how many people are eating, but generally it's one chicken breast per person. Serve this with steamed green beans, then drizzle the lot with gravy. (See pic page 106.)

2 tbsp olive oil, plus extra for pan-frying
1 thyme sprig, leaves picked
1 garlic clove, finely chopped
4 boneless, skinless free-range or organic chicken breasts
12 slices prosciutto

Breadcrumbs
¾ cup (85 g/3 oz) dry breadcrumbs
10 g (¼ oz) butter
2 garlic cloves, finely chopped or crushed
grated zest of 1 lemon
¼ bunch flat-leaf (Italian) parsley, leaves finely chopped

Gravy
30 g (1 oz) butter
1 tbsp plain (all-purpose) flour
2 cups (500 ml/17 fl oz) chicken stock
¼ cup (60 ml/2 fl oz) white wine

01 In a bowl, mix together oil, thyme and garlic. Add chicken breasts and turn to coat completely in the marinade. Take one piece of chicken, leaving as much marinade on it as possible, and place it on a board. Wrap chicken evenly in 3 slices of prosciutto, to cover most of breast. (You can secure it with a piece of kitchen string, if you like.) Repeat with remaining chicken and prosciutto slices. Wrap each fillet in plastic wrap and refrigerate for 2–3 hours.

02 Preheat oven to 190°C (375°F). Meanwhile, cook breadcrumbs. Heat a frying pan over medium–high heat, add breadcrumbs, butter and garlic and stir until golden. Add lemon zest and parsley, then tip mixture into a small bowl.

03 In the same frying pan, heat a small drizzle of olive oil still over medium–high heat. Remove chicken from plastic (leaving string still on, if you tied it up). Pan-fry chicken, rotating it several times, until golden brown. Transfer chicken to a roasting tin, keeping frying pan handy, and bake for 10–12 minutes.

04 Meanwhile, make the gravy. In the same frying pan (don't clean it out: the juices will help make a yummy gravy), melt butter over medium heat. Stir in flour and cook, stirring, for 3 minutes, or until light brown. Add stock and simmer, stirring constantly, until thickened slightly. Stir in wine and season with a pinch of sea salt and freshly ground black pepper. Simmer gravy for 5 minutes, until it has reduced slightly (the alcohol will burn off).

05 When chicken is done, remove it from oven and let it rest for 5 minutes. Cut off string, if you tied chicken up, and slice each breast into 1 cm (½ inch) slices. Arrange on four plates.

06 Pour any chicken pan juices into the gravy. Scatter each plate with breadcrumbs and serve with the gravy for pouring.

Serves 4

TUSCAN THIGHS WITH POTATO AND ROASTED TOMS *

This one-pot roast chicken is rich with flavour. The combination of potatoes, ripe tomatoes and lots of fresh lemon with the sticky chicken is otherworldly. Try growing your own rosemary so you constantly have it on hand for this sort of thing—it's one of the easiest things to grow, in a pot in the sun.

8 free-range or organic chicken thighs, bone in, skin on
⅓ cup (80 ml/2½ fl oz) olive oil
5 desiree potatoes, skin on, cut into slices 5 mm (¼ inch) thick
1 rosemary sprig, leaves chopped
4 garlic cloves, skin on
1 red capsicum, sliced
juice of 2 lemons
250 g (9 oz) cherry tomatoes

01 Preheat oven to 190°C (375°F). Season chicken pieces with sea salt and freshly ground black pepper, then drizzle with 2 tbsp olive oil. Heat a roasting tin on stove over medium–high heat.

02 Once tin is hot, add chicken pieces, skin side down, and sear the meat for 3–5 minutes, or until just golden brown. Transfer chicken to a plate.

03 Now layer potatoes in roasting tin to brown, turning once to give both sides colour—about 2 minutes each side. Add remaining oil as needed.

04 Add chicken, skin side up, and garlic cloves and capsicum. Pour lemon juice over and bake for 25 minutes. Add tomatoes to tin and roast for another 10–15 minutes. Serve straight out of the tin, at the table with a green salad.

Serves 4–6

FRENCH ROAST CHICKEN **

The trick of pushing butter under the skin of the chicken protects the breast from drying out, while also infusing it with herby flavours. The result is worth the effort. I've cooked this with a seven-year-old, and he totally managed the whole raw-plucked-bird touching thing, so I have no doubt you'll be able to do it too.

1 large free-range or organic chicken
70 g (2½ oz) butter, softened
zest and juice of 1 lemon, lemon halves reserved
½ cup (30 g/1 oz) finely chopped flat-leaf (Italian) parsley
olive oil, for drizzling
8 thyme sprigs
3 garlic cloves, smashed, peeled

01 Preheat oven to 190°C (375°F). Wipe chicken cavity with a paper towel and remove excess fat. Combine butter, lemon zest and parsley in a small bowl and season.
02 With clean hands, slip two fingers under skin of chicken around cavity and, being careful not to tear skin, create a space between skin and chicken breast. Push three-quarters of butter mixture into space under skin, as evenly as possible. Spread remaining butter mixture over chicken skin, drizzle with lemon juice and a little olive oil, and season with more salt and pepper. Fill cavity with thyme sprigs, garlic and reserved lemon halves, then tie legs with kitchen string.
03 Place chicken in a roasting tin and roast for 50–60 minutes, basting chicken with pan juices every 20 minutes, until skin is crisp and golden and chicken is cooked through.
04 Remove chicken from oven, cover with foil and leave to rest. Serve with a green salad, a crispy potato galette or steamed green beans.
Serves 4

LEMON FISH PARCELS *

This super simple, fresh and healthy dish can be served on plates, straight from the little paper parcels that are unwrapped with great anticipation at the table. Serve with simple steamed potatoes and asparagus, or a green leaf salad. The tasty juices run out onto the plate . . . delicious mopped up with crusty bread.

4 x 200 g (7 oz) ocean trout fillets or white fish fillets, skin removed
juice of 1 lemon, plus finely grated zest of ½ lemon
8 cherry tomatoes, halved
2 tbsp extra virgin olive oil
lemon wedges, to serve

01 Preheat oven to 180°C (350°F). Lay each fish fillet on an individual square of baking paper large enough to wrap around it twice. Place them on a baking tray.
02 Scatter lemon zest over each fillet. Scatter with 4 tomato halves each, then drizzle each fillet with a little oil and lemon juice. Season with sea salt and freshly ground black pepper. Wrap each parcel tightly, with open side at top so juices can't escape.
03 Bake for 12–15 minutes, or a little less if you prefer your fish rare. Serve in parcels on plates, ready to be unwrapped at the table like yummy presents for all, with lemon wedges for squeezing over.
Serves 4

BASIC PASTA DOUGH **

Why cook pasta when there are perfectly good packets out there waiting to be bought, and ready on your fork within 20 minutes? Because sometimes it's really satisfying making things from scratch. This recipe can be used for ravioli (see page 143) or lasagne sheets, or cut into long lengths about 1.5 cm (5/8 inch) thick to make your own pappardelle.

2⅔ cups (400 g/14 oz) Italian 00 flour, plus extra for dusting
3 eggs

01 Sift flour and a pinch of sea salt onto a clean bench or a large wooden board, into a mound.
02 Make a well in the centre and break eggs into the well. Use a fork to beat eggs together and gently bring sides of well in on eggs.
03 Draw mixture together using your hands, then gently knead to form a solid mass. It shouldn't feel too dry and crumbly; add 1 tbsp water if needed. Wash and dry your hands to prepare for kneading.
04 Sprinkle about 1 tbsp flour over your work surface. Place dough on top, then knead it by pressing down with the heel of one hand, pushing dough away from you. Fold dough in half, then turn it over and give it a half-turn. Repeat this process, using two hands if needed, pushing dough away from you, and always turning in the same direction.
05 Knead for about 10 minutes, until dough is quite elastic. Test it has been kneaded enough by pressing it with your finger—it should spring back. If it doesn't, keep kneading until it does.
06 Make a thickish patty with the dough, then wrap it up in plastic wrap. Refrigerate for at least 30 minutes, and up to 24 hours.
07 The dough is now ready to turn into pasta, either using a pasta machine or a rolling pin, or whatever you have planned for it.
Makes a good portion for at least 6–8 people

BASIC FRESH TOMATO SAUCE **

Cookbook author Marcella Hazan invented this method of easy tomato sauce in her bible of Italian recipes, *Essentials of Classic Italian Cooking*. It's the easiest possible sauce to make, with no chopping even involved. This is your go-to sauce for pasta and lasagne, or any time you need a delicate, fresh and sweet sauce.

2 x 400 g (14 oz) tins whole peeled tomatoes
1 onion, peeled and halved
70 g (2½ oz) unsalted butter

01 Heat tomatoes, onion halves and butter in a heavy-based saucepan over medium heat. Bring to a simmer, reduce heat and simmer gently for 45 minutes, stirring occasionally. Use a wooden spoon to crush tomatoes against side of the pan.
02 Remove sauce from heat. Discard onion, then season sauce to taste with sea salt.
03 Store in sterilised glass jars, or use immediately.
Makes enough to magic up 4–6 bowls of pasta

in my world

TWIRLY PASTA

ITALIAN FOOD RULE #1: Don't use a knife to eat pasta, even lasagne—it suggests you think the pasta isn't cooked. Spaghetti is eaten with a fork, twirled with one hand: spoons are for children.
ITALIAN FOOD RULE #2: Spaghetti bolognese is a bit of a no-no. If you ever wander around Rome, be much more adventurous! There is a dish called pasta ragù, but it's never with spaghetti.
ITALIAN FOOD RULE #3: Italians never have cappuccinos or lattes after 11 a.m. Milky coffee is strictly a morning thing in Italy—after that it's just espressos or something closer to the 'vino' variety.

try me *

TOO-EASY HOMEMADE PIZZA **

So, so much easier than you're imagining right now. When you weigh up satisfaction versus effort, homemade pizza is about the best thing to cook from scratch. Add to that a rich dollop of tomato sauce that takes less time to make than your pizza dough does to rise, and this recipe will be engraved in your mind, ever the clever solution to what-should-I-cook.

Basic pizza dough

2¼ cups (280 g/10 oz) plain flour (Italian 00 flour is best)
1 tsp salt
½ tsp sugar
2 tsp dried yeast
3/4 cup (185 ml/6 fl oz) lukewarm water (plus a little extra)
¼ cup (60 ml/2 fl oz) olive oil

Pizza tomato sauce

¼ cup (60 ml/2 fl oz) olive oil
400 g (14 oz) tin chopped tomatoes
5–8 basil leaves

01 Sift flour into a large bowl with salt and stir in sugar and yeast. Make a little well in the centre and add water and oil. Use a wooden spoon and then your hands to mix a dough, and turn out onto a well-floured bench or board. The dough should come together but still be very flexible. Add another tbsp or two of lukewarm water if it's a little crumbly.
02 Knead lightly for 4–5 minutes, until dough is smooth and elastic. Transfer to an oiled bowl, turn it to coat with oil and cover with a clean tea towel. Set aside in a warm place for about 1 hour to rise. It should double in size.
03 To make the pizza sauce, heat oil in a saucepan over medium heat, then add tomatoes and basil. Simmer gently for 10 minutes, stirring until sauce has reduced a little. Season with sea salt and freshly ground black pepper. Remove herbs.
04 Preheat oven to 230°C (450°F). Turn dough out onto a floured bench, divide it in half and roll out thinly to fit two pizza trays.
05 Top pizza as desired, starting with a smear of pizza sauce and then just one or two other ingredients. Don't overfill pizza or it will go soggy.
06 Bake for 10–15 minutes until crisp and golden. Serve on a big wooden board.
Makes 2 medium pizzas

TIP: Can you go past a Margherita pizza? Just a smear of tomato sauce, a few knots of fresh mozzarella, and a scattering of fresh basil leaves (from your own garden?). I think not. Add a few slices of pepperoni or free-range ham to this faultless pizza if you must.

ANOTHER TIP: Leftover pizza sauce will last about 5 days, covered, in the fridge.

SAUSAGE AND BROCCOLI PASTA *

Something often rather ordinary, a sausage, turns into something truly delicious. Keep the heat on high here, and toss the sausage meat around with a light hand, being careful not to let all the juices out with too much playing around.

1 tbsp olive oil
4 good-quality sausages—any variety
375 g (13 oz) fusilli pasta
1 small head of broccoli, cut into small florets
¼ cup (30 g/1 oz) grated parmesan cheese or cheddar cheese

01 Heat oil in a frying pan over high heat. Squeeze meat from skin of sausages into small chunks and fry until cooked.
02 Meanwhile, add pasta to a saucepan of boiling water. Cook for about 11 minutes, or until al dente, adding broccoli in last 4 minutes of cooking time. Drain pasta and broccoli together.

03 Add pasta and broccoli to frying pan with sausage meat, then toss together to combine. Season to taste with sea salt and freshly ground black pepper. Serve in bowls, sprinkled with grated cheese.
Serves 4

SPAGHETTI PESTO **

The word pesto comes from the Italian word 'pestare', which means 'to crush' or 'to grind'. Originally this fresh basil sauce was made using a mortar and pestle, but we're skipping all the hard work by using that great kitchen time-saver, the food processor It's basically a case of throwing everything together and whizzing it up. Pesto is great tossed through hot spaghetti. You can also spread it over bread, use it as a dip, or drizzle it over pizza or grilled vegetables or meats, so keep some extra pesto handy and store it in a jar in the fridge.

4 garlic cloves, peeled
1 bunch basil
125 g (4½ oz) rocket (arugula)
¼ cup (20 g/¾ oz) grated parmesan cheese
1½ tbsp pine nuts
½ cup (125 ml/4 fl oz) olive oil
375 g (13 oz) spaghetti

01 Peel garlic cloves, then cut in half lengthways. Remove and discard any green sprouts in the centre as they are bitter.
02 Pick leaves from basil and place in a food processor with garlic cloves. Add rocket, parmesan, pine nuts and oil. Pour in 100 ml (3½ fl oz) water and process until mixture is creamy and thick. Add sea salt and freshly ground black pepper to taste.
03 Meanwhile, add pasta to a saucepan of boiling, salted water. Cook following packet instructions until al dente, then drain. Toss pesto through hot spaghetti and serve.
Serves 4

TIP: Basil is really, really good for you. It's packed with antioxidants and mineral salts. Garlic, meanwhile, helps prevent allergies and strengthens the immune system. Not too shabby for one little sauce!

ANOTHER TIP: Chef Neil Perry recommends not toasting the pine nuts, because that makes their flavour too strong for pesto. You want them subtle but still nutty. Plus, it's less work. Hooray!

in my world

A GASTRONOMIC MULTI-LINGUIST

I'm not bilingual but do I know a lot of Italian food words. Here are some good ones and how to pronounce them (stress on the caps).
AL DENTE (ahl DEN-tay) A cooking term that means 'to the tooth' in Italian. It's used to indicate pasta that is not overcooked but 'to the bite'.
CACCIATORA (kah-chyah-TOE-rah) Italian for 'hunter style' stew, often done with chicken and the addition of tomatoes, olives and capsicum.
DIAVOLA (dee-ah-VOL-ah) It may be your favourite pizza topping, but it refers to 'devil's style', because there's always some fiery chilli in these Italian dishes.
RIPIENO (ree-PYAY-no) This is a good one. It means stuffing, but when it finishes with an 'i' it is an adjective which means 'stuffed', such as '*pomodori ripieni*', or stuffed tomatoes.

BEETROOT RAVIOLI ***

I only first made a dish along these lines quite recently—so you're already a few steps ahead of me if you do these now. I'd written a newspaper article about how hard chef's recipes really are, and this one involved a recipe by Lucio Galletto and David Dale. A friend and I expected this recipe to be really hard to make, but it turned out to be totally do-able. I've simplified and tweaked it a bit, but the result is a very pretty, very chef-like, and very impressive ravioli.

1 portion Basic pasta dough (see page 138)
extra virgin olive oil, for drizzling
fresh herbs (such as chervil or parsley), for sprinkling
shavings of parmesan cheese, to serve

Beetroot filling
500 g (1 lb 2 oz) beetroot (beets)
40 g (1½ oz) butter, melted
2 tbsp dry breadcrumbs
⅓ cup (80 g/2¾ oz) ricotta cheese
1 egg
freshly grated nutmeg, to taste

01 Roll pasta dough into very thin sheets, using the thinnest possible setting on the pasta machine. Make each sheet about the same size and shape. Set aside.
02 Next, make the beetroot filling. Put beetroot in a saucepan, cover with cold water, bring to the boil and cook for 25 minutes, or until a knife can be easily inserted all the way through. Drain beetroot and allow to cool a little, then slip off and discard skins. Roughly chop beetroot.
03 Place beetroot in a food processor with remaining filling ingredients. Process to form a slightly lumpy paste. Allow to rest for 5 minutes, then spoon some out – it should be a little firm, so add more breadcrumbs if needed. Season to taste with sea salt and freshly ground black pepper.
04 Lay out one sheet of pasta on a lightly floured work surface. Place 1 tbsp filling for each ravioli in rows on the pasta, spacing them 3–4 cm (1¼–1½ inches) apart, and leaving a 2 cm (¾ inch) border at edge of pasta.
05 Brush a little water onto pasta around each mound of filling, then lay a second sheet of pasta over top, using your fingers to press it down around each filling mound to push out any air.
06 Use a knife or round cookie cutter to cut out ravioli, then pick up each one and push around edges to ensure all air has come out.
07 Cook ravioli in a large saucepan of boiling salted water. They are cooked when they rise to surface.
08 'Plate up' about three ravioli per person. Drizzle with a little oil, scatter with herbs, if using, top with a few parmesan shavings and serve.
Serves 4

Blueberry pavlova * Meringues * Downright Eton mess * Queensland mess * Crunchy apple tarts * Apple cherry crumble * Mango frozen yoghurt * Chocolate pots de crème * Rhubarb rice pudding * Chocolate-dipped strawberries * Chilled lemon sago * Lemon-meringue-in-a-glass * Chewiest chocolate brownies * Raspberry chocolate sundae * Chocolate fudge sundae sauce * Rhubarb and strawberry fool * Choc raspberry bread and butter pudding * Lemon curd * Chocolate mousse * Real custard * Coconut panna cotta with mango and lime syrup

DESSERT

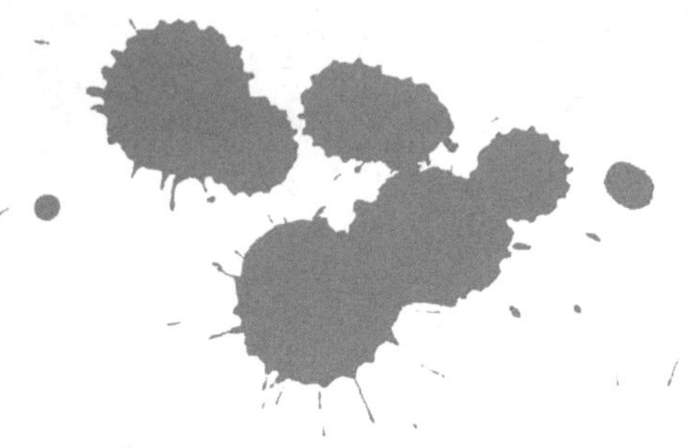

Dessert is an awesome thing. It's romantic, splendid, and at the epicentre of delicious eating and cooking ...

... There are worse things in the world than a deflated pavlova. Nobody should shed tears over a collapsed panna cotta, or an overly oozing chocolate brownie. After all, a messy catastrophe is still going to taste marvellous. Is there anything more spectacular, more epic, and more woo-worthy than a sugar-sprinkled, cream-laden, sweet-nooked finale to a meal?

I'm not going to pretend dessert is the easiest course in the world. It calls for good organisation, and a knack with timing. It's not the time to muck around and take enormous risks, but takes patience and a bit of practice. It's where cooking meets science, so recipes should be followed. My grandmother has always emphasised the importance of reading a recipe through once or twice before anything else is done. If you don't want your chocolate fudge sauce to be grainy, then follow the recipe. If you like your chocolate mousse properly set, follow the recipe. The French concept of *mise en place*—everything in its place—is especially important with dessert. Measure out everything and check all ingredients are on hand before you start cooking.

In our household, dessert was a 'special occasion' thing. We'd have it once a week, maybe. As much as I tried to rebel against this philosophy at the time, moderation made dessert something to look forward to. I never had weight issues as a teen, I never got spots, sugar didn't cause mood slumps or cravings—quite simply because it didn't feature in my life all that much. I wasn't perfect, and nor was my diet as a teen, but it did give me a healthy respect for dessert as being a food, rather than a great big sugar hit. From chocolate ice cream to lemon sorbet, some wobbling jelly or a bowl of custard with fruit, I'm all about the world having pudding. Just not every day, in a greedy sugar-craving whim.

Roald Dahl once said that if you have good thoughts they will shine out of your face like sunbeams and you will always look lovely. I say, if you make delicious desserts for your loved ones and serve them up in great blooming bowlfuls, you will always, always, be lovely too.

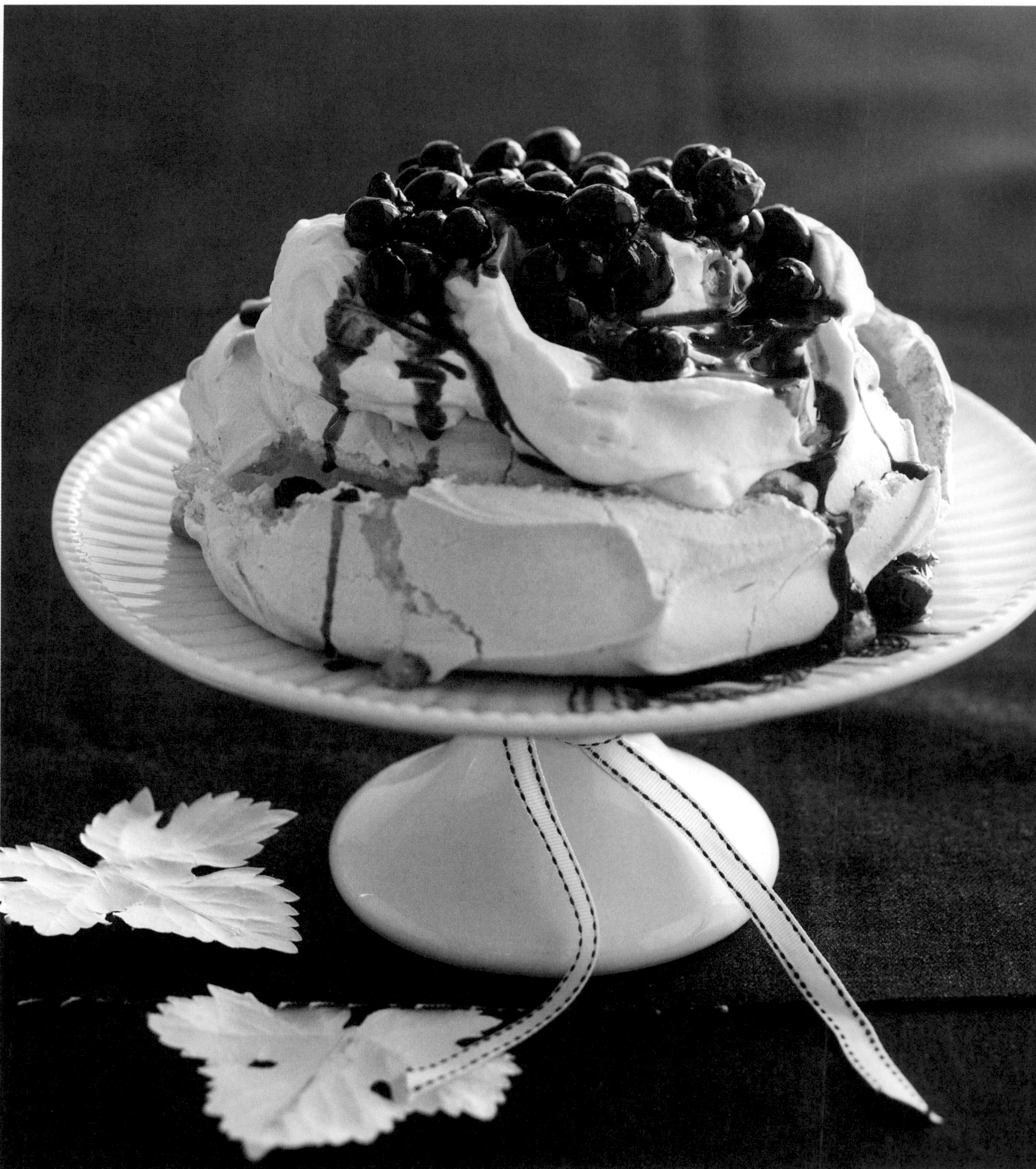

BLUEBERRY PAVLOVA ***

If we don't get dessert we can be fragile creatures. Sometimes we can wander to the dark side if there's no pudding, erring on wicked-witch-of-the-west, mean and strutty, little blighter behaviour. Which is why a recipe like this is such a saviour. So we can whip up some egg whites with sugar, pile on the blueberries and start apologising for our behaviour after the first creamy, billowing, crunchy mouthful.

4 large free-range egg whites
pinch of sea salt
1½ cups (330 g/11½ oz) caster (superfine) sugar
1½ tsp vinegar
1 tsp vanilla extract
300 ml (10½ fl oz) pouring (whipping) cream
175 g (6 oz) blueberries
2 tbsp blueberry syrup (optional)

01 Preheat oven to 200°C (400°F). Line a baking tray with baking paper, then mark an 18 cm (7 inch) circle on the paper with a pencil—use a compass, or find a bowl with the right sized rim and use it as a guide.
02 Beat egg whites and salt using electric beaters until they form stiff peaks (see 'how to' over the page). With beater at its lowest speed, gradually add 1 tbsp sugar at a time. Beat at full speed once all sugar has been added. Lastly, fold in vinegar and vanilla.
03 Spoon large dollops of mixture on the inside of your pencil circle. Keep everything light and be careful not to flatten the egg whites—the meringue should look quite tall and fluffy, with lots of pointy swirly bits. It's OK if it all looks a bit mad—just try to keep everything inside the circle. Smooth the top a little using the back of a spoon, so you'll have somewhere to plop your cream and blueberries later.
04 Place in oven for only 5 minutes, then reduce oven temperature to 150°C (300°F) and bake for 1 hour. (If you're using a gas oven, bake at 150°C/300°F for 1 hour, then reduce heat to 110°C/225°F for another 20 minutes.)
05 Now turn off oven, but leave pavlova in oven until it is completely cool.
06 Meanwhile, whip cream until stiff. Put blueberries in a small bowl, with syrup if using, then crush lightly with a spoon to release blueberry juices a little.
07 When you're ready to serve, place pavlova on a platter. Dollop on cream and top with blueberries, allowing syrup and juices to run wild all over pavlova. Serve it up in big crunchy dollops.
Serves 8

MERINGUES **

Individual meringues are great for dessert. Use them in the Downright Eton mess and Queensland mess recipes in this chapter, or make your own creations by adding peaches, plums or other favourite fruits.

3 large free-range or organic egg whites
pinch of cream of tartar
1 cup (220 g/7¾ oz) caster (superfine) sugar

01 Preheat oven to 120°C (235°F). Line two baking trays with baking paper.
02 Using electric beaters (or a bowl and whisk if you're energetic!), beat egg whites on medium speed until light and a little frothy.
03 Add cream of tartar, then beat on highest speed until stiff, still-wet peaks form. Gradually add sugar, beating until egg whites are very stiff and glossy.
04 Using two large spoons or a piping (icing) bag, dollop mixture onto baking trays to form meringue shapes, leaving a space of at least 2 cm (¾ inch) between each. Remember they will expand a little when cooking.
05 Bake for 1½ hours, then remove from the oven and allow to cool. Store in an airtight container at room temperature for 4–5 days.
Makes 12–24 meringues, depending on size. The bigger they are, the chewier they will be on the inside.

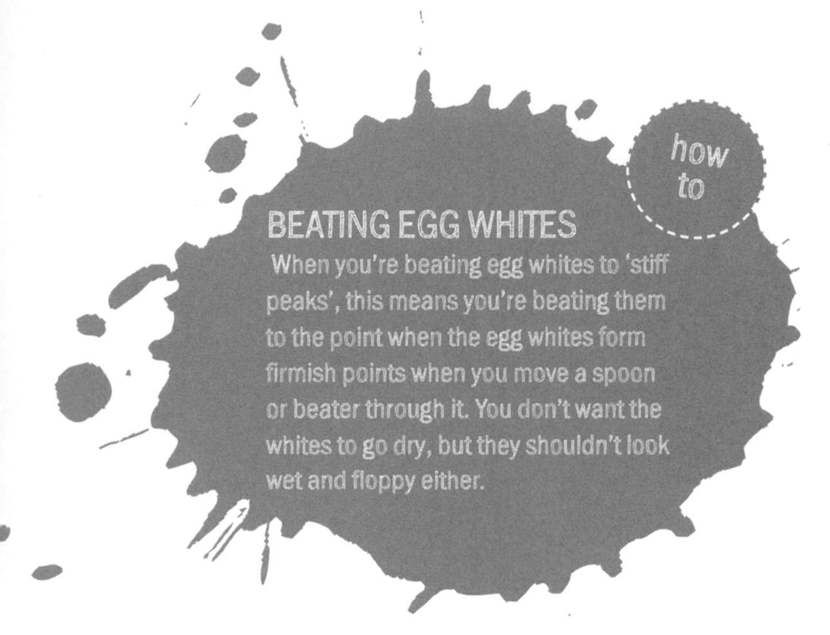

how to
BEATING EGG WHITES
When you're beating egg whites to 'stiff peaks', this means you're beating them to the point when the egg whites form firmish points when you move a spoon or beater through it. You don't want the whites to go dry, but they shouldn't look wet and floppy either.

DOWNRIGHT ETON MESS **

Boys at the famous English school of Eton invented this dish. Apparently the kids (who wear top hats as part of their school uniforms) smashed up their school pudding of meringues, strawberries and cream to make this downright Eton mess. Let the juice of the crushed strawberries and raspberries dribble down the insides of the glasses, and add less cream for a healthier version.

4–6 large Meringues (see page 149)
1 cup (125 g/4½ oz) frozen raspberries
250 g (9 oz) strawberries, stalks removed
1 cup (250 ml/9 fl oz) pouring (whipping) cream, whipped

01 Place meringues in a plastic bag and crush into 2–3 cm (¾–1¼ inch) pieces.
02 Thaw raspberries in a bowl. Add half the strawberries and mash with a fork, until berries are juicy but still chunky. Add cream and broken meringues and gently fold together.
03 Carefully spoon mixture into four or six glasses. Thinly slice remaining strawberries, scatter over the top and serve immediately.
Serves 4–6

QUEENSLAND MESS **

Mango, coconut, passionfruit and crunchy meringue. It's the sunnier, Australian, tropical version of the British classic.

4–6 large Meringues (see page 149)
3 tbsp shredded or shaved coconut
1 cup (250 ml/9 fl oz) pouring (whipping) cream, whipped
1 mango, peeled and cut into 1 cm (½ inch) cubes
pulp from 2 passionfruit
1 tbsp maple syrup

01 Place meringues in a plastic bag and crush into 2–3 cm (¾–1¼ inch) pieces.
02 Heat a small frying pan over medium heat. Gently toast coconut until fragrant and starting to turn a little golden. Remove from heat and set aside.
03 Gently fold crushed meringues through cream, then divide mixture among four or six glasses.
04 Add mango cubes, then drizzle with passionfruit pulp. Sprinkle with toasted coconut, drizzle with maple syrup and serve.
Serves 4–6

in my world

WHAT'S WITH SILVER SERVICE?

What exactly is silver service, apart from a bit over-the-top and expensive and formal? Oh darling, it's just darling, actually. This is the world of London's Savoy, New York's Plaza or Paris' Ritz. Specifically, it is the art of using a spoon and fork as though they were chopsticks to serve guests at the table. Silver service is part of the ritual of dining in the Classic (la-de-da) manner. For the chef, it is the opportunity to display her best creations, and a style which the great chefs like Careme and Escoffier helped establish. In silver service, the mark of a good waiter's skill is to be unobtrusive. Yes, no elbowing, no interruptions, no 'excuse me miss can you move your iPhone so I can put down your food'. These highly skilled waiters are members of a proud profession that demands speed, dexterity, organisation and an unbeatable knowledge of food and wine. A first-class waiter combines some of the qualities of an actor, a diplomat and, on occasion, a helpful nanny.

CRUNCHY APPLE TARTS *

These apple tarts are basic assembly. Do them when you need an easy dessert, quick.

6–8 sheets filo pastry
80 g (2¾ oz) unsalted butter, melted
1 cup (270 g/9½ oz) apple purée
3 apples, cored and very thinly sliced
⅓ cup (35 g/1¼ oz) flaked almonds
1–2 tbsp raw or demerara sugar
ice cream or yoghurt, to serve

01 Preheat oven to 190°C (375°F).
02 Unwrap filo pastry and peel off one sheet. Cover remaining pastry with a clean, damp tea towel (dish towel). Brush one half of pastry sheet with some melted butter, then fold it in half and brush top with more butter. Crumple sheet loosely at edges, shaping it into a rough, round shape, gathering in sides. Repeat with more sheets of pastry.
03 Dollop about 1 tbsp apple purée in centre of each round, then arrange apple slices in centre so that each tart is filled. Scatter with almonds, sprinkle with sugar, then place on a baking tray.
04 Bake for about 20 minutes, or until pastry is golden brown and crispy. Serve warm, with a scoop of ice cream or yoghurt.
Makes about 6–8

APPLE CHERRY CRUMBLE **

The nubbly old favourite, apple crumble, delivers deliciousness with ease. It's the page in my cookbooks stuck together from years of dinner parties and last-minute dessert requests. Crumble recipes are often the first to get handed down the generations because they're such a lovely reminder that home cooking is the most comforting and rewarding. Make any berry substitutions you like here, and use fresh berries if you have them. Serve with whipped cream, yoghurt or vanilla ice cream.

3 apples, peeled and cored
20 g (¾ oz) butter
1 tbsp sugar
⅓ cup (80 ml/2½ fl oz) lemon juice
2 cups (400 g/14 oz) tinned cherries, drained

Crumble topping
1 cup (150 g/5½ oz) plain (all-purpose) flour
½ cup (50 g/1¾ oz) rolled (porridge) oats
80 g (2¾ oz) butter
¼ cup (45 g/1½ oz) brown sugar
1 tsp ground cinnamon
½ tsp ground ginger
large pinch of ground nutmeg

01 Preheat oven to 180°C (350°F).
02 Cut each apple into quarters, then into eight pieces. Place in a saucepan with butter, sugar and lemon juice. Cover and cook over medium heat for 5 minutes, or until just soft.
03 Remove from heat and gently fold in cherries. Tip fruit mixture into a baking dish.
04 To make the topping, combine ingredients in a bowl. Use your fingers to rub butter into the dry ingredients until mixture resembles large crumbs, being careful not to melt butter too much with your warm hands. Evenly sprinkle crumble over fruit.
05 Bake for 30 minutes, or until topping is golden brown.
Serves 4

MANGO FROZEN YOGHURT *

Summer, with its awesome sunshine, beachy weather and summer fruits, doesn't have to end completely each season. This frozen yoghurt is how we keep the summer months going just a little bit longer.

500 g (1 lb 2 oz) frozen mango flesh
2 cups (500 g/1 lb 2 oz) natural yoghurt
1 tbsp honey
6–10 mint leaves, torn
1 cup (155 g/5½ oz) blueberries

01 Place four serving glasses in freezer to get chilled and icy.
02 Place frozen mango, yoghurt, honey and mint in a food processor and blend until combined.
03 Divide blueberries among chilled glasses, then dollop yoghurt mixture over the top in large scoops. Drizzle with extra honey, if you like.
Serves 4

TIP: When mangoes are in season and cheap, freeze some to use for later. Peel off the skin using a vegetable peeler, then cut the mango cheeks off in two large pieces, discarding the stone. Wrap the mango in plastic wrap, slip them into little snap-lock bags, and freeze.

CHOCOLATE POTS DE CRÈME **

This easy dessert fits the just-looking-for-something-little-and-sweet demand. These are little pots of cream custard, basically, either had with a little spoon as a sneaky afternoon snack, or served with proud pomp and ceremony after a special occasion dinner. Not crazy about chocolate? You can leave it out altogether. Add a few drops of vanilla extract instead, or even a small, strong shot of espresso coffee.

1 cup (250 ml/9 fl oz) pouring (whipping) cream
1½ cups (375 ml/13 fl oz) milk
150 g (5½ oz) good-quality dark chocolate, roughly chopped
1 vanilla pod, or 1 tsp vanilla extract
1 tbsp caster (superfine) sugar
4 free-range egg yolks
1 free-range egg
brandy snaps or sweet wafers, to serve

01 Preheat oven to 150°C (300°F).
02 In a small saucepan, slowly bring cream, milk, chocolate, vanilla and sugar to scalding point (not yet simmering), stirring gently until chocolate has melted. Remove from heat.
03 Beat egg yolks and egg lightly in a bowl until combined, then pour into scalded cream mixture. Mix together well, then pour into a jug.
04 Pour mixture carefully into six ½ cup (125 ml/4 fl oz) individual heatproof dishes. Place them in a roasting tin, then pour in enough hot water to come three-quarters of the way up the sides of pots. Cover roasting tin with a lid or foil.
05 Transfer to oven and cook until custards have set, which could take 20–40 minutes, depending on thickness of pots.
06 Turn oven off, then leave pots in oven to cool for 30 minutes.
07 Lift pots out of roasting tin, removing lid or foil quickly so that no water falls into creams. Leave to cool completely.
08 Once cooled, cover with plastic wrap and store in refrigerator until ready to serve. Serve with a crisp dessert biscuit, such as a brandy snap or sweet wafer.
Makes 6

by the way

HOSTESS WITH THE MOST-ESS

My friend Nicole is a superstar of desserts, and just when you think you can't eat another thing she comes out with some great tiramisu sprinkled with hazelnuts and grated chocolate. We recently decided we'd all have a very chilled evening at home, and get takeaway for dinner–nobody cooking, nobody washing up. But Nicole, ever the dessert master, afterwards surprised us all with a platter of chocolate-covered strawberries. For heaven's sake, they were completely awesome.

how to

WHIP CREAM

The luscious billowing stuff that turns a simple dessert into a knock-'em-out extravaganza–whipped cream–demands a few tricks:

- # Chilled cream whips more quickly.
- # For soft peaks, whisk until cream just clings to whisk, and a little longer for firm peaks.
- # Don't whip so much that the cream gets firm–it will go grainy and horrible.
- # Save slightly grainy, over-whipped cream by adding a dash of un-whipped cream, then fold through. If this doesn't work just start all over again.

RHUBARB RICE PUDDING **

A rice pudding with bright pink stripes through it. This really creamy rice pudding serves two, so make double quantities if you're cooking for four. I've made this recipe for one on a rainy day—me curled up on the sofa and dipping into it with a spoon, while a storm carries on outside. Then there's always some left over the next day, which is nice cold, packed for lunch in a little container.

4 cups (1 litre/35 fl oz) milk
¾ cup (150 g/5½ oz) basmati rice
1 tsp ground cinnamon
2 tbsp brown sugar
350 g (12 oz) rhubarb, cut into 2.5 cm (1 inch) lengths
2 tbsp honey
2 slices orange peel, white pith removed

01 First, make the rice pudding. Heat milk and rice in a saucepan over medium heat; add cinnamon and bring to a simmer. Cook gently for 30 minutes, stirring frequently. The rice will absorb the milk, but it should still be soft and wet, not dry. Add sugar and stir for 2 minutes, or until sugar has dissolved. Add more milk if rice looks too dry.
02 Meanwhile, cook the rhubarb. Place rhubarb in a heavy-based saucepan with honey and orange peel slices. Add ½ cup (125 ml/4 fl oz) water and bring to a gentle simmer. Cook gently for 8 minutes, or until rhubarb is soft, but not dissolved. Use tongs to remove orange peel, then discard.
03 Scoop large dollops of rice pudding into two bowls, then spoon rhubarb over the top. Ask people to swirl it all together as they like.
Serves 2

TIP: Serve with cream (or Real custard, page 166) for just a little more creamy goodness.

CHOCOLATE-DIPPED STRAWBERRIES **

These are great for parties because they can be done ahead. Dipping food into melted chocolate is only going to make life better, really.

20 medium-sized strawberries, stalks on
200 g (7 oz) dark chocolate or milk chocolate

01 Line a baking tray with baking paper. Wash and dry strawberries.
02 Break chocolate into even pieces, then place in a small heatproof bowl that fits snugly over a small saucepan. Leave bowl out of saucepan for now, and fill pan one-third full of water.
03 Bring water to the boil over high heat. Reduce heat to low, then place chocolate bowl over saucepan. Be careful not to let bowl touch the water, or it will overheat. Stir chocolate with a metal spoon until it is melted and smooth. Turn off heat. Be really careful not to let even a drop of water get in the chocolate.
04 Dip one strawberry two-thirds into chocolate, then gently shake it over bowl so any excess chocolate drips back into bowl. Carefully place strawberry on baking tray, and don't move it once you've placed it.
05 Repeat with remaining strawberries. Stir chocolate every now and then, and turn heat to low if it starts to harden.
06 Refrigerate strawberries for at least 1 hour, until set. Serve on a platter or in a big bowl.
Makes 20

Top left: Meringues (page 149)
Bottom left: Lemon-meringue-in-a-glass (page 158)

try me

CHILLED LEMON SAGO **

'Those are eel's eyes you're eating, you know.' When my dad was a boy, this is what his older brother would say when their mum served up lemon sago for dessert. Mean trickery, of course: they're not eel's eyes at all. The story carried down to me and my sister Louise, and we'd make the same joke every time. I've always loved this lemon dessert—it's like eating tiny soft pearls, or a bowl full of lemony jelly balls.

1 cup (195 g/6¾ oz) sago
grated zest of 2 lemons
juice of 3 lemons
2 tbsp golden syrup
⅓ cup (75 g/2½ oz) sugar
pouring (whipping) cream, for drizzling

01 Soak sago in 3 cups (750 ml/26 fl oz) water for 30 minutes.
02 Stir in lemon zest, lemon juice, golden syrup and sugar, then pour mixture into a saucepan.
03 Bring to the boil, then reduce heat to medium-high. Simmer, stirring, for about 8 minutes, or until mixture is quite thick and sago is tender all the way through.
04 Pour into dessert bowls, then chill until set. Serve drizzled with cream.
Serves 4–6

LEMON-MERINGUE-IN-A-GLASS **

Half cheesecake, half lemon meringue pie. My grandmother, Margaret Fulton, is an expert on the cheesecake. Her New York cheesecake is about my favourite dessert—light and fluffy concoction on a biscuit base, a thin layer of sour cream adding a gorgeous gilded topping. This isn't that, but it's a fun take on that traditional dessert, with a touch of billowing lemon meringue pie, all spooned into a glass so you can see the pretty layers.

⅓ cup (50 g/1¾ oz) whole hazelnuts, skin on
5 ginger nut biscuits (cookies)
50 g (1¾ oz) butter
1½ cups (195 g/6¾ oz) frozen raspberries
4–5 tbsp Lemon curd (see page 165)
250 g (9 oz) mascarpone cheese
1 tsp vanilla extract
2 tbsp milk

01 In a food processor, blend together hazelnuts and biscuits, so they're roughly chopped (not too fine).
02 Melt butter in a small saucepan over medium heat, then add nut mixture. Stir and let mixture cook for 1 minute, or until it is slightly fragrant. Turn off heat.
03 Reserve about 1 tbsp mixture for topping. Divide the rest among four glasses, pressing down a little with a spoon.
04 Scatter a few frozen raspberries in each glass. Dollop lemon curd over the top, then top with remaining raspberries. Leave to sit for 10 minutes at room temperature.
05 In a bowl, combine mascarpone, vanilla extract, and some of the milk. Mix well with a wooden spoon, until cheese is soft and very smooth. Add a splash more milk if it's too firm. Dollop mixture into glasses, making it pretty and dollopy and not pushing it down into the glass.
06 When you're ready to serve, sprinkle reserved ginger crumble over each glass.
Serves 4

Poids net 10 Kilos

CHEWIEST CHOCOLATE BROWNIES **

Prunes make things chewy, and you'll barely taste them through all that excellent chocolate. You can fold a handful of roasted, crushed hazelnuts through the mixture at the last minute, if you prefer your brownies nutty. Personally I like mine all chocolate and chew.

1 cup (250 ml/9 fl oz) apple juice
1 cup (200 g/7 oz) pitted prunes, quartered
1/3 cup (50 g/1 3/4 oz) plain (all-purpose) flour
1/3 cup (40 g/1 1/2 oz) unsweetened cocoa powder, plus extra for dusting
2 tsp baking powder
300 g (10 1/2 oz) dark chocolate, roughly chopped
75 g (2 1/2 oz) unsalted butter
1 1/3 cups (295 g/10 1/4 oz) caster (superfine) sugar
4 free-range eggs
150 g (5 1/2 oz) sour cream

01 Preheat oven to 180°C (350°F). Find yourself a 23.5 cm (9 inch) square baking tin, or a 20 cm x 30 cm (8 inch x 12 inch) rectangular baking tin, with 4 cm (1 1/2 inch) sides. Grease tin, then line base with baking paper.
02 Heat apple juice in a small saucepan or in the microwave, until very hot. Remove from heat, then soak prunes in juice for at least 1 hour.
03 Sift flour, cocoa and baking powder into a bowl. Set aside.
04 Melt chocolate, butter and sugar in a heatproof bowl set over a saucepan of simmering water, being careful not to let base of bowl touch water. Stir until chocolate has melted—about 8–10 minutes. The mixture should be soft and look almost fudgy. Remove bowl from heat and allow to cool to room temperature.
05 Beat chocolate mixture with a wooden spoon, adding 1 egg at a time and beating well after each addition.
06 Add flour mixture and stir to combine. Then add sour cream and fold together. Drain prunes, discarding juice, and fold them into mixture.
07 Spoon mixture into baking tin and bake for 50 minutes. Test brownies are ready by pressing top lightly with your finger. It should be soft but not runny—the mixture will firm up as it cools.
08 When mixture is cool, use a hot knife to cut it into squares. Dust with a little extra cocoa powder and have a slice with a glass of cold milk.
Makes about 20

RASPBERRY CHOCOLATE SUNDAE *

So retro caravan, milk-bar America. So 1950s hairdos and pastels and drawling accents and space shuttle planning. Yet still so totally modern. (See pic page 144.)

1/2 portion Chocolate fudge sundae sauce (see page 162)
1 cup (125 g/4 1/2 oz) raspberries
4 scoops vanilla ice cream, softened
1 handful of toasted nuts, such as almonds, hazelnuts, pistachios or a mixture

01 Get sauce ready and let it reach room temperature.
02 Crush raspberries a little in a bowl using a fork. If you're using frozen raspberries, let them thaw and then lightly smash.
03 Pour a drizzle of chocolate sauce into two tall glasses. Divide half the raspberries between glasses, then add ice cream balls, more raspberries and more chocolate sauce.
04 Lightly crush nuts using a mortar and pestle or wrap in a clean tea towel (dish towel) and beat gently with a rolling pin. Sprinkle on top and serve.
Serves 2

CHOCOLATE FUDGE SUNDAE SAUCE **

This is your ultimate dark glossy chocolate fudge sauce for drizzling over ice cream, ladling over banana splits, or stirring wildly into a glass of milk. (See pic page 167.)

175 g (6 oz) good-quality dark chocolate
50 g (1¾ oz) butter
50 g (1¾ oz) caster (superfine) sugar
2 tbsp golden syrup
200 ml (7 fl oz) milk

01 To melt chocolate, break into squares and place in a heatproof bowl set over a small saucepan of simmering water, being careful not to let base of bowl touch water. Add butter and stir gently until chocolate melts and mixture is smooth.
02 Stir in sugar and golden syrup until sugar has dissolved, then pour in milk and continue to cook, stirring often, until sauce is thick and perfectly saucy. Store in the fridge in an airtight container for up to 1 week.
Makes about a cup (250 ml/9 fl oz)

in my world

MOST EXPENSIVE DESSERTS

Fancy a slice of $1000 Sultan's Golden Cake? It's served in Istanbul, Turkey. It's laden with apricots, pears, quince and figs that have been marinating in rum for 2 years and flavoured with shaved caramelised black truffles. It's then wrapped in edible gold leaf and served in a sterling silver handcrafted box with a gold seal.

RHUBARB AND STRAWBERRY FOOL **

Growing up, I thought this dish was a bit rude. Ah, la-de-da, we grow up and we realise there's more than one meaning to some words. So, this is a fool. And it's not a bit foolish to make it.

1 bunch rhubarb, trimmed and cut into 5 cm (2 inch) lengths
½ cup (110 g/3¾ oz) sugar
grated zest of 1 orange
250 g (9 oz) strawberries, stalks removed, or 1 cup (150 g/5½ oz) frozen strawberries, thawed
1½ cups (375 ml/13 fl oz) pouring (whipping) cream
2 egg whites

01 Place rhubarb, sugar, orange zest and about 1 tbsp water in a saucepan that has a lid. Bring to a gentle simmer and cook for 5–8 minutes, or until sugar has dissolved and rhubarb is tender.
02 Drain mixture, then purée in a blender or food processor. If you're using frozen strawberries, add these to the blender too. If you're using fresh ones, thinly slice them, and set aside.
03 Whip cream until firm peaks form. Set aside.
04 Whip egg whites until stiff peaks form. Add egg whites to whipped cream and fold to completely combine. Add puréed rhubarb and strawberries, then gently fold through so there are swirls of fruit. Dollop fool into chilled wine glasses and serve immediately.
Serves 6

like me *

CHOC RASPBERRY BREAD AND BUTTER PUDDING *

This gorgeous take on the old-fashioned bread and butter pudding has a tart yet sweet choc-raspberry ribbon running through the middle. It's also completely easy to make, and is just about layering the ingredients together, pouring over the soon-to-be custard, and popping it in the oven to work its oozing, gooey, crispy-topped magic.

80 g (2¾ oz) butter, softened, plus extra for brushing and topping
8 thick slices white bread
3 tbsp good-quality jam
150 g (5½ oz) fresh or frozen raspberries
⅓ cup (50 g/1¾ oz) dark or milk chocolate melts (buttons)
5 free-range eggs
4 cups (1 litre/35 fl oz) milk
2 tsp vanilla extract
½ tsp ground cinnamon
½ tsp freshly grated nutmeg
1 tbsp sugar
pouring (whipping) cream, to serve (optional)

01 Preheat oven to 180°C (350°F).
02 Butter bread slices thickly on one side, then spread a little jam on top. Cut bread into triangles. Arrange half the slices in a deep buttered pie dish or shallow casserole dish. Scatter with half the raspberries and all the chocolate melts. Cover with remaining bread triangles. Set aside.
03 Crack eggs into a large bowl and beat with a fork until foaming. Beat in milk, vanilla extract, cinnamon and nutmeg, mixing well. Pour mixture evenly over bread, then scatter with remaining berries. Leave to stand for 15 minutes.
04 Dot generously with a little more butter and sprinkle with sugar. Cover with a piece of buttered baking paper. Bake for about 25 minutes.
05 Remove paper and bake for another 30 minutes, until top is golden brown and crisp.
06 Serve hot straight from dish, with or without a drizzle of cream.
Serves 6

LEMON CURD **

Lemon curd can be spread onto bread or toast like jam, spooned over ice cream (yum), folded through whipped cream to use as a filling for sponge cakes or pavlova, or to fill tiny pastry cases. Swap lemons for limes if you like. And swirl some passionfruit pulp through at the last minute if you fancy.

125 g (4½ oz) butter
1 cup (220 g/7¾ oz) sugar
grated zest and juice of 3 lemons
3 free-range eggs

01 Place the butter, sugar, lemon zest and juice in a heatproof bowl. Set bowl over a saucepan of barely simmering water, over medium–low heat—be careful not to let base of bowl touch the water. Stir continuously until sugar has dissolved and butter has melted.
02 In a small bowl, whisk eggs with a fork.
03 Slowly add eggs to hot lemon mixture, stirring continuously over very low heat until mixture thickens—do not allow it to boil or it will curdle. The lemon curd is ready when it is thick enough to coat the back of a spoon.
04 Pour curd into one or two hot, sterilised jars and seal. Label and store in the fridge for up to 2 weeks.
Makes about 2 cups (500 ml/17 fl oz)

CHOCOLATE MOUSSE **

Velvet spoonfuls, great soft pillows of chocolate, melting bubbles of richness. Yep, chocolate mousse. The trickiest part here is melting the chocolate—a job easily done over a low heat, in a bowl that fits snugly just above a small saucepan. Serve the mousse with a dollop of cream and a dusting of cocoa powder, if desired.

130 g (4½ oz) dark chocolate (about 55% cocoa), chopped
1 tbsp strong black coffee
4 free-range eggs, separated
½ tsp vanilla extract

01 Get all ingredients ready, because this recipe needs to be made quickly.
02 Fill a small saucepan one-third full of water and bring to a gentle simmer. Place a heatproof bowl on top, ensuring it does not touch the water. Let water simmer slowly underneath.
03 Add chocolate and coffee to bowl and melt chocolate, stirring until smooth. Remove from heat.
04 Mix in egg yolks one at a time, stirring until blended, then stir in vanilla extract. Allow to cool.
05 Use an electric beater to beat egg whites until stiff peaks form, being careful not to overbeat them or they will dry out. Pour in chocolate mixture and gently fold it through with a wooden spoon, being careful not to let out the air.
06 Spoon mousse into four small teacups or ramekins. Chill in the refrigerator for at least 4 hours, or overnight. Serve each with a dollop of cream and a dusting of cocoa, if desired.
Makes 4

Right: Chocolate fudge sundae sauce (page 162)

REAL CUSTARD **

The world's best chefs have been using custard in desserts for hundreds of years. And it's still a crowd pleaser. Custard is a foundation recipe for chefs, and is an excellent skill to master, as you can use it to fill pies and tarts, as a sauce in trifles, on Christmas puddings, or just straight up.

2 cups (500 ml/17 fl oz) milk
2 tbsp caster (superfine) sugar
1 vanilla pod, or 1 tsp vanilla extract
5 large free-range eggs, separated

01 Combine milk and half the sugar in a saucepan. Split vanilla pod and scrape seeds from pod. Add seeds and pod to milk, or add vanilla extract. Bring to the boil, then remove pan from heat and let mixture cool a little.
02 Meanwhile, in a bowl, combine egg yolks and remaining sugar and whisk until pale.
03 Remove vanilla pod from milk. Pour one ladle of warm milk into egg mixture, then whisk well. Add another ladle of milk and whisk, and repeat until all the milk is added.
04 Pour everything back into saucepan and cook over low heat for a few minutes, stirring constantly with a rubber spatula or wooden spoon. Watch custard carefully as you stir: after a minute or so it will begin to thicken, at which point remove it from heat. Stir to check its thickness—it should be shiny and coat the back of the spoon. It may need to cook a little longer over low heat to thicken a little more.
05 Once custard is thick enough, immediately take it off heat. Serve hot or cold.
Makes about 2½ cups (625 ml/21½ fl oz)

TIP: It you cook custard too fast or for too long, it may turn lumpy or grainy. If you see lumps of egg in your custard, pour the mixture into a cold saucepan to cool it down a little, then strain the custard through a sieve into a clean jug.

COCONUT PANNA COTTA WITH MANGO AND LIME SYRUP **

The panna cotta sounds all glam and fabulous—and looks it—but in fact it's a foolproof dessert, destined to become one of your signature dishes.

2 cups (500 ml/17 fl oz) pouring (whipping) cream
2 cups (500 ml/17 fl oz) coconut cream
¼ cup (55 g/2 oz) sugar
2 tsp vanilla extract or paste
3 sheets (6 g/⅛ oz) gold-strength gelatine
rice bran oil, for brushing
1 mango, peeled, stone removed, cut into 1 cm (½ inch) cubes

Lime syrup
½ cup (110 g/3¾ oz) sugar
finely grated zest of 1 lime
3 tbsp lime juice

01 Bring cream, coconut cream and sugar to a gentle simmer in a saucepan over low heat. Cook for 5 minutes, or until sugar has dissolved. Remove from heat and stir in vanilla.
02 Soak gelatine in a bowl of cold water until it has softened. Squeeze out excess water with your hand, then whisk gelatine into warm cream mixture, until it has dissolved.
03 Lightly oil eight ½ cup (125 ml/4 fl oz) cups, glasses or ramekins. Pour mixture into cups, not quite filling each one. Place on a tray and refrigerate for 4 hours.
04 To make the lime syrup, heat sugar and ½ cup (125 ml/4 fl oz) water in a small saucepan over medium heat, stirring for about 8–10 minutes until sugar dissolves and liquid reduces a little. Remove from heat, stir in lime zest and juice, then set aside to cool.
05 Serve panna cotta either straight from their pots, topped with cubes of mango and mint leaves, and a small jug of lime syrup on the side—or turn them out onto individual plates, scatter over mango cubes and drizzle with lime syrup.
Serves 8

in my world

GOATS DISCOVERED COFFEE

Yes it's true: coffee, one of the most popular drinks on earth, was actually discovered by goats. Back in the 9th century, a goat herder in Ethiopia noticed his goats becoming agitated and full of energy after eating coffee beans. The story goes that the herder, named Kaldi, then tried the red berries himself. His exhilaration (or 'caffeine hit', as we now know it) prompted him to bring the berries to a nearby monastery. But the disapproving holy man threw them in a fire in a rage. An amazing aroma floated up from the fire, so the roasted beans were quickly raked from the embers, ground up, and dissolved in hot water. The first cup of coffee ever was brewed.

PAPRIKA

Shichimi popcorn * Spiced crispy chickpeas * Sugar-and-spice nuts * Sticky soy chicken wings * Vegie crisps * Meatballs for dipping * Niçoise crostini * Glazed apple lamb cutlets * {on the side} Mayonnaise * {on the side} Tapenade * Grilled prawns with creamy dill and lime dressing * Peanut chicken san choy bau * Lemongrass beef skewers in mini baguettes * Cheesy chicken schnitzel with caponata * Not-from-Kentucky deep-fried chicken * Sticky BBQ pork skewers with pineapple salsa * Steamed Asian dumplings * Chilli Mex * Proper lasagne * Roast fillet of beef * Béarnaise sauce * Banoffee cups * Tiramisu * Singapore swinging spider * Happy hour ice cubes * Watermelon cosmo cocktail * Creaming berry spider * All about the chocolate loaf * Chocolate fudge sauce cake * Chocolate frosting * Lemony cupcakes with lemon icing * Honey, banana and pepita loaf * Strawberry shortcakes * Carrot cupcakes with orange icing * Jam thumbprint cookies * White chocolate, cranberry and macadamia cookies * Chocolate crackles * Honey nut joys

PARTIES & FRIENDS

Dear Life of the Party, I hope you are having a nice day...

. . . I hope the weather is sparkling and everyone has RSVP'd. Awesome! I assume the outfit has been picked out. Hmm, what else. Someone should probably run a vacuum over the floor at some point today. And let's get some amazing food together that just makes everyone think you're some kind of master of the culinary. Not fussy—but not just packets of chips either.

If this gathering is going to be a 'mates' eats' kind of thing—a few friends chilling and unfussed—then think about things you can do ahead, or hearty things that you can just pop in the middle of the table for everyone to help themselves: things like lasagne, meatballs for dipping, little rolls stuffed with excellent barbecued things. The barbecue will probably be lit; you're wearing jeans, maybe a towel a bit later on if you get down to the beach or pool. There will be ice cubes and tunes and chilling. But in an organised lovely way. Pick a few things to cook, and do plenty of each. People don't need 100 different things to eat.
We have, as well, food for more sophisticated gatherings. This is more refined fare, but things are still fun. Set the table ahead, make one big awesome drink. You want to be relaxed, and for the guests to actually see you, so do as much as possible beforehand. There should be flowers and some cool little tunes in the background. I might wear tulle, and put flowers in my hair.

I like something happily sweet and celebratory at a gathering. Pick a cake, or some cookies, some biscuits, something sweet to have, no matter what the occasion. Even chocolate crackles will do, or go for joyous orange-crusted carrot cupcakes for the summery soirée. Or a thick gooey chocolate thing, which is impossible not to love. Your guests are gooey with love. For you. And your cake.

Best regards,

Your gathering accomplice
xoxo

VANS
"OFF THE WALL"

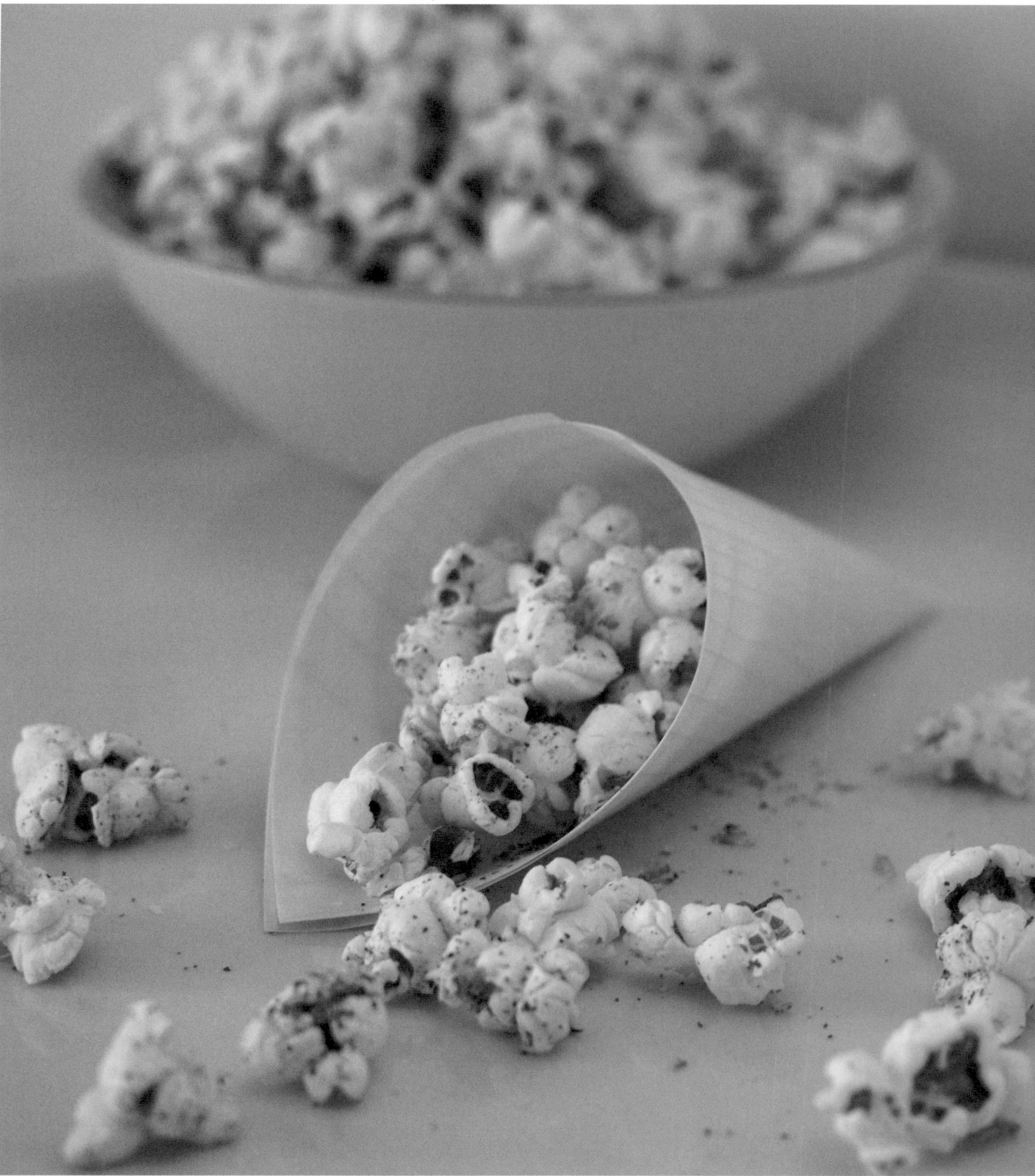

SHICHIMI POPCORN *

Shichimi is a Japanese spice mix that's kind of spicy, kind of acidic, and just pretty darned amazing. Its full name, shichimi togarashi, is Japanese for 'seven-flavour chilli pepper'. Usually it's a dried powder containing red chilli pepper, ground Sichuan pepper, roasted orange peel, sesame seeds, hemp seeds, ground ginger and nori. I've sprinkled shichimi on popcorn, both as a mid-afternoon snack, and to have with drinks at fancy dinner parties. Use it on rice crackers as a lunch snack, too.

¼ cup (60 ml/2 fl oz) vegetable oil
2 tbsp toasted sesame oil
½ cup (115 g/4 oz) popping corn
2 tsp shichimi togarashi, or to taste
finely grated zest of 1 lime

01 In a large saucepan with a tight-fitting lid, heat both oils over medium–high heat. Once oil is hot, add popcorn kernels, fit lid and hold it down as you shake pan well to coat kernels.
02 Cook popcorn for about 5 minutes, or until all kernels are popped, shaking pan every now and then but not removing lid.
03 Transfer popcorn to a serving bowl, removing any burnt or unpopped kernels.
04 Sprinkle with shichimi, 1 tbsp sea salt and the lime zest, to taste. Toss together, serve and munch.
Serves a group of friends–makes more than you'd think

TIP: Shichimi is available from most Asian supermarkets. If you can't get any, a decent alternative are these ingredients, ground up using a mortar and pestle: 1 tsp finely grated orange zest, 2 tsp sesame seeds, 2 pinches of cayenne pepper, 2 pinches of ground ginger.

SPICED CRISPY CHICKPEAS **

Just like round, spicy chips. These are great done ahead so your friends have something to nibble when they arrive. Omit the cayenne pepper if you're worried about it being overly spiced, and add just half the spice quantities—do a taste test, then add more if you like. We all love something crunchy and salty with a drink, and this one's pretty awesome. (See pic page 170.)

2 x 400 g (14 oz) tins chickpeas
½ cup (125 ml/4 fl oz) rice bran oil or vegetable oil
2 tsp smoked paprika
1 tsp ground cumin
2 tsp curry powder (optional)
½ tsp cayenne pepper
finely grated zest of 1 lime

01 Drain and thoroughly rinse chickpeas, then dry with paper towels. Set aside to dry even more.
02 Heat oil in a large, heavy-based, deep-sided frying pan until very hot. Fry half the chickpeas in the oil, stirring well, until crispy and golden, about 10–15 minutes. Be really careful with hot oil, it will spit.
03 Remove chickpeas with a slotted spoon, then transfer to paper towels. Repeat with remaining chickpeas.
04 Place all chickpeas in a serving bowl, then sprinkle with spices and lime zest. Season to taste with sea salt and serve.
Serves a handful or two each for 6–8 people

TIP: Make larger quantities if you're catering to a big crowd. Just remember to do the chickpeas in batches—about one tin of chickpeas in the pan at a time is the max.

SUGAR-AND-SPICE NUTS **

You've probably realised before why some brands of take-away burgers, some packets of chips, and so many bought things taste so good. Yep, it's all that sugar and all that salt. Together they're a match made in tastebud heaven. So, why not skip the fat-laden bought things and make these instead?

½ cup (100 g/3½ oz) brown sugar
½ cup (110 g/3¾ oz) sugar
¼ tsp paprika
pinch of cayenne pepper
1 tsp ground cinnamon
1 egg white
450 g (1 lb) mixed peeled walnuts, hazelnuts and almonds

01 Preheat oven to 150°C (300°F). Line a baking tray with baking paper.
02 In a mixing bowl, combine sugars, spices and a few pinches of sea salt. Set aside.
03 In a small bowl, whisk egg white with 1 tbsp water, until frothy but not stiff. Stir in nuts to evenly coat. Add the nuts to sugar and spice mixture and toss until evenly coated.
04 Spread nuts in a single layer on baking tray, then bake for 30 minutes. Toss nuts around a couple of times during cooking.
05 Remove tray from oven and use two spoons to separate nuts before they cool completely. Allow to cool, then serve, or you can make them a day or two ahead.
Makes enough for 6–8 people as a snack

STICKY SOY CHICKEN WINGS *

The good thing about marinated chicken wings is that you don't have to be too rigid about it all. No need to wince when the honey overflows from the measuring cup, or the soy gives out too many glugs; here or there is just fine. The point here is getting enough of these sticky numbers to please the gang. These are also great served on top of steamed rice for a sit-down affair.

1.5 kg (3 lb 5 oz) chicken wings, about 12
2 tbsp brown sugar or honey
½ cup (125 ml/4 fl oz) soy sauce
1 small knob of fresh ginger, finely grated
2 garlic cloves, crushed
pinch of coarsely ground Sichuan pepper (optional)
cucumber sticks, to serve

01 Preheat oven to 180°C (350°F). Cut chicken wings into two at the largest joint, keeping wing tips attached.
02 In a bowl, combine brown sugar or honey, soy sauce, ginger, garlic and Sichuan pepper, if using. Add chicken wings, tossing to coat.
03 Place wings in a roasting tin in a single layer. Roast for 25 minutes, or until crisp and cooked through. To test, stick a knife in one wing; the juices should run clear. Pop them in the oven for another 5–8 minutes if you're unsure.
04 Serve on a big platter with sticks of cucumber, for a great crunch on the side.
Serves about 6, or make double quantity for a larger crowd

VEGIE CRISPS ***

There is one tricky part to making your own crisps, but the crunchy result is well worth it. These numbers get fried in hot, hot oil—so please be careful. Wear an apron and don't let the hot oil touch you. If you like, you can sprinkle the crisps with ground cumin or smoked paprika while they're still hot.

2 parsnips, peeled
2 carrots, peeled
2 desiree potatoes
2 cups (500 ml/17 fl oz) rice bran oil or vegetable oil
2 tsp paprika or ground cumin (optional)

01 Using a sturdy peeler, shave vegies into very thin, long slices. Keep different vegetables separate, because parsnips cook really quickly compared with carrots and potatoes. Pat raw slices with paper towels to dry them completely.
02 Heat oil in a deep saucepan or flat-bottomed wok. When oil is very hot, use tongs to carefully lower in batches of vegetable slices. Use tongs to stir them around a little, being careful not to knock pan or splash oil.
03 When they start to turn golden, fish them out with tongs or a slotted spoon. Drain on paper towels, then sprinkle with a little sea salt and some paprika or cumin, if using.
04 Repeat with remaining vegetables and serve when cool.
Serves 6–8 as a nibble

NOTE: A mandoline, one of those graters that makes transparent slivers of anything with great ease, is also great for shaving the vegies here. Ask for a hand from someone who's used it before. Seriously, do—I've almost taken the tip off one of my fingers using one of these.

MEATBALLS FOR DIPPING **

These meatballs are great as they are, dipped in tomato ketchup or chutney and served on a big plate for a gathering. Or do a big bowl of spaghetti, a Basic fresh tomato sauce (see page 138), and toss these through. This serves 4–6 as a nibble, so double the recipe if you're throwing a bigger bash.

500 g (1 lb 2 oz) good-quality minced (ground) beef
3/4 cup (85 g/3 oz) dry breadcrumbs
1 tbsp Dijon mustard
grated zest of 1 lemon
1 tbsp dried oregano
1/2 cup (30 g/1 oz) flat-leaf (Italian) parsley leaves, roughly chopped
1 free-range egg
1 tbsp olive oil, plus 2 tbsp extra, for pan-frying
tomato ketchup or tomato chutney, for dipping

01 In a bowl, combine all ingredients except oil. With clean hands, squish mixture together until it's well combined.
02 Divide mixture into four balls, then divide each of those into six small balls, to make 24 balls. If the mixture is sticky, use wet hands to shape balls.
03 Place balls in a bowl, drizzle with 1 tbsp oil, then gently turn to coat them all. Cover with plastic wrap and place in the fridge (for up to 24 hours), until you're ready to cook them.
04 Heat remaining 2 tbsp oil in a large frying pan over medium–high heat. Cook balls in two or three batches, turning them with tongs so they turn golden brown all over, about 8–10 minutes for each batch. Serve with tomato ketchup or tomato chutney.
Makes 24 balls

NICOISE CROSTINI *

Imagine telling your buddies you've made 'Niçoise crostini': how amazing are you? If you like fresh tuna (much less fishy than the tinned variety), and you like olives, this is your clever little starter for when everyone arrives. Completely sophisticated, but a breeze to make.

½ baguette, cut into 10 thin slices
200 g (7 oz) spreadable cream cheese
250 g (9 oz) yellowfin tuna, mid loin
1 tbsp olive oil
80 g (2¾ oz) kalamata olives, pitted and roughly chopped
½ lemon
chopped flat-leaf (Italian) parsley, basil, or whatever herbs you can find
extra virgin olive oil, for drizzling

01 Toast baguette slices. Spread each slice with a little stripe of cream cheese, and arrange them on a serving platter.
02 Season tuna with sea salt and freshly ground black pepper.
03 Heat olive oil in a frying pan over medium heat. Sear tuna for no more than 10 seconds on each side, until lightly coloured on the outside, but still raw inside. Allow to cool, then slice into 10 pieces acrossways.
04 Top each of the toasts with olives. Squeeze over a little lemon juice, then add one slice of tuna to each.
05 Scatter with chopped herbs and drizzle with a tiny bit of extra virgin olive oil before serving.
Makes 10

TIP: If you've made Tapenade (see page 180), use it here instead of the olives.

GLAZED APPLE LAMB CUTLETS **

A mate of mine once said lamb cutlets are perfect for parties because they're basically food with handles. It's true, too: they're great to just have on a big platter so people can help themselves, or wander around with them. Plus, there are no crumbs. But paper napkins will be handy.

1 cup (250 ml/9 fl oz) no-sugar-added apple juice
¼ cup (60 ml/2 fl oz) balsamic vinegar
grated zest and juice of ½ lemon
10 lamb cutlets
olive oil, for drizzling
roughly torn mint leaves, to serve

01 Combine apple juice, vinegar, lemon zest and juice with a pinch of sea salt in a small, heavy-based saucepan. Bring to the boil over high heat, then reduce heat to medium and simmer for about 20 minutes, or until liquid has reduced to about ¼ cup (60 ml/2 fl oz) of syrupy glaze.
02 Heat a large chargrill pan or heavy-based frying pan over high heat. Season lamb cutlets with sea salt, freshly ground black pepper, and a small drizzle of olive oil.
03 When pan is very hot, cook lamb until it is just seared, about 1 minute on each side. Brush cutlets on both sides with some of the glaze, then cook for another 1 minute on each side. Be careful not to overcook lamb—it should be medium-rare.
04 Transfer the lamb to a board or serving dish, cover loosely with foil and leave to rest for 5 minutes.
05 Brush lamb again with more glaze, scatter with mint leaves and serve.
Makes 10

MAYONNAISE **

What? Not from a jar? Are you kidding? This whole cooking thing is getting serious. This real mayonnaise leaves all others in the dust. Use a food processor and you'll be laughing. Serve with crisp carrot and celery sticks, blanched asparagus or little radishes for dipping and you'll wow everyone with your incredible mayonnaise.

2 free-range egg yolks
2 tsp Dijon mustard
2 tsp white wine vinegar or lemon juice
1 cup (250 ml/9 fl oz) olive oil

01 Process egg yolks, ½ tsp sea salt, a good grinding of black pepper, Dijon mustard and 1 tsp vinegar or lemon juice in a food processor for a few seconds.
02 With motor running, very slowly pour in oil, in the thinnest stream you can manage. Make sure oil is mixing properly, and stop pouring every now and then to check it's really blended before adding more.
03 When all oil has been incorporated, add remaining vinegar or lemon juice. Serve immediately or store in the fridge in an airtight container.
Makes a medium-sized jar

TIP: Please don't be disheartened if the mayo doesn't work the first time you make it. Read through the entire recipe again and double check you added the oil really slowly, and that you added the ingredients in the right order. Good luck!

TAPENADE **

Some people hate hate hate olives, and think they're nasty, dark and salty things. Personally, I adore them, and have done since I was a baby. Before I could even walk I'd find a way to get to them. I'd crawl across a room and reach up onto a coffee table if they were on offer for adults. Odd child, perhaps. If you're like me, you'll love this olive tapenade paste. It's great on sandwiches, used in place of the olives in our Niçoise crostini recipe on page 178, or as a salty dip with crusty bread at a gathering with friends. Make this ahead and keep it in the fridge in an airtight container for a few days.

¾ cup (125 g/4½ oz) pitted black olives
3 anchovy fillets, drained (optional)
2 tbsp capers, drained and rinsed
100 g (3½ oz) tin tuna in oil, drained
juice of 1 lemon
⅓ cup (80 ml/2½ fl oz) extra virgin olive oil

01 In a food processor, blend olives, anchovies, capers, tuna and half the lemon juice until a fairly smooth paste forms.
02 With motor still running, add oil in a slow stream.
03 Turn processor off, taste tapenade and add more lemon juice if you like.
Makes 1 small jar

HOW TO HOST A SOPHISTICATED GATHERING

- # Tidy up, but don't go overboard. You're having friends over, not the Queen. So, sure clean the bathroom and run a vacuum over the carpets. Get a bunch of flowers, if you like, and pop them in a large jar. Your friends are there to eat and to hang out, not judge you on the sparkle of your cutlery.
- # But, also, your house should be a pleasure to be in. Get rid of chip packets and wipe down the tables, let some air in the house and even up piles of books and magazines. Get enough seating.
- # Remember, the people you invite are more important than the food you serve. Think about who the really lovely ones are. Invite people you actually like. Invite people with something to say, with something to offer other than a nice tan and good hair. Mix it up a bit. Don't invite people you want to impress–invite people who impress you just because they're so nice, funny and interesting.

GRILLED PRAWNS WITH CREAMY DILL AND LIME DRESSING **

Leaving myself open to Australian stereotypes here, we're going to throw another 'shrimp' on the barbie, but this time with some elegant flair. This is the typical Aussie barbecue taken up a notch. It's a summer must-have, basically. Buy fresh prawns and only buy local, sustainable varieties. Omit the brandy or gin if you like, but rest assured all the alcohol completely burns off when cooked.

- 1/3 cup (80 ml/2 1/2 fl oz) olive oil
- 2 tbsp brandy or gin (optional)
- 4 golden shallots, finely chopped
- 1 small bunch dill, finely chopped
- 20 large raw local prawns (shrimp), peeled except for tails
- 125 g (4 1/2 oz) spreadable cream cheese
- juice of 1 lime
- 2 tbsp rice bran oil
- 1 lime, cut into wedges, to serve

01 Soak 20 bamboo skewers in water for at least 30 minutes, to stop them burning on barbecue.

02 Meanwhile, lightly combine olive oil, brandy or gin, half the shallot and half the dill in a large flat bowl or flat plastic container big enough to fit skewers.

03 Thread a prawn onto each skewer, running skewer through length of the prawn, from head to tail. Place skewers in bowl or container with marinade.

04 Toss together so prawns are completely coated, then cover and leave to marinate in the fridge for at least 1 hour.

05 To make the dressing, in a little serving bowl mix together cream cheese, lime juice, and remaining shallot and dill, to make creamy dill and lime dressing. Add a drizzle of olive oil if you like.

06 Heat a barbecue plate or chargrill pan to high. Drizzle half the rice bran oil on the hot plate and cook prawns for 2 minutes, then turn and cook for another 1–2 minutes, until light golden.

07 Place prawns on a serving platter, with a little bowl of dressing for dipping, and lime wedges for squeezing over.

Serves 4–6 for nibbles

PEANUT CHICKEN SAN CHOY BAU **

Little peanut chicken balls served in crunchy lettuce cups—it's all so cute you'll want them every day. Just trim the edges of the lettuce cups with scissors a bit, so they're not all shabby, and serve on a great platter. Finger food, but with feeling.

- 600 g (1 lb 5 oz) free-range or organic minced (ground) chicken
- 2 tbsp olive oil
- 1/4 cup (45 g/1 1/2 oz) water chestnuts, roughly chopped
- 2 garlic cloves, finely chopped
- 1 egg, lightly beaten
- 3 kaffir lime leaves, thinly sliced
- 1 lemongrass stem, white part only, finely chopped
- 1 small iceberg lettuce, leaves carefully removed (be careful not to tear them!)
- 1/2 cup (65 g/2 1/4 oz) peanuts, roasted and roughly chopped

Peanut butter and lime dressing

- 1/2 cup (140 g/5 oz) smooth peanut butter
- juice of 1 lime
- 1/3 cup (80 ml/2 1/2 fl oz) good-quality chicken stock
- 2 chillies, seeds removed, finely sliced

01 Preheat oven to 180°C (350°F). Line a baking tray with baking paper.

02 In a little serving bowl, mix together ingredients for peanut butter and lime dressing. Set aside.

03 In another bowl, combine chicken, oil, water chestnuts, garlic, egg, lime leaves and lemongrass. Mix together well, until mixture binds together—add a little more oil and another egg if needed.

04 Roll mixture into walnut-sized balls and place on baking tray. Roast for 20 minutes, turning once or twice with tongs during cooking.
05 Meanwhile, lay lettuce cups out on a serving platter, trimming any ratty lettuce edges with scissors.
06 When meatballs are cooked, remove them from oven, divide among lettuce cups and drizzle with dressing. In a final flourish, scatter with peanuts and serve immediately.
Makes about 30 balls

TIP: This one's too messy for words, so offer plates and paper napkins.

LEMONGRASS BEEF SKEWERS IN MINI BAGUETTES **

This tasty meal-in-a-roll is perfect for when friends are over because it's a one-hand dish. You can have a drink in one hand and the roll in the other. I made these once for a street party in London—it was really cool just having them sitting on a massive platter so everyone could help themselves, and eat while standing up and chatting. Just leave a pile of paper napkins out for sticky fingers. This recipe makes eight rolls, so double the quantities for a larger crowd, or for seconds.

500 g (1 lb 2 oz) rump steak, thinly sliced
1 brown onion, finely chopped
4 garlic cloves, roughly chopped
3 lemongrass stems, white part only, roughly chopped
1 red chilli, seeds removed, roughly chopped, plus extra to serve
1 tbsp sesame seeds, toasted
2 tsp fish sauce
8 small baguette rolls, or 1 proper baguette cut into 8 pieces
½ iceberg lettuce, roughly chopped
3 Lebanese (short) cucumbers, peeled and diagonally sliced
1 handful coriander (cilantro) leaves

01 Place steak slices in a bowl. In a food processor or using a mortar and pestle, grind together onion, garlic, lemongrass and chilli to form a paste. Add paste to meat, along with sesame seeds and fish sauce. Toss together and marinate in the fridge for 1 hour.
02 Meanwhile, soak 16 bamboo skewers in water to stop them burning on the barbecue.
03 Loosely thread the meat onto the skewers, then cook in a hot chargrill pan or on a barbecue for 2–3 minutes each side. Don't overcrowd hotplate or they won't char properly.
04 Split baguettes lengthways and layer lettuce, cucumber and coriander in rolls. Place two cooked skewers inside each baguette. Hold onto baguette and gently pull bamboo skewers from the meat and discard them.
05 Close rolls and serve, with some extra chopped chilli in a little bowl on the side.
Makes 8

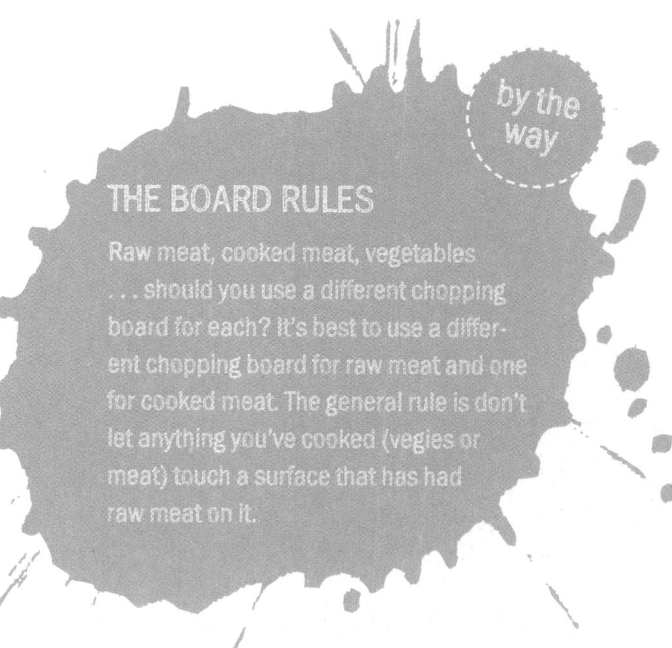

by the way
THE BOARD RULES
Raw meat, cooked meat, vegetables . . . should you use a different chopping board for each? It's best to use a different chopping board for raw meat and one for cooked meat. The general rule is don't let anything you've cooked (vegies or meat) touch a surface that has had raw meat on it.

make me *

CHEESY CHICKEN SCHNITZEL WITH CAPONATA ***

This is a whole meal that you can pretty much do ahead for a handful of friends, or just have the family 'for dinner' and make it a sophisticated affair. They probably deserve it. Do the caponata ahead, and finish it off very gently when you pop the schnitzel in the oven. Caponata is a soft, slightly sweet and acidic vegetable dish that is great with the crunchy schnitzel. Of course the pairing isn't essential, and you can enjoy the chicken schnitzel or caponata with other things (hint: mashed potatoes or creamy polenta).

4 boneless, skinless free-range or organic chicken breasts
2 cups (220 g/7¾ oz) dry breadcrumbs, lightly toasted
½ cup (50 g/1¾ oz) finely grated parmesan cheese
2 free-range eggs, lightly beaten
3 tbsp rice bran oil or vegetable oil
chopped flat-leaf (Italian) parsley, for sprinkling
1 lemon, cut into wedges

Caponata
½ cup (125 ml/4 fl oz) olive oil
1 kg (2 lb 4 oz) eggplants (aubergines), cut into 2 cm (¾ inch) cubes
1 onion, chopped
4 celery stalks, roughly chopped
2 tbsp drained capers
1 cup (125 g/4½ oz) pitted green olives, halved
400 g (14 oz) tin chopped tomatoes
2 tsp caster (superfine) sugar
⅓ cup (80 ml/2½ fl oz) red wine vinegar

01 Preheat oven to 200°C (400°F). Line a baking tray with baking paper.
02 Slice chicken breasts in half through the centre, to form eight flat breasts. Place a couple of breasts between two sheets of plastic wrap, then use a rolling pin to gently beat breasts until they are less than 5 mm (¼ inch) thick. Repeat with remaining breasts, then set them aside on a plate.
03 To make the caponata, heat half the oil in a large, heavy-based saucepan over medium-high heat and fry half the eggplant, turning once or twice, until golden brown. Transfer to a plate. Repeat with remaining oil and eggplant and transfer to plate.
04 In the same pan, cook onion and celery for 5–8 minutes, or until soft and translucent. Add remaining caponata ingredients, stir gently, then add browned eggplant. Reduce heat to medium-low and cook, stirring frequently, for 20–25 minutes, or until eggplant is cooked through.
05 Meanwhile, finish the schnitzel. Combine breadcrumbs and parmesan on a large plate and season with freshly ground black pepper. Dip each chicken fillet into the beaten egg, then into the breadcrumb mixture.
06 Heat oil in a large heavy-based frying pan over medium-high heat. Lightly fry two schnitzels on both sides for 2 minutes, or until just golden. Transfer to baking tray, then repeat with remaining schnitzels.
07 Bake schnitzels for 10 minutes, or until chicken is cooked through.
08 Dollop caponata onto plates and top with one or two chicken schnitzels. Sprinkle with chopped parsley and serve with lemon wedges for squeezing.
Serves 6–8

NOT-FROM-KENTUCKY DEEP-FRIED CHICKEN ***

Fried chicken has a bad rap. But that's all because of the oil-blistered takeaway stuff, while we've almost forgotten that a fried chook is a little bit awesome. Almost any food is OK in moderation, after all. Basically, if it comes from your own kitchen instead of from a takeaway tub—and yes I'm talking to you, naughty indulger—we're OK with a piece or two of fried chicken. A squeeze of lemon or some homemade dipping sauce, too, instead of mash and gravy please. These are also fab packed up for lunch the next day.

1 kg (2 lb 4 oz) small free-range chicken pieces, such as drumsticks and wings, cut at a joint, skin on
2 tbsp sweet paprika
1 tbsp finely ground black or white pepper
2 cups (500 ml/17 fl oz) buttermilk
800 ml (28 fl oz) rice bran oil or peanut oil
3 cups (450 g/1 lb) plain (all-purpose) flour
½ cup (60 g/2¼ oz) tapioca or arrowroot flour
4 cups (440 g/15½ oz) dry breadcrumbs
lemon or lime wedges, to serve

01 First, marinate the chicken. Place chicken pieces in a deepish dish and season with paprika, pepper and a couple of pinches of sea salt. Add the buttermilk and turn chicken to coat it. Marinate for 15–30 minutes outside the fridge, so chicken reaches room temperature.
02 Meanwhile, heat oil in a deep-fryer, wok or deep-sided frying pan to 180°C (350°F), or until a cube of bread sizzles and spits when dropped in.
03 Combine plain flour, tapioca or arrowroot flour and breadcrumbs in a plastic bag (check it doesn't have any holes in it!).
04 Drain chicken, discard marinade, then add chicken pieces to bag. Shake bag to coat chicken in mixture, tie a loose knot in the top and leave bag on bench for 5 minutes.
05 Remove chicken from bag, onto a plate. Press any excess crumbs into chicken.
06 Use tongs to carefully immerse one-quarter of chicken pieces into the hot oil. Don't let the oil splash on your skin. Cook for 4–5 minutes, then turn chicken using tongs and cook for another 3–5 minutes, until golden brown and cooked through.
07 Use tongs to remove chicken from oil and place on paper towels. Repeat with remaining chicken. Serve with citrus wedges and paper napkins. You'll need them for greasy fingers!

Serves 6–8. Break up the pieces before cooking as much as possible for easy finger food

TIP: Try a simple dipping sauce of 3 tbsp mayonnaise, the juice from ½ lime and 1 tsp smoked paprika mixed together well to go with this recipe.

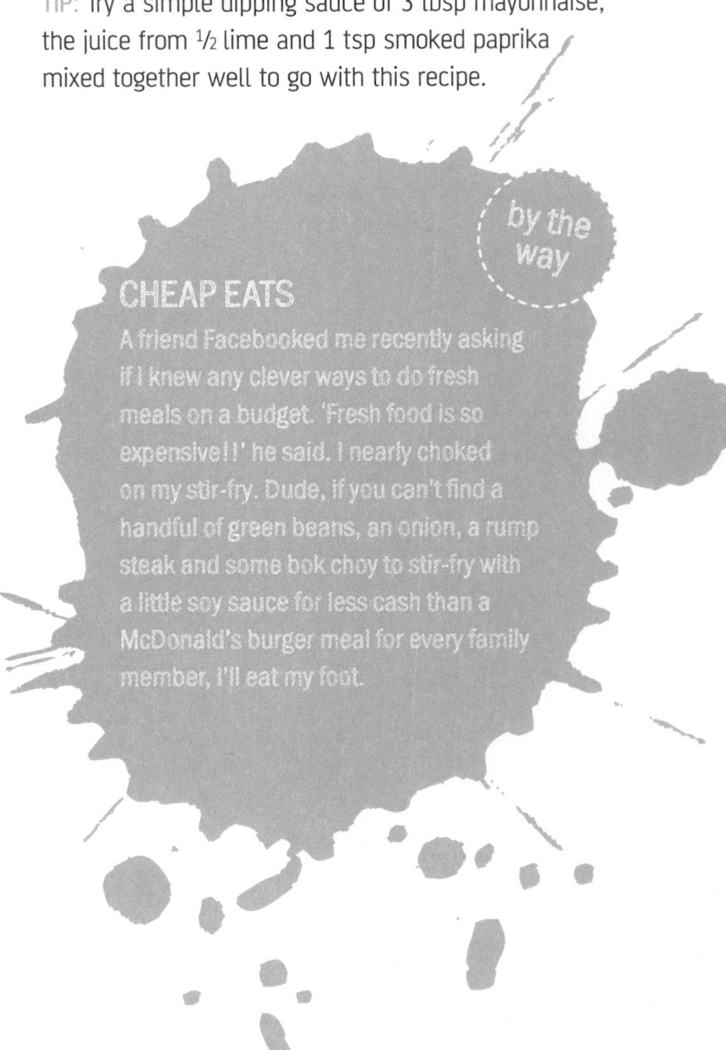

CHEAP EATS

A friend Facebooked me recently asking if I knew any clever ways to do fresh meals on a budget. 'Fresh food is so expensive!!' he said. I nearly choked on my stir-fry. Dude, if you can't find a handful of green beans, an onion, a rump steak and some bok choy to stir-fry with a little soy sauce for less cash than a McDonald's burger meal for every family member, I'll eat my foot.

STICKY BBQ PORK SKEWERS WITH PINEAPPLE SALSA **

If you're into the slightly sweet, smoking, spit-roasting, barbecuing flavours of the American Deep South, this might be your bag. These are totally simple to do, too. Once you have the marinade and pineapple salsa ready, all you need to do is fire up the barbecue. Just arrange the skewers on a big platter for people to help themselves. Serve with a big salad and the pineapple salsa, which gives a sweet and sour punch. Try it with other grilled meats too. British chef Jamie Oliver is behind the excellent 'meat lollipop' invention.

4 x 300 g (10½ oz) free-range or organic pork fillets
lemon or lime wedges, to serve

Marinade
½ tsp ground cumin seeds
1 tsp ground fennel seeds
1 tbsp smoked paprika
1 tbsp brown sugar
2 tbsp olive oil
zest and juice of 1 orange
3 garlic cloves, finely chopped
¼ cup (60 ml/2 fl oz) tomato ketchup
100 ml (3½ fl oz) balsamic vinegar

Pineapple salsa
200 g (7 oz) pineapple, peeled and cut into 1 cm (½ inch) cubes
10–12 large mint leaves, thinly sliced
1 small handful coriander (cilantro), roughly chopped
1 small red chilli, seeds removed, thinly sliced
1 golden shallot, thinly sliced
1 tsp tamarind paste (optional)
juice of ½ lime
½ tbsp brown sugar
2 tsp fish sauce

01 Combine marinade ingredients in a large bowl. Season with sea salt and freshly ground black pepper. Add pork fillets and turn to completely coat them in marinade. Cover and marinate for at least 1 hour in the refrigerator.
02 About 30 minutes before you're ready to eat, heat barbecue to high. Combine all pineapple salsa ingredients in a bowl.
03 Line up pork fillets on a board. Skewer them acrossways with four metal skewers—so each skewer runs through all four pieces of pork.
04 Cook skewers on barbecue for 15–20 minutes, until blackened and golden. During this time, turn skewers a few times, and spoon or brush with leftover marinade each time to give them a nice sticky glaze.
05 Remove from heat and let the pork rest for about 5 minutes.
06 Slice meat between the skewers, so you get four skewers with four pieces of pork on each one. Remove the meat from skewers and pile on a platter.
07 Serve with pineapple salsa for spooning over, and lemon or lime wedges for squeezing over.
Serves 6–8

STEAMED ASIAN DUMPLINGS **

Steamed dumplings have become the go-to unfussy starter at my place.

1 packet egg wonton wrappers, thawed
1 red chilli, thinly sliced
light vegetable oil, for dipping
juice of ½ lime
soy sauce, for dipping
Chinese chilli sauce, for dipping

Filling
500 g (1 lb 2 oz) free-range or organic minced (ground) chicken
½ bunch coriander (cilantro), including stalks, chopped
¼ cup (45 g/1½ oz) drained sliced water chestnuts, roughly chopped
3 spring onions (scallions), white parts and some green bits thinly sliced
1 small knob of fresh ginger, finely chopped
2 tsp sesame oil
1 tbsp soy sauce

01 In a bowl, combine all filling ingredients. Use a 1 tbsp measure to make individual balls. Don't make the balls too dense.
02 Place a ball in the centre of a wonton wrapper, then top with a slice of chilli. Bring sides of wrapper around filling so that it forms a money-bag shape. Repeat.
03 Bring a wok containing 5 cm (2 inches) of water to a simmer.
04 Working in batches of about eight, dip base of dumplings in the vegetable oil, then place in a steamer (don't overcrowd it). Cover, place steamer in wok and steam each batch for about 6 minutes. Serve hot, with soy and chilli dipping sauces on the side.
Makes about 25

CHILLI MEX **

Not as hot as it sounds, just as spicy as you. This is a bastardised version of a classic dish, and now it's more Tex-Mex than plain Mex. Those spicy favourites, cumin, coriander and cinnamon, pack in the flavour, while chorizo sausage takes things to a whole new level. Serve on a big platter with basmati or brown rice. Guys absolutely love this. I'm with them: it's completely awesome.

1 tsp olive oil
1 large chorizo sausage (the soft, non-cured kind)
500 g (1 lb 2 oz) minced (ground) beef
1 tsp ground cumin
1 tsp ground cinnamon
1 tsp ground coriander
400 g (14 oz) tin peeled whole tomatoes
400 g (14 oz) tin red kidney beans, rinsed and drained
¼ tsp dried chilli flakes
steamed rice, to serve
½ bunch coriander (cilantro), roughly chopped
sour cream, to serve
Tabasco sauce or smoked paprika, to serve

01 Heat oil in a large saucepan over high heat. Squeeze meat out of the chorizo into saucepan, breaking it up with a wooden spoon. Fry for 3 minutes, or until golden brown.
02 Add beef, stirring to combine meat and break up any lumps. Cook for 5 minutes, or until browned.
03 Stir in spices and cook for 30 seconds, or until aromatic. Add tomatoes and their juice, kidney beans and chilli flakes. Stir well, then simmer, uncovered, for 15–20 minutes.
04 Serve on a large platter with cooked rice, scattered with coriander. Dollop with sour cream and sprinkle with Tabasco or a pinch of paprika, or serve these on the side.
Serves 4–6

PROPER LASAGNE ***

The Italian staple that needs no introduction. You can easily prepare it ahead and then just pop it in the oven when your friends arrive. There are two main elements to lasagne—the meat sauce and cheese filling, which are made separately and then assembled into layers before baking. Forty minutes later you can slice it into hearty squares and serve it up. I'll fight you for a corner slice.

8 large fresh lasagne sheets
3 cups (300 g/10½ oz) grated mozzarella cheese

Meat sauce
2 tbsp olive oil
500 g (1 lb 2 oz) minced (ground) beef
1 garlic clove, chopped
¼ bunch basil, roughly chopped
400 g (14 oz) tin chopped tomatoes
1 cup (250 ml/9 fl oz) tomato passata (puréed tomatoes)

Cheese filling
3 cups (690 g/1 lb 8 oz) fresh ricotta cheese
½ cup (60 g/2¼ oz) grated parmesan cheese
2 free-range eggs, lightly beaten

01 Preheat oven to 180°C (350°F). Cook lasagne sheets in a large saucepan of boiling salted water, according to packet instructions, then set aside.
02 To make the meat sauce, heat oil in a large frying pan over medium heat, add beef and cook until well browned. Add remaining sauce ingredients, then cover and simmer for 25 minutes, stirring occasionally.
03 Meanwhile, make the cheese filling. Add all ingredients to a bowl, season with sea salt and freshly ground pepper and mix well with a wooden spoon.
04 To assemble the lasagne, place a layer of lasagne sheets in a 33 cm x 23 cm x 5 cm (13 inch x 9 inch x 2 inch) baking dish. Spread with half the cheese filling, then spoon over half the meat sauce, and sprinkle with half the mozzarella. Repeat with remaining ingredients, finishing with a layer of mozzarella.
05 Bake for 30 minutes. Remove from oven, then stand for 5–10 minutes before serving, to allow lasagne to set a little.
Serves 6–8

TIP: It's easy to experiment with this recipe. Add a layer of raw baby spinach leaves or thinly sliced raw tomatoes before cooking, if you like.

ROAST FILLET OF BEEF **

Two long, crusty sourdough baguettes, cut into thick slices, a smear of buttery béarnaise or mustard, one single slice of rare roast beef on top. This is my party. This is what I made when I came back to Australia from London and had all my friends over for a long evening of Champagne catch-ups. This is what I made at my own 21st birthday party. This, to me, is the ultimate in joyous celebration when you feel like your heart just might explode from the gladness of it all.

1.5 kg (3 lb 5 oz) fillet of grass-fed beef
90 g (3 1/4 oz) butter
¼ cup (60 ml/2 fl oz) brandy

01 Preheat oven to 200°C (400°F). Trim beef fillet and remove any stringy tissue bits with a sharp knife. Rub meat with a generous amount of sea salt and freshly ground black pepper.
02 Heat a large heavy-based frying pan over medium–high heat. Add butter and sauté fillet, turning occasionally with tongs, for 8 minutes, or until brown on all sides.
03 Pour brandy into a measuring cup (do not skip this step). Pour the brandy over the fillet in the pan—the brandy will catch alight. Shake the pan until the flames subside. Use a spoon to ladle juices over beef a few times, then turn off heat.

04 Transfer beef and juices to a roasting tin. Bake for 15–20 minutes. Remove from oven, cover loosely with foil and stand for at least 5 minutes.

05 Carve the fillet into slices. Serve hot or at room temperature.

Serves 8

BÉARNAISE SAUCE ***

This is roast beef's great love. If ever there was a saucy match made in heaven, it's this buttery sauce with that great roast. This is a bit tricky to master, but you will not believe your tastebuds once you do. Serve it with a simple roasted fillet (see above) and crusty sourdough baguette slices for a totally fancy gathering. People can help themselves to a slice of baguette, a slice of rare beef, and a plop of sauce. As always, read through the entire recipe a few times so you understand every step completely, get all your ingredients measured, whisk and saucepan ready, and then let the cooking begin.

3 tarragon sprigs, or ½ tsp dried tarragon
2 golden shallots, finely chopped
¼ cup (60 ml/2 fl oz) white wine vinegar
¼ cup (60 ml/2 fl oz) white wine
3 free-range egg yolks
250 g (9 oz) unsalted butter, at room temperature, cut into 1 cm (½ inch) cubes
1 tbsp chopped flat-leaf (Italian) parsley, chervil or tarragon

01 Combine the tarragon, shallot, vinegar and wine in a saucepan. Cook over low heat until mixture reduces by two-thirds. Turn off heat and allow to cool slightly. Strain mixture into a small bowl that fits snugly over a small saucepan.

02 Fill saucepan with 1 cup (250 ml/9 fl oz) of hot, but not boiling, water. Place bowl over saucepan. Add egg yolks and 1 tbsp water and stir briskly with a whisk, until mixture is light and fluffy.

03 Still resting the bowl over the saucepan and low heat, add about one-third of the butter and whisk constantly until the mixture thickens slightly. Add remaining butter in small pieces, stirring well and allowing mixture to thicken a little after each addition.

04 Remove from heat and season to taste with sea salt and a pinch of ground white pepper. Stir in chopped herbs. Béarnaise sauce . . . well done!

Makes a good bowlful. This lasts as long as butter, a few days in the fridge at least

by the way

COLONEL MUSTARD

Mustard is the yellowish condiment made from the seeds of a mustard plant ground up, cracked or bruised then mixed with other spices, salt, water, lemon juice and sometimes mayonnaise. It ranges from really hot hot, to a little spicy, to barely punchy at all.

HOT ENGLISH is the hot stuff. It's great with roast beef and used in small quantities to give a kick to sauces.

DIJON is the French mustard almost everyone loves because it's milder, which means we can use more of it. It's great in salad dressings or with a steak.

DRY MUSTARD is a powder—I recommend Keen's brand. Mix with a little water to make hot mustard, or use in dry rubs for beef with other spices.

GERMAN MUSTARD is mild and great on hot dogs and sandwiches.

SEEDED MUSTARD is where the seeds are mixed in whole instead of being ground. It often has a similar punch to Dijon.

BANOFFEE CUPS *

You'll break hearts with these. Totally cute little in-a-cup puddings, which are also a pip to make. They're packed with pastry, ice cream, creamy toffee and banana—toothachingly sweet of course, but completely gorgeous. We're using shop-bought dulce de leche (pronounced 'dol-say de le-chay') . . . oh my goodness it's so good.

250 g (9 oz) packet ready-rolled shortcrust pastry
1 scoop vanilla bean ice cream per person
100 g (3½ oz) hazelnuts, toasted and roughly chopped
3–4 ripe bananas, thinly sliced
450 g (1 lb) jar dulce de leche

01 Preheat oven to 200°C (400°F). Unroll pastry and place it on a baking tray lined with baking paper. Bake for 15 minutes, or until golden.
02 Remove pastry from oven and set aside to cool completely.
03 Snap the cooled pastry into pieces about half the size of the palm of your hand. Divide pastry crisps among 8–10 teacups with saucers.
04 Fill up the cups with one scoop of ice cream each, then layers of hazelnuts (reserve some to decorate the tops), banana slices and dollops of dulce de leche. Sprinkle the remaining hazelnuts over the top and serve with a little spoon resting in the saucer.
Makes 8–10

TIP: You can use whipped cream instead of ice cream if you like.

TIRAMISU **

Literally 'pick-me-up' in Italian, this creamy coffee-spiked dessert is a voluptuous, billowing thing to be spooned out at the table. There's often a nip each of alcoholic Tia Maria and Marsala in tiramisu, which would obviously 'pick-us-up' a little more. But even without you'll have everyone on the edge of their seats. You'll need an espresso machine (or a local coffee shop).

2 cups (500 ml/17 fl oz) hot strong coffee, espresso is best
½ cup (110 g/3¾ oz) sugar, plus 1 tbsp sugar kept aside
4 egg yolks
1¾ cups (400 g/14 oz) mascarpone
2 tsp natural vanilla extract or vanilla essence
½ cup (125ml/4½ oz) thickened cream, for whipping
about 36 savoiardi (lady finger) biscuits
1 tbsp cocoa, for topping
grated chocolate, for topping

01 Stir together hot coffee and 1 tbsp sugar in a large flat bowl until sugar has dissolved. Set aside.
02 Beat egg yolks and sugar with electric beaters until thick and pale. Beat in mascarpone and vanilla extract until just combined.
03 In a bowl, whip cream until soft peaks form. Use a metal spoon to fold cream into mascarpone mixture.
04 Dip both sides of half the savoiardi into coffee mixture, and place in the bottom of a two-litre capacity serving dish. Spread half the mascarpone cream filling on top. Repeat with remaining savoiardi and pour over remaining mascarpone cream. Dust with cocoa, cover and chill. When ready to serve, scatter grated chocolate over tiramisu.
Serves 6–8

SINGAPORE SWINGING SPIDER *

I don't know, don't ask. I can't explain the name. Maybe it's the ginger-and-therefore-Asian thing. Do make this, it's positively swinging.

2 scoops lemon sorbet
2 scoops vanilla ice cream
about 400 ml (14 fl oz) ginger beer
4–5 mint leaves, to serve

01 Chill two tall glasses in the freezer for 30 minutes.
02 When you're ready for the fizz, place one scoop of sorbet and one scoop of ice cream in each glass. Slowly fill the glasses with ginger beer, letting it fizz and bubble with glee. Decorate with mint leaves and serve with straws and long spoons.
Serves 2. Make more for a crowd

HAPPY HOUR ICE CUBES *

These are great little things for your sparkling water—so much more interesting than cola.

1 cup (220 g/7¾ oz) sugar
1 cup (125 g/4½ oz) raspberries or blueberries, or a mix

01 In a small saucepan, combine sugar and 2 cups (500 ml/17 fl oz) water. Simmer over low heat for about 5 minutes, until sugar dissolves.
02 Remove from heat and add berries, gently mixing them up a bit. Allow to cool completely.
03 Pour mixture into an ice cube tray, dividing berries evenly between the compartments.
04 Freeze for at least 4 hours before serving one cube in each bubbling, sparkling-water-filled glass.
Makes 1 tray

WATERMELON COSMO COCKTAIL *

This could be the greatest cocktail out there that is not a Manhattan or a Cosmopolitan. This recipe was actually inspired by one I had in New York, at a little nook in Brooklyn called Bubby's that also does hot honey lemonade, peach lemonade, and of course pink lemonade. At $8 a pop in New York though, they're worth doing at home. If making this for a thirsty crowd, use a whole watermelon and times the other ingredients by four. Garnish with mint leaves, or a slice of lemon if you're feeling fancy.

¼ watermelon, flesh only, seeds removed
¼ cup (60 ml/2 fl oz) lemon juice
2 tbsp agave nectar (a very sweet, healthy syrup from Mexico) or sugar syrup
2 cups (500 ml/17 fl oz) cold water

01 Cut watermelon into chunks and process in a blender or food processor until completely liquid. Add remaining ingredients and blend again.
02 Pour into a tall glass filled with ice and serve.
Serves 4–6

TIP: For a spritzy alternative, blend the watermelon with the lemon juice and agave syrup, then pour into a jug with 2 cups (500 ml/17 fl oz) soda water (club soda). Stir to combine and serve over ice.

CREAMING BERRY SPIDER *

When I was a kid I had a sip of a shop-bought drink you'll know as creaming soda. It nearly knocked me out in a sugar rush. My teeth still hurt thinking about it. It's crazily pink and I don't even know what flavour it was, but I think it was aiming for a very eye-boggling raspberry. In a bid to recreate the nonsense, without the giddying sugar hit, I do this instead.

2 scoops raspberry sorbet
2 scoops vanilla ice cream
150 g (5½ oz) raspberries or other berries
about 400 ml (14 fl oz) soda water (club soda)

01 Chill two tall glasses in the freezer for 30 minutes.
02 Place 1 scoop of sorbet and 1 scoop of ice cream in each glass. Top with berries, then very slowly fill to the top with soda water. It will fizz and bubble like some gorgeous cauldron, so be careful not to let it spill over. Suck it and see . . . pretty darned good.
Serves 2, with straws and spoons. Just double or triple quantities for more peeps

ALL ABOUT THE CHOCOLATE LOAF ***

This cake improves with age. It tests our patience as well, because it tastes even better after a day or two. As if you can wait that long.

1⅓ cups (200 g/7 oz) plain (all-purpose) flour
1 tsp bicarbonate of soda (baking soda)
130 g (4½ oz) dark chocolate
200 g (7 oz) unsalted butter, softened
1½ cups (285 g/10 oz) brown sugar
2 large free-range eggs
1 tsp vanilla extract
1 cup (250 ml/9 fl oz) boiling water
1 portion sesame and almond praline (optional)

01 Preheat oven to 190°C (375°F) (fan-forced). Grease a 23 cm x 13 cm (9 inch x 5 inch) loaf (bar) tin and line with baking paper.
02 Sift flour with bicarbonate of soda and set aside. Break up chocolate and melt it in the microwave for 1 minute on Medium.
03 Cream butter and sugar in a bowl using electric beaters, then add eggs and vanilla and beat well.
04 Carefully fold in slightly cooled melted chocolate. Then, one spoon at a time, add flour mixture and boiling water alternately, stirring gently after each addition, until batter is smooth and quite runny.
05 Pour into loaf tin and bake for 30 minutes. Reduce oven temperature to 170°C (325°F) and bake for another 15 minutes.
06 The cake will still be quite wobbly when removed from oven, so hold it carefully with oven mitts and place on a wire rack. Leave until it is completely cool—at least 2 hours—before turning it out of the tin.
07 Turn cake out onto a serving plate. If you like, scatter with sesame and almond praline pieces (see below). Top with Chocolate frosting (see page 203), if you like. Serve in thick, toast-like slices.
Makes about 8–10 thick slices

Sesame and almond praline *

Line a baking tray with a large square of baking paper. Gently toss ⅓ cup (55 g/2 oz) almonds in a dry frying pan over medium heat for 1 minute. Add 3 tbsp sesame seeds and 2 tbsp white sugar, and stir gently until the sugar has melted and the nuts and seeds are coated in syrup. Pour and spread the mixture out onto the tray, being careful not to touch the extremely hot syrup. Cool for 10 minutes, until hard, then chop the praline with a knife into small crunchy pieces.

Right: Creaming berry spider (page 200) and Singapore swinging spider (page 199)

CHOCOLATE FUDGE SAUCE CAKE **

Ah the names me and my mate Jess came up with for this cake as teenagers. Chewy, screaming fantastic delicious, oozing messy sauce cake, chocolate melting lava fudge happy-making sauce cake . . . the list goes on and on, testament to how many times we made it. We perfected the cake, never mind the name. I have my grandmother to thank for this recipe.

250 g (9 oz) plus butter, plus softened butter for greasing
1/4 cup (35 g/1 1/4 oz) plain (all-purpose) flour, plus extra for dusting
250 g (9 oz) good-quality dark chocolate, roughly chopped
6 free-range eggs, separated
3/4 cup (165 g/5 3/4 oz) caster (superfine) sugar
3/4 cup (60 g/2 1/4 oz) brown sugar
1/4 cup (25 g/1 oz) ground almonds
1/2 tsp cream of tartar
1 tbsp sifted icing (confectioners') sugar or cocoa, for dusting
whipped cream, to serve

01 Preheat oven to 180°C (350°F). Generously butter sides and base of a 23–25 cm (9–10 inch) spring-form cake tin. Line base with baking paper and dust very lightly with a sprinkling of flour.
02 Melt butter and chocolate in a large heavy-based saucepan over low heat, stirring constantly until just melted and smooth. Do not overheat. Set aside.
03 Put egg yolks in a bowl, then beat in sugars until just mixed. While chocolate is still warm, whisk egg yolk mixture into it, then stir in flour and almonds. (If the chocolate mixture has cooled, warm it a little over low heat.)
04 Add egg whites to a bowl, add cream of tartar and beat until they form rounded peaks. Gently fold into chocolate mixture, keeping mixture light and airy.
05 Pour batter into cake tin. Bake for 35–45 minutes, or until cake is completely set around the sides, but still has a soft and creamy circle—about 12 cm (4 1/2 inches) across—in the centre. The cake should be wobbly in the centre.
06 Remove cake from oven and cool completely in tin.
07 When cooled, remove cake from tin. Dust with icing sugar or cocoa, and serve with dollops of whipped cream.
Serves 8 (or just two teenage girls)

TIP: This cake keeps really well in the tin, covered loosely with foil, for 2–3 days. Do not refrigerate or freeze.

CHOCOLATE FROSTING *

Here's a super-easy frosting for decorating cupcakes and large fabulous birthday cakes.

125 g (4 1/2 oz) butter, softened
1 1/2 cups (185 g/6 1/2 oz) icing (confectioners') sugar mixture, sifted
60 g (2 1/4 oz) dark chocolate, melted

01 Place butter in a bowl. Using electric beaters set to low-medium speed, cream the butter, whipping it until soft. Gradually beat in half the icing sugar mixture. Beat in melted chocolate, then beat in remaining icing sugar mixture.

* try me

LEMONY CUPCAKES WITH LEMON ICING **

The best part of the cupcake needn't be the icing. There's no issue with that here, as the cakes themselves are light and slightly lemony, delicious in their own right. That said, the lemon icing is pretty special too—a smooth, elegant and simple icing for cupcakes. I got this recipe from my grandma, who can basically do it with her eyes closed. And soon, so will you!

125 g (4½ oz) butter, softened
¾ cup (165 g/5¾ oz) caster (superfine) sugar
1 tsp vanilla extract
grated zest of 1 lemon
2 free-range eggs
2 cups (300 g/10½ oz) self-raising flour
⅔ cup (170 ml/5½ fl oz) milk

Lemon icing
60 g (2¼ oz) unsalted butter, softened
1 tsp grated lemon zest
1 tbsp lemon juice
1 tsp vanilla extract
about 1 cup (220 g/7¾ oz) sifted icing (confectioners') sugar

01 Preheat oven to 190°C (375°F). Line a 12-hole patty pan or mini muffin tin with paper cases.
02 Cream the butter in a bowl using electric beaters, then gradually add sugar, beating until soft and creamy. Add vanilla extract and lemon zest. Add eggs, beating well between each addition.
03 Sift flour and a pinch of sea salt and lightly fold into the mixture a little at a time, alternating with the milk, to make a smooth consistency. Spoon mixture into paper cases and bake for 15 minutes, or until cupcakes are a pale golden brown.
04 Remove from oven and leave to cool completely.
05 To make the icing, cream the butter, lemon zest, lemon juice and vanilla extract in a bowl using electric beaters, until soft and creamy. Gradually beat in icing sugar until thick and smooth. Don't add all the icing sugar if you're happy with the consistency, or add a little more if it's too thin. It should be soft and easily spreadable using a butter knife or spatula.
06 Decorate cooled cupcakes with lemon icing. Store in an airtight container.
Makes 12

HONEY, BANANA AND PEPITA LOAF **

This half-cake, half-bread is fabulous sliced and packed for lunch, or toasted for breakfast. It's the thing to bake-and-take to Grandma to have with tea and stories of love, loss, laughter and sparkling days in her youth spent sewing her own clothes and shucking oysters straight from the rocks.

2 cups (250 g/9 oz) self-raising flour
½ tsp ground cinnamon
pinch salt
½ cup (100 g/3½ oz) brown sugar, plus 1 tbsp for topping
175 g (6 oz) unsalted butter, softened and diced
2 free-range eggs, lightly beaten
3 tbsp runny honey
⅓ cup (100 g/3½ oz) pitted prunes, chopped
2 ripe bananas, mashed
½ cup (70 g/2½ oz) pepitas

01Preheat oven to 160°C (315°F). Grease and line a 21 cm x 11 cm (9 inch x 5 inch) loaf tin, leaving a little baking paper overhanging the edges.
02 Place all ingredients, reserving 2 tbsp pepitas and 1 tbsp brown sugar, in a mixing bowl and beat until well combined.
03 Pour mixture in tin, smooth the top and sprinkle with reserved pepitas and brown sugar. Bake for 1 hour, until golden brown and a skewer inserted in the middle comes out clean. Cook for another 10 minutes

if needed. Cover with foil in last 15 minutes if top is browning too much.

04 Cool in the tin for 15 minutes, then turn out and cool completely on a wire rack. Slice and serve, or store in an airtight container for up to 3 days.

Makes 1 loaf

STRAWBERRY SHORTCAKES **

This gorgeous old-fashioned American classic, crumbly and creamy, is the real thing. It's basically a sandwich of the world's best pairing, strawberries and cream, giving a grand twist to a simple thing.

1⅔ cups (250 g/9 oz) self-raising flour
¼ cup (55 g/2 oz) golden caster (superfine) sugar, plus extra for sprinkling
1 tsp baking powder
2 hard-boiled egg yolks
90 g (3¼ oz) cold unsalted butter, cut into 1 cm (½ inch) cubes
⅔ cup (170 ml/5½ fl oz) cold pouring (whipping) cream or buttermilk, plus extra for brushing

To fill

250 g (9 oz) strawberries, hulled (green caps removed) and sliced
1 tbsp strawberry jam
1 cup (250 ml/9 fl oz) pouring (whipping) cream, beaten to soft peaks

01 Preheat oven to 180°C (350°F). Line a baking tray with baking paper.

02 Place flour, sugar, baking powder, egg yolks and butter in a food processor. Pulse to combine. Add cream or buttermilk and pulse until the dough comes together.

03 Turn dough out onto a lightly floured work surface and gather together lightly. Knead a couple of times, then pat it into a rough circle, about 15 cm (6 inches) across, and 4 cm (1½ inches) thick.

04 Using a round cutter, cut it into about 8 circles and arrange them on baking tray. Chill dough for at least 20 minutes and up to 2 hours in the refrigerator.

05 Brush tops of shortcakes with some extra cream or buttermilk, then sprinkle lightly with extra sugar. Bake until golden brown, 18–20 minutes, then cool shortcakes on a wire rack.

06 Once cool, slice shortcakes in half horizontally. Toss strawberries in a bowl with jam, then heap them over the bottom halves of the shortcakes. Spoon whipped cream generously over the strawberries and replace the shortcake tops.

07 Serve immediately, with remaining whipped cream on the side.

Serves 6, including seconds for some

TIP: The hard-boiled egg yolks are a novel addition, but they give the dough a richer, crumblier texture without adding water, as a raw yolk would. Literally hard-boil a couple of eggs, peel them, discard the whites and use the whole egg yolks in the recipe.

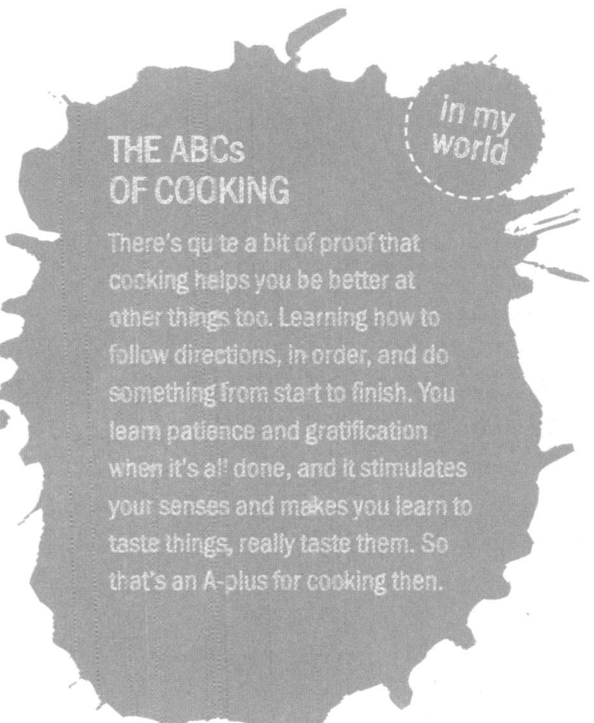

in my world
THE ABCs OF COOKING
There's quite a bit of proof that cooking helps you be better at other things too. Learning how to follow directions, in order, and do something from start to finish. You learn patience and gratification when it's all done, and it stimulates your senses and makes you learn to taste things, really taste them. So that's an A-plus for cooking then.

CARROT CUPCAKES WITH ORANGE ICING **

These are your reliable pretty treat to serve at any party or gathering because they can be made a day ahead—and taste even better if you do. Which leaves you more time to get a playlist sorted, wash your jeans and do other essential pre-party jobs.

1½ cups (220 g/7¾ oz) wholemeal (whole-wheat) plain (all-purpose) flour
1½ tsp baking powder
½ tsp bicarbonate of soda (baking soda)
1½ tsp ground cinnamon
½ tsp ground ginger
good pinch or two of freshly grated nutmeg
¾ cup (185 ml/6 fl oz) vegetable oil
3 large free-range eggs
1 cup (185 g/6½ oz) light brown sugar
2 cups (310 g/11 oz) coarsely grated carrot
1 tsp vanilla extract

Orange icing
1¼ cups (155 g/5½ oz) icing (confectioners') sugar
½ tsp grated orange zest
2–3 tbsp orange juice

01 Preheat oven to 180°C (350°F). Line a 12-hole muffin tin (with ½ cup/125 ml/4 fl oz holes) with paper cases.
02 In a bowl, combine flour, baking powder, bicarbonate of soda, spices and a pinch of sea salt.
03 In a large bowl, whisk together oil, eggs, sugar, carrot and vanilla extract, then stir in flour mixture until just combined. Don't over-mix, or the cupcakes will be tough.
04 Divide batter among cupcake cases and bake for 20–25 minutes, or until golden. A skewer inserted into the centre of a cupcake should come out clean.
05 Cool in the tin on a wire rack for 10 minutes, then remove the cupcakes to a wire rack to cool completely.
06 To make the icing, sift icing sugar into a bowl and whisk in orange zest and 2 tbsp juice until smooth. The icing should be quite runny. If it is too thick, add more juice.
07 Dip the tops of each cooled cupcake into the icing, letting any excess drip off. Leave the cakes on a wire rack for about 15 minutes to allow the icing to set.
Makes 12

TIP: The cupcakes can be made and iced one day ahead, then kept in one layer in an airtight container at room temperature.

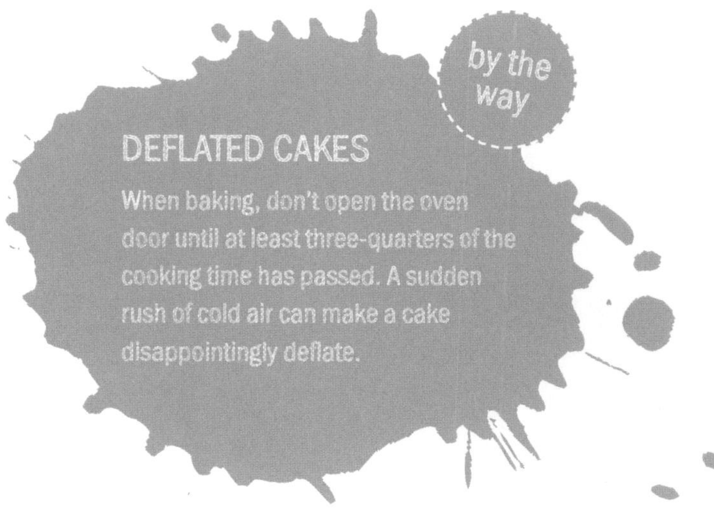

by the way
DEFLATED CAKES
When baking, don't open the oven door until at least three-quarters of the cooking time has passed. A sudden rush of cold air can make a cake disappointingly deflate.

JAM THUMBPRINT COOKIES *

Thumbprint cookies are age-old, previous-generation things, but you can give them your own thumbprint by choosing your favourite jam and spicing them up a bit. They're pretty healthy, though sweet, so you can eat them almost any time.

250 g (9 oz) buckwheat flour
1 ⅓ cups (200 g/7 oz) plain (all-purpose) flour
450 g (1 lb) whole unblanched almonds, roughly chopped
1 tsp ground cinnamon
1 tsp ground allspice
½ tsp ground ginger
generous grating of fresh nutmeg
1 cup (250 ml/9 fl oz) rapeseed oil or vegetable oil
1 cup (250 ml/9 fl oz) maple syrup
jam, such as raspberry, cherry, blueberry or rhubarb, for filling

01 Preheat oven to 180°C (350°F). Line a baking tray with baking paper.
02 In a bowl, combine all ingredients except jam and mix well with a wooden spoon.
03 Use a heaped 1 tbsp measure to form dough into balls. Roll each one and space them evenly on baking tray. Use your thumb or index finger to make indents in the top of each ball. Use a teaspoon to fill each indent with a little jam.
04 Bake for 20 minutes, or until golden brown. Leave to cool before eating. Store in an airtight container for up to a week.
Makes about 50

WHITE CHOCOLATE, CRANBERRY AND MACADAMIA COOKIES **

The cookie dough can be stored in the fridge for up to a week, so you can slice off and bake at least six or so cookies as you want them. Once baked, they also keep well in the fridge, in an airtight container. Speckled with white and red, these cookies are perfect for Christmas or a red-and-white themed party.

1¼ cups (185 g/6½ oz) plain (all-purpose) flour
½ tsp baking powder
115 g (4 oz) unsalted butter, softened
⅓ cup (75 g/2½ oz) caster (superfine) sugar
⅓ cup (60 g/2¼ oz) brown sugar
1 free-range egg, lightly beaten
½ tsp vanilla extract
⅓ cup (55 g/2 oz) macadamia nuts, roughly chopped
⅓ cup (55 g/2 oz) dried cranberries
⅔ cup (100 g/3½ oz) white chocolate melts (buttons), roughly chopped

01 Sift together flour, baking powder and a pinch of sea salt.
02 Cream the butter with both sugars using a wooden spoon, or electric beaters with a paddle attachment on high speed. Turn off the beaters, if using, then beat in egg and vanilla extract by hand.
03 Fold in flour in two batches, until well combined. Fold in nuts, cranberries and chocolate.
04 Form the dough into a log shape on a lightly floured surface, then wrap in plastic wrap. Refrigerate for at least 2 hours, until firm.
05 Heat oven to 170°C (325°F). Line two baking trays with baking paper, if you're cooking all the cookies. Unwrap dough and slice it into about 20 slices, placing them on trays.
06 Bake for 15 minutes, or until golden and still soft. Cool cookies on their trays. They will harden slightly as they cool.
Makes 20

CHOCOLATE CRACKLES *

I can't go past these at a gathering. They're just so kiddie, which only makes them more hilarious. They're almost too retro to be true, and I love them for it. Crunchy, crackling, chocolate morsels that shouldn't be reserved for little kids.

4 cups (120 g/4¼ oz) puffed rice cereal
1 cup (125 g/4½ oz) icing (confectioners') sugar
1 cup (90 g/3¼ oz) desiccated coconut
5 tbsp unsweetened cocoa powder
250 g (9 oz) Copha (white vegetable shortening)

01 Double-line a 24-hole patty pan or muffin tin with small paper cases.
02 In a bowl, combine puffed rice, icing sugar, desiccated coconut and cocoa powder.
03 Melt Copha in a saucepan over low heat, stirring very gently. Remove from heat, then add puffed rice mixture and fold through to completely combine.
04 Use two spoons to dollop mixture into paper cases. Refrigerate until firm.
Makes 24

HONEY NUT JOYS *

It's the texture of these that is so addictive. They're pretty and crunchy golden, super sweet in all ways.

90 g (3¼ oz) butter
⅓ cup (75 g/2½ oz) sugar
1 tbsp honey
3 tbsp flaked almond
4 cups (120 g/4¼ oz) plain corn flakes

01 Preheat oven to 150°C (300°F). Line a 24-hole patty pan or muffin tin with small paper cases.
02 Melt butter, sugar and honey together in a small saucepan over low heat until sugar has dissolved. Add almonds and corn flakes and fold through to fully coat.
03 Quickly spoon mixture into paper cases, then bake for 10 minutes. Remove from oven and cool before serving. Store in an airtight container.
Makes 24

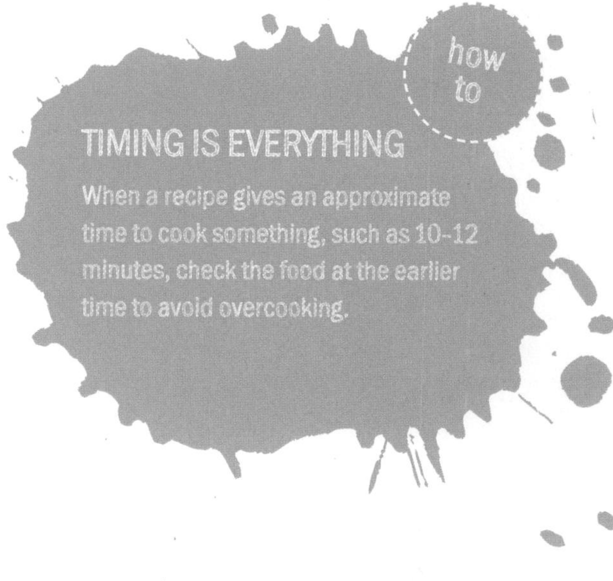

how to
TIMING IS EVERYTHING
When a recipe gives an approximate time to cook something, such as 10–12 minutes, check the food at the earlier time to avoid overcooking.

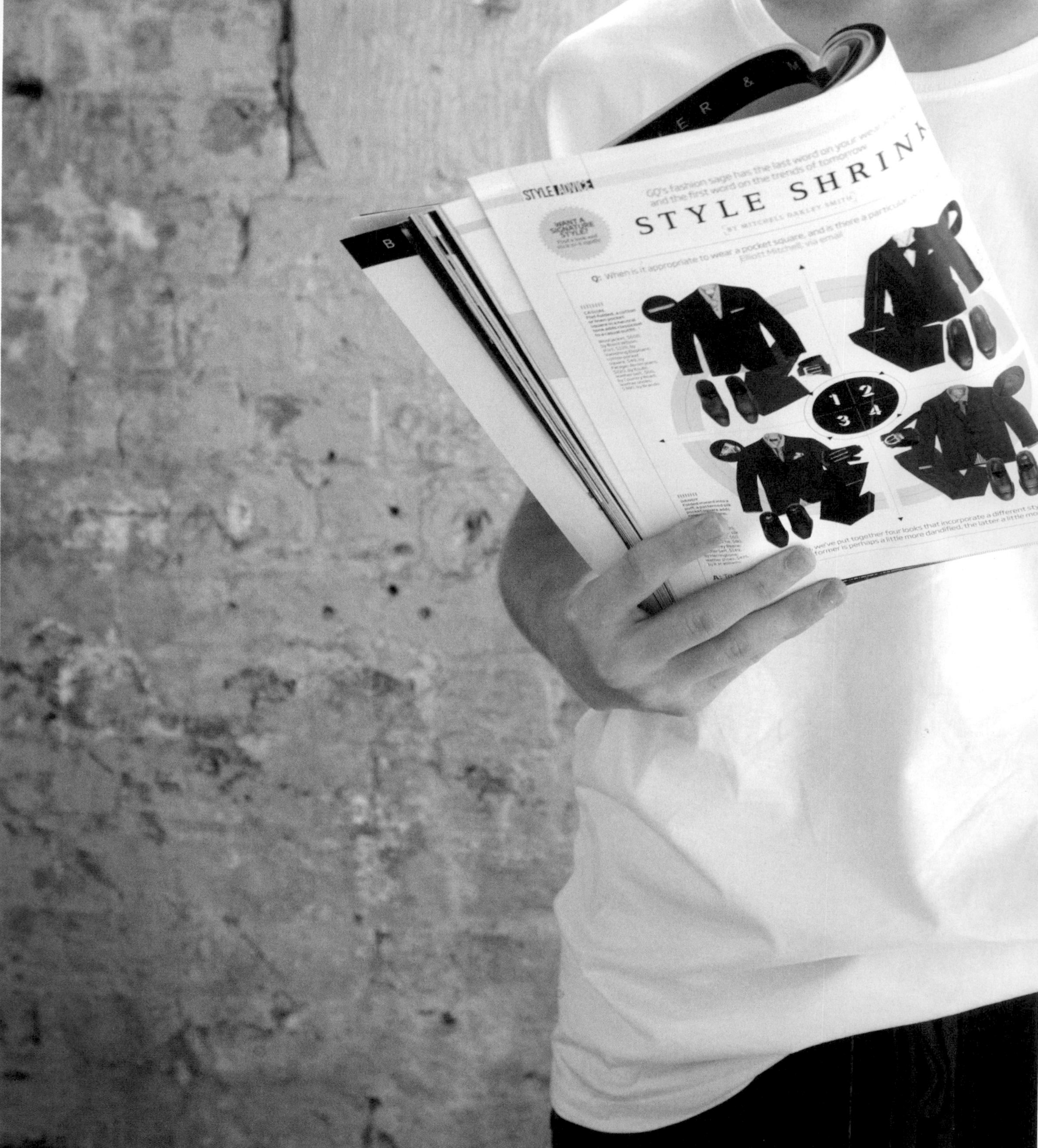
STYLE ADVICE
GQ's fashion sage has the last word on your wear
and the first word on the trends of tomorrow
STYLE SHRIN
BY MITCHELL OAKLEY SMITH
Q: When is it appropriate to wear a pocket square, and is there a particular
Elliott Mitchell, via email
1 2
3 4

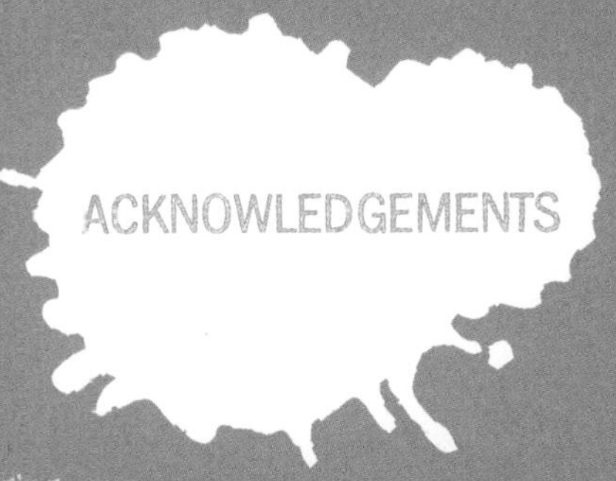

ACKNOWLEDGEMENTS

THANK YOU to my publisher TRACY O'SHAUGHNESSY, a guru of books, for your wholehearted and passionate belief in all this, your ideas and patience. LOUISE LISTER, photographer extraordinaire–thank you for bringing your light and expertise into these pages. ANDREW BALLARD, the cook, whose fascination with food and produce made recipe testing a breeze. To KRISTIAN TAYLOR WOOD, thank you for bringing your camera and self into this book.

And thank you KRISTIN HOVE, friend, photographer and miracle worker of style and cool, whose creative touch is always magic.

My editor KATHRYN KNIGHT, wordsmith and gracious diplomat, whose expertise left me reassured, and the book so so much better–thank you.

My designer KRISTINE LINDBJERG, for making everything look so absolutely beautiful and for your hard work and wonderful ideas.

Thank you, so much, to my various newspaper and food guide editors, whose trust in my writing and impeccable editing enables me to follow my dreams and just explore, ask questions, cook and tap away at my laptop as a career. In particular, thank you SARAH OAKES, NATALIE REILLY and KATE COX at Fairfax and *Sunday Life* magazine, SUE BENNETT on *Good Living* at *The Sydney Morning Herald*, JILL DUPLEIX, LYNNE WHILEY at *Traveller*, *The Sydney Morning Herald*, PAUL MCNALLY at Hardie Grant, DANNY MCCUBBIN at *Jamie Oliver* and ANDREW VAILLE at *The Wall Street Journal*. Thank you too to SIMON THOMSEN, friend and food writer, whose standards and wise words keep me on my toes and spurred on to continue with this food-writing caper.

Thank you to EL LOCO, JOHN and PETER CANTEEN and the EVELEIGH MARKETS for giving us space to photograph. Thanks to QUINTESSENTIAL duckeggBLUE for the chairs and stools on our cover.

And finally, a huge thank you to the fabulous people who modelled for this book, who traipsed through markets and parks and woke up in the wee hours to be photographed–LILLIE and HARRY, CHARLIE and ANNELISE, JORDAN, FERN, ROXY and RHAYN.

IN THIS BOOK

MEASUREMENTS

IN SHORT: ABBREVIATIONS

In this book, we use accepted abbreviations in lists of ingredients. These are handy to know, no matter which book you cook from.

- tbsp = tablespoon
- tsp = teaspoon
- ml = millilitres
- L = litres

TABLESPOONS: MEASURE FOR MEASURE

1 tbsp = 4 tsp (about 20 ml/½ fl oz)
3 tbsp = ¼ cup (about 60 ml/2 fl oz)
4 tbsp = ⅓ cup (about 80 ml/2½ fl oz)

LIQUIDS: WEIGHT VS. VOLUME

1 cup = 250 ml (9 fl oz)
¾ cup = 185 ml (6 fl oz)
⅔ cup = 170 ml (5½ fl oz)
½ cup = 125 ml (4 fl oz)
⅓ cup = 80 ml (2½ fl oz)
¼ cup = 60 ml (2 fl oz)

CUPS VS. GRAMS AND OUNCES—OH MY!

Cookbooks often list ingredients by weight, instead of in cups, just because this is more precise. You might pack flour really tightly into a cup, for example, or make it light and loose so there's less, but both measures of flour will fill up the cup. That's why we often go for weight, especially with baking where exact measurements are very important.

INGREDIENTS

BUTTER. When a recipe says to use butter, it generally means unsalted butter, unless otherwise stated. The other rather quirky thing we see in cookbooks is the term butter as a verb—so, for example, 'butter the baking dish'. This means to rub the inside of the dish with butter so it's all greasy and ingredients won't stick. When a recipe says 'grease and line with baking paper', this means running butter around all the insides, then cutting a sheet of baking paper to fit exactly in the bottom of the dish. The butter will help the paper stick to the bottom of the dish, instead of your food.

ONIONS. When we say 'onions' in this book, we mean *brown onions*. When we say *white onions*, we mean those white onions. *Golden shallots* are walnut-sized, golden-brown onions. Some people call them French shallots or eschallots. In this book, *spring onions* (scallions) are long, skinny things, made up mostly of green stem; there is no bulbous white bit on the end. In some parts of the world they're also called shallots or green onions. *Salad onions* are small, white, bulbous onions with long green stems attached. They're lovely thinly sliced, or used in a famous French dish called *coq au vin* ('chicken with wine'). *Red onions* are those big reddish-purple onions that you often see cut—too thickly!—raw in salads. They are also called Spanish onions.

SALT-SAVVY. Think again next time you buy salt. When it comes to flavour and texture, not all salts are created equal. All salt is either mined or extracted from sea water. Most table salt is mined, and potassium iodine and magnesium silicate are added to prevent caking. I recommend kosher salt or sea salt, which contains no additives. Sea salt has naturally occurring iodine and a great flavour. Get rid of the salt shaker and find a small dish and tiny spoon for having good sea salt at the table.

TEMPERATURES

In this book we've used degrees Celsius and degrees Fahrenheit to describe cooking temperatures. If your oven uses gas marks, use the following conversion table to work out which setting to use.

Gas mark	Fahrenheit	Celsius	Description
¼	225	110	Very cool
½	250	130	Cool/slow
1	275	140	Cool/slow
2	300	150	Cool/slow
3	315/325	160/170	Very moderate
4	350	180	Moderate
5	375	190	Moderately hot
6	400	200	Moderately hot
7	425	220	Hot
8	450	230	Very hot
9	475	240	Very hot

INDEX

E

F

G

H

I

J

L

M

N

O

P